for Aaron

By the same author:

Carpenters – All The Top 40 Hits
ABBA – All The Top 40 Hits
Michael, Janet & The Jackson Family – All The Top 40 Albums
Michael, Janet & The Jackson Family – All The Top 40 Singles
Whitney Houston: For The Record

Fiction:

The Secret Library
Shadow Of Death
Tyranny

With Chris Cadman:

Janet Jackson: For The Record
Michael Jackson: For The Record
ABBA Gold Hits
Jacksons Number Ones
Michael Jackson – The Early Years
Michael Jackson – The Solo Years

www.craighalstead.com

Donna Summer

For The Record

Craig Halstead

Second Edition

ISBN-10: 1508416966
ISBN-13: 978-1508416968

CONTENTS

INTRODUCTION

'Donna Summer is one of the most underrated singers in the history of pop music'

Dick Clark

LaDonna Adrian Gaines was born on New Year's Eve, 31st December 1948 in Boston, Massachusetts, the daughter of Andrew Gaines & Mary Ellen Gaines (née Davis).

Donna was the third of seven children, six girls and one boy, and in her autobiography, *Ordinary Girl: The Journey*, she described her mixed heritage as 'something like African, Indian, and Dutch-Irish'.

'I was raised in a three family house that was like an orphanage,' said Donna. 'Besides the seven kids in my family, there were eight children on the two other floors of the house. We always had the best back yard in the neighbourhood – all the others would come to our house to play.'

As a young girl, Donna joined the Grant A.M.E. (African Methodist Episcopal) Church's junior choir. 'I never wanted to do anything but sing,' she said. 'And that's all I ever tried to do well. I was never a good student – unless my parents said that I couldn't sing unless I got this or that grade. *Then* I studied.'

The church choir director refused Donna's pleas to sing a solo, 'because when I screamed, I screamed *loud*. I just wasn't getting it out right. So that's when I would go to my parents' bedroom to do breathing exercises, and listen to Mahalia Jackson records.' Finally, aged 10, she got her opportunity to sing in public for the first time, when the Grant A.M.E. Church choir's soloist was taken ill, and her mother volunteered Donna to sing in her place. Donna sang a popular Christian gospel song, *I Found The Answer*.

Seven years later, during her last year at high school, Donna joined a rock band. 'I was in a rock 'n' roll band called the Crow,' she said, 'not to be confused with Counting Crows. You can guess who the crow was – I was the only black one in the group … we were kind of in the vein of Janis Joplin. We wrote songs with very hippy, kind of psychedelic lyrics.'

After she turned 19, Donna travelled to New York with the Crow, where she – but not the other band members – was offered a recording contract by RCA. The band cut a few demos for RCA in August 1968, but Donna was spared having to make a difficult decision when a friend introduced her to Bertrand Castelli, the Broadway producer of the musical, *Hair*. She auditioned to join the cast, and was offered the role of understudy to Melba Moore – but Donna wanted to be onstage, not watching from the wings.

When she was offered the chance to join the cast of one of three European productions of *Hair*, Donna plumped for Germany ahead of England and France, as her father had served in Germany during World War II, and both her parents spoke fluent German. She accepted a six month contract without telling her parents; when he found out, her father was furious, and he only agreed to his daughter travelling abroad after he had spoken at length to Bertrand Castelli.

On 28th August 1968, three months shy of her twentieth birthday, Donna boarded a plane bound for Munich, Germany. Six months later, she re-signed for another 18 months, and travelled from Berlin to Vienna with the cast of *Hair*. On her return to Vienna, she performed on stage in two more musicals, *Porgy And Bess* and *Showboat*.

In Vienna, Donna met an Austrian actor called Helmuth Sommer – the pair had actually met before, briefly, when Donna joined the Berlin cast of *Hair*, at the same time Sommer was in the choir. Donna was offered a lead part in the Hamburg production of *The Me Nobody Knows*, and Sommer joined the cast as well; the two grew closer, and eventually became lovers.

Together, Donna and Helmuth joined the cast of *Godspell*, and toured through German speaking countries with the musical. They went on to do a show in Italy, called *The Black Experience*, but neither enjoyed the experience and when the show closed, they returned to Vienna – and married. Their daughter, Mimi, was born in Munich on 16th February 1973.

The marriage didn't last. 'It was simply that he and I come from very different backgrounds,' said Donna, explaining why she and Helmuth split up, 'and we never really got to know each other well enough to stay together, but we're still good friends.'

Donna was contemplating how she could juggle her career and being a single mother, when a friend told her about a producer, who was on the look-out for new voices. His name: Giorgio Moroder. Donna sang a few songs from *Hair*, and other shows she had appeared in, for Moroder and he liked what he heard. Donna sang on demos for Three Dog Night, and although she wasn't really looking to get into the business at a recording level at the time, she cut three solo songs with Moroder and his partner, Pete Bellotte.

Moroder took the songs to the MIDEM international music festival in Cannes, France, and sold all three. One, *The Hostage*, became a Top 10 hit in several European countries. The follow-up, *Lady Of The Night*, was also a hit in several countries. However, it wasn't until early 1975 that Donna came up with the one line that would change her life: 'I'd love to love you.'

Moroder immediately had Donna cut what she thought was a three minute demo of *Love To Love You*, which he took to MIDEM in January. At the music festival, he met Neil Bogart, founder and owner of Casablanca Records.

Bogart liked the demo, and he took it home with him and played it at a party – over and over again, such was the demand. After sitting on the demo for a while, Bogart contacted Moroder – and asked for an extended, twenty minute version of the song; and Bogart insisted the only person who could sing the song was whoever had sung the demo.

So *Love To Love You Baby*, as the song was re-titled, was born – and Donna was on her way to becoming an international superstar.

This book follows the same format as the previous *For The Record* books I have written/co-written with Chris Cadman, and documents Donna's career under a number of headings:

- Part 1: The Songs.

- Part 2: The Albums.

- Part 3: The Home Videos.

- Part 4: The Musicals, Films & TV Shows.

- Part 5: The Concerts.

- Part 6: The Autobiography

- Part 7: Chartography & Chart Runs.

- Part 8: USA Discography.

- Part 9: UK Discography.

Sadly, since the first edition of this book was published, Donna Summer has left us. Typically, she kept her battle against lung cancer a closely guarded secret, so it came as a great shock to hear she had passed away on 17th May 2012 at her home in Naples, Florida. Here are just a few of the tributes that poured in, following her passing.

'Michelle and I were saddened to hear about the passing of Donna Summer.
A five-time Grammy Award winner, Donna was truly the Queen of Disco. Her voice
was unforgettable and the music industry has lost a legend far too soon.'
President Barack Obama

'She was a queen, the Queen of Disco, and we will be dancing to her music forever.'
Liza Minnelli

'Donna, like Whitney, was one of the greatest voices ever. I loved her records. She was the disco queen and will remain so. I knew her and found her to be one of the most likable and fun people ever.'
Dolly Parton

'My wife and I are in shock and are truly devastated. Donna changed the face of pop culture forever. There is no doubt that music would sound different today if she had never graced us with her talent. She was a super-diva and a true superstar who never compromised when it came to her career or her family. She always did it with class, dignity, grace and zero attitude.'
David Foster

'Donna Summer made music that moved me both emotionally and physically to get up and dance. You could always hear the deep passion in her voice. She was much more than the Queen of Disco she became known for, she was an honest and gifted singer with flawless vocal talent.'
Beyoncé Knowles

'I loved doing the duet with her. She had an amazing voice and was so talented.'
Barbra Streisand

'Her voice was the heartbeat and soundtrack of a decade.'
Quincy Jones

'She changed the world of music with her beautiful voice and incredible talent.'
Janet Jackson

'Donna and I had a friendship for over thirty years. She is one of the few black women I could speak German with, and she is one of the few friends I had in this business.'
Chaka Khan

'Rest in peace, Donna. You are a pioneer and you have paved the way for so many of us. You transcended race and gender. Respect.'
Lenny Kravitz

I wholeheartedly agree with Dick Clark: Donna was and is one of the most underrated singers in the history of pop music. She is my no.1 female singer of all-time, and I have thoroughly enjoyed researching and writing this book about her music ~ I hope you enjoy reading it.

Craig Halstead.

PART 1:
THE SONGS

Donna, although best known as the 'Queen of Disco', was a prolific song-writer, as well as being an amazingly versatile singer.

In this chapter, the numerous songs Donna was involved with in her musical career are listed alphabetically, and each listing includes details of the connection to Donna, together with other interesting snippets of information.

A number of sources were consulted in compiling this listing. The starting point, naturally, were the officially released singles and albums by Donna, including the many collaborations she has been involved with over the years.

The listing includes songs Donna is known to have performed live, for example in concert or on TV, but which she hasn't recorded (or, if she has, remain unreleased), plus unreleased songs registered with one or more of the following professional bodies:

- The American Society of Composers, Authors And Publishers (ASCAP).

- The American Performing Rights organisation, BMI.

- The United States Copyright Office.

Also included and detailed:

- Official Versions.

- Cover versions & other hit versions.

- Chart positions achieved in the USA (Pop & R&B), UK and other countries.

- USA sales awards by the RIAA (Recording Industry Association of America).

- UK sales awards by the BPI (British Phonographic Industry).

- American Music Awards, Grammy Awards & selected other awards and nominations.

1960s MEDLEY

This is a medley Donna performed with Brooklyn Dreams, when they appeared on *The Midnight Special* on 26th May 1978. Donna also performed a similar medley on her Bad Girls Tour in 1979.

The medley featured: *So Fine, Maybe, My Girl, My Guy, The Way You Do The Things You Do, Good Lovin', I Heard It Through The Grapevine* and *Heat Wave*.

A DIFFERENT ROAD

Song performed by Donna on her Live & More Encore Tour in 1999 – however, the song wasn't included on Donna's *LIVE & MORE ENCORE!* album, or on the accompanying home video.

A GIRL LIKE YOU

Written by Bruce Sudano & B. Incorvaia, and recorded by Sudano for his 1981 album, *FUGITIVE KIND* – backing vocals by Donna (credited as Donna Sudano).

Donna & Bruce Sudano married on 16th July 1980, and remained man and wife for over thirty years, until Donna's passing in May 2012.

A LOVER IN THE NIGHT

Song recorded by Brooklyn Dreams for their 1980 album, *WON'T LET GO* – backing vocals by Donna.

Brooklyn Dreams = Bruce Sudano, Joe 'Bean' Esposito & Eddie Hokenson.

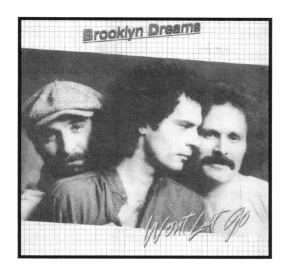

A MAN LIKE YOU

Written by Donna with Giorgio Moroder & Pete Bellotte, and recorded by Donna for her 1977 album, *ONCE UPON A TIME* – produced by Moroder & Bellotte.

A SONG FOR YOU

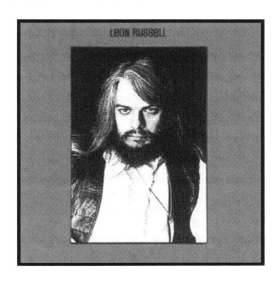

Written and recorded by Leon Russell, for his self-titled debut album, issued in 1970.

Donna performed the song when she appeared as a guest on the TV special, *Mac Davis... Sounds Like Home*, in 1977.

Donna also performed the song regularly on her Once Upon A Time Tour in 1977-1978, and at select dates during later concert tours.

A WHOLE NEW WORLD

Written by Alan Menken & Tim Rice, for Disney's 1992 animated film, *Aladdin* – originally performed by Brad Kane & Lea Salonga, but better known for the hit version recorded by Peabo Bryson & Regina Belle.

Recorded by Donna for Dave Koz's 2007 album, *AT THE MOVIES* – produced by Phil Ramone.

Peabo Bryson & Regina Belle took the song to no.1 on the Hot 100 and no.21 on the R&B chart in the States, and to no.12 in the UK.

ADONAI

This is a song Donna mentioned, in an interview in 1999, she had recorded with Metro for her next album – produced by Graham Stack.

An audio clip on the song was posted on Donna's official website, however, the song remains unreleased.

AFTER THE LOVE HAS GONE

Written by David Foster, Jay Graydon & Bill Champlin, and recorded by Earth, Wind & Fire for their 1979 album, *I AM*.

Donna performed the song, with Kenny Rogers, as part of a Grammy nominations medley, when she appeared at the Grammy Awards, staged at the Shrine Auditorium, Los Angeles, on 27th February 1980.

Earth, Wind & Fire took the song to no.2 on the Hot 100 and R&B chart in the States, and to no.4 in the UK.

See also: *Grammy Nominations Medley*.

AIN'T NO MOUNTAIN HIGH ENOUGH

Written by Nickolas Ashford & Valerie Simpson, and originally recorded by Marvin Gaye & Tammi Terrell for their 1967 album, *UNITED*.

Performed by Donna with Diana Ross, the Supremes, Mariah Carey, Faith Hill, Destiny's Child & RuPaul, on *VH1 Divas 2000: A Tribute To Diana Ross, An Honors Concert For VH1's Save The Music*, staged at New York's Madison Square Garden on 9th April 2000 and aired by VH1 two days later.

Donna was also scheduled to perform a Supremes medley with Diana Ross and Mariah Carey, however, she reportedly wasn't happy with the lack of rehearsal time, so Diana and Mariah sang the medley as a duo.

VH1 Divas 2000 has never been released on CD or home video, as Diana Ross refused to give her consent – she didn't feel her performance on the night was one of her best.

Hit Versions:
Marvin Gaye & Tammi Terrell – no.3 on the R&B chart and no.19 on the Hot 100 in the States in 1967.
Diana Ross – no.1 on the Hot 100 and R&B chart in the States, and no.6 in the UK, in 1970.
Boystown Gang (medley) – no.46 in the UK in 1981.
Jocelyn Brown – no.35 in the UK in 1998.

Whitehouse – no.60 in the UK in 1998.

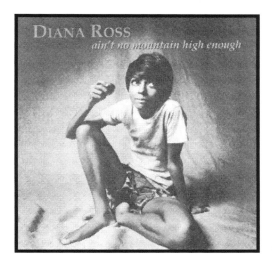

See also: *Bad Girls*, *Love Is The Healer* & *Reflections*.

ALL SYSTEMS GO

Written by Donna & Harold Faltermeyer, and recorded by Donna for her 1987 album with the same title – produced by Faltermeyer.

'I wrote that song for the astronauts on the space shuttle Challenger, before it crashed,' said Donna. 'Out of respect, we held it back as a single – but I still really love that song.'

The song was released as a single in select European countries, including the UK, where it charted at no.54.

Donna performed the song when she appeared on the *Solid Gold* TV show in 1987.

Official Versions:
Album Version.
7" / Single Edit
Dance Mix / Extended Remix.

ALL THROUGH THE NIGHT

Written by Donna & Bruce Roberts, and recorded by Donna for her 1979 album, *BAD GIRLS* – produced by Pete Bellotte & Giorgio Moroder.

AMAZING GRACE

Popular Christian hymn written by John Newton, and first published in 1779.

Donna revealed, in her autobiography *Ordinary Girl: The Journey*, this is one of the songs she often sang as a young girl – sometimes, for elderly people from the nursing home next to her home.

Donna performed the song, as a medley with *Operator* and *How Great Thou Art*, on her Rainbow Tour in 1984, and her Silver Girl Tour two years later.

Donna also included the song in the set list of her All Systems Go Tour in 1987-88.

Donna, as the character Aunt Oona, performed the opening lines of the song, when she fronted a church choir in Season 8, Episode 22 – *Pound Foolish* – of the American sitcom, *Family Matters*. The episode aired on 25th April 1997.

Hit Versions:
Judy Collins – no.5 in the UK in 1970,

and no.15 on the Hot 100 in the States in 1971.
Royal Scots Dragoon Guards (instrumental version) – no.1 in the UK, and no.11 on the Hot 100 in the States, in 1972.

Other artists to have recorded the song include the Byrds, Johnny Cash, Sam Cooke & the Soul Stirrers, Aretha Franklin, Mahalia Jackson, Willie Nelson, Elvis Presley and Rod Stewart.

AMERICA THE BEAUTIFUL

Patriotic American song written by Katharine Lee Bates (lyrics) & Samuel A. Ward (melody) – the combined lyrics and melody were first published in 1910.

Donna performed the song on her Silver Girl Tour in 1986.

ANGELS NEVER SLEEP AT NIGHT

Song former model Twiggy recorded for her shelved 1979 album, *HEAVEN IN MY EYES* – produced by Donna & Juergen Koppers.

The album was finally released in 2007, and also included an up-dated remix by OUTpsiDER.

ANY WAY AT ALL

Written by Donna with Bruce Sudano & E. Silver, and recorded by Donna for her 1994 compilation album, *ENDLESS SUMMER* – produced by Michael Omartian.

The song was originally written for Oleta Adams. 'I've always been a fan of

Oleta's,' said Donna, 'and I wanted to write something for her. But when we played it for the label, they loved it so much they insisted I keep it for myself.'

Released as a single in a limited number of countries, with a medley of *Dim All The Lights*, *Hot Stuff*, *Bad Girls* & *Last Dance* on the B-side.

ANYTHING FOR YOU

Written by Gloria Estefan, and recorded by Estefan & Miami Sound Machine for their 1987 album, *LET IT LOOSE*.

Donna performed the song on her Spanish concert dates in 1990.

Gloria Estefan & Miami Sound Machine took the song to no.1 on the Hot 100 in the States, and to no.10 in the UK.

AQUARIUS

See: *Wassermann (Aquarius)*.

ARE YOU BRAVE

Written by the popular children's show host Fred 'Mister Rogers' Rogers, and recorded by Donna for the various artist 2005 tribute album, *SONGS FROM THE NEIGHBOURHOOD – THE MUSIC OF MISTER ROGERS* – produced by Dennis Scott.

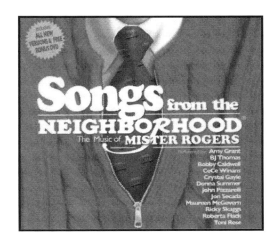

Other artist to contribute to the album included Jon Secada, Amy Grant, B.J. Thomas, CeCe Winans, Crystal Gayle and Roberta Flack.

The album won a Grammy Award, for Best Musical Album For Children.

ARMS AND LEGS

Written by Donna with Al Kasha & Michael Omartian, for the as yet unpublished play Donna worked on with Bruce Sudano, Kasha & Omartian, *Ordinary Girl* – remains unreleased.

AUTUMN CHANGES

Written by Donna with Pete Bellotte & Giorgio Moroder, and recorded by Donna for her 1976 album, *FOUR SEASONS OF LOVE* – produced by Bellotte & Moroder.

BABY I LOVE YOU

Written by Jimmy Holiday & Ronnie Shannon, and recorded by Aretha Franklin for her 1968 album, *ARETHA ARRIVES*.

This was one of the songs the Crow, with Donna as lead singer, regularly sang live in 1965-66.

Aretha Franklin took the song to no.1 on the R&B chart and no.4 on the Hot 100 in the States, and to no.39 in the UK, in 1967.

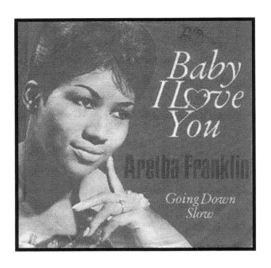

BACK IN LOVE AGAIN

Written by Donna with Pete Bellotte & Giorgio Moroder, and recorded by Donna for her 1977 album, *I REMEMBER YESTERDAY* – produced by Bellotte & Moroder.

The song is a re-working, with new lyrics, of an earlier song titled, *Somethings In The Wind*, which was the B-side of *Denver Dream*, issued in Belgium and the Netherlands.

On the album, this song represented the 1960s.

Released as a single in a limited number of countries, including the UK, where it charted at no.29.

B-side of *I Feel Love* in Germany.

BACK OFF BOOGALOO

Written by Richard Starkey (*aka* Ringo Starr), and released as a single by Starr in 1972 – produced by George Harrison.

One of nine tracks Donna recorded, as a member of the multi-national Veit Marvos Red Point Orchestra, for an album released in Germany circa 1972-73. The full track listing was:

Fun Street/Little Marie/Shout It Out/They Can't Take Away Our Music/Back Off Boogaloo/Jeannie/Nice To See You/Na

Na Hey Hey Kiss Him Goodbye/Do What Mother Do

In 1983 the album was re-released, and remixed, and since then it has appeared in numerous (over 30) different guises, including:

- *DONNA SUMMER AND FRIENDS*
- *DONNA SUMMER*
- *BACK OFF BOOGALOO*
- *NA NA HEY HEY*
- *FUN STREET*
- *SUPER STARS*
- *NICE TO SEE YOU*
- *REMIXED & EARLY GREATS*

Each release has featured the same nine tracks, but not necessarily in the same running order – the original album was 37:16 minutes, while the extended remix album runs to 52:20 minutes.

Ringo Starr took the song to no.2 in the UK, and to no.9 on the Hot 100 in the States.

BACK WHERE YOU BELONG

Written by Harold Faltermeyer & Keith Forsey, and recorded by Donna for her shelved 1981 album, *I'M A RAINBOW* – produced by Pete Bellotte & Giorgio Moroder.

The album was finally released in 1996.

BAD GIRLS

Written by Donna with Bruce Sudano, Joe Esposito, Eddie Hokenson, Harold Faltermeyer & Keith Forsey, and recorded by Donna for her 1979 album of the same title – produced by Pete Bellotte & Giorgio Moroder.

'Bad Girls started with a lyric,' said Donna, 'and we went into the studio, and they played guitars and I wrote the whole song that way, singing it over and over again. I think I sang that verse a hundred times and we added things, chopped things, moved them here and there.'

'A lot of people think I'm glorifying prostitution,' she acknowledged, 'which is absolutely not correct at all. It's totally the opposite. You know, I would come out of Casablanca Records, which is on Sunset Boulevard, and there would be a lot of girls, you know, soliciting on the street.

'I wrote *Bad Girls* because I had a friend who had an experience on Sunset Boulevard. The police stopped her, and they were going to arrest her because they thought she was a "bad girl" – quote, unquote. And she was a secretary at Casablanca Records at the time, and I was really affected by it. I felt really kind of appalled by the whole thing, and *Bad Girls* started off as a social statement about prostitution really and became finally, at the time, my biggest hit.'

Casablanca's owner, Neil Bogart, initially wanted Donna to give the song to Cher. 'When I first played it to him (Bogart),' said Donna, 'he asked if he could have it for Cher, and I said "I love Cher, but she can't have my song!" And then, a couple of years later, an engineer was in a studio in L.A. and found the song, and we dusted it off and worked on it and it just evolved. We added the toot-toots and beep-beeps and stuff. Then Neil loved it. It was a big record for me.'

Released as the second single from the album, the song went to no.1 on the Hot 100, R&B chart and Hot Dance Club Play chart simultaneously in the States – it was Donna's first R&B chat topper, and her third on the Hot 100.

The single was less successful outside the USA, charting at no.1 in Canada, no.5 in Switzerland, no.6 in New Zealand, no.7 in the Netherlands, no.8 in Norway, no.9 in Germany, no.13 in Sweden, no.14 in Australia & the UK, no.23 in Austria & Ireland and no.35 in Japan.

With *Hot Stuff* and *Bad Girls*, Donna became the only female artist to have two singles in the Top 3 of the Hot 100 at the same time – she repeated the trick a few months later, with *Dim All The Lights* and *No More Tears (Enough Is Enough)*.

RIAA Award: Platinum (September 1979) = 2 million.

BPI Award: Silver (July 1979) = 250,000.

No.5 best-selling single of 1979 in the USA.

Grammy Award nominations:
Best Pop Vocal Performance, Female.
Best Disco Recording.

Donna performed the song at the Grammy Awards ceremony, staged at the Shrine Auditorium, Los Angeles, on 27th February 1980.

The song featured in Donna's *The Donna Summer Special* TV movie, which aired in the States on 27th January 1980.

A live version, recorded at the Hammerstein Ballroom, New York, in February 1999, was included on the 1999 album, *LIVE & MORE ENCORE!*

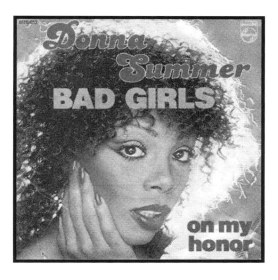

A demo version featured on the Deluxe Edition of *BAD GIRLS*, issued in 2003.

Official Versions:
Album Version.
7" / Single Edit.
12" Extended Mix.
Live Version.
Demo Version.

Performed by Donna, with Queen Latifah, on a TV show in 1999, to promote her album, *LIVE & MORE ENCORE!*

Performed by Donna on *VH1 Divas 2000: A Tribute To Diana Ross, An Honors Concert For VH1's Save The Music*, staged at New York's Madison Square Garden on 9th April 2000 and aired two days later.

Featured as the theme song to ITV1's *Bad Girls Most Wanted* TV show in the UK in 2004.

Performed by Donna when she appeared at the Nobel Peace Prize Concert, staged in Oslo, Norway, on 11th December 2009.

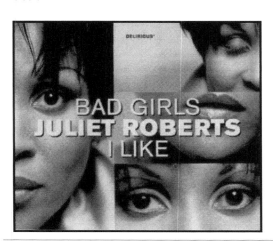

A cover version by Juliet Roberts, featured in the music video arcade game, *Dance, Dance Revolution 2nd Mix*, was released as a single in 1999 and charted at no.17 in the UK.

BAD REPUTATION

Written by Donna with Peter Bunetta & Joe Erickson, and recorded by Donna for her 1987 album, *ALL SYSTEMS GO* – produced by Bunetta & Rick Chudacoff.

B-side of *All Systems Go*.

BE MYSELF AGAIN

Written by Donna with Lester Mendez & Wayne Hector, and recorded by Donna for her 2008 album, *CRAYONS* – produced by Mendez.

'What I wanted to do,' said Donna, about *Be Myself Again*, 'is strip down a song. I wanted it to be *a cappella*. There's always so much hoopla around the voice, I wanted to do a song where there's no hoopla. There's just you and the audience listening to somebody who's just singing to themselves, singing about the intimate parts of what it has taken to do what they do. The thing is to stay connected to the true self, and that's really difficult in show business. That's what the song is about.'

BEGIN AGAIN

Written by Donna with Bruce Sudano, Al Kasha & Michael Omartian, for the as yet unpublished play Donna worked on with Sudano, Kasha & Omartian, *Ordinary Girl* – remains unreleased.

BITTER END

Written by Donna & Michael Omartian, for the as yet unpublished play Donna worked on with Bruce Sudano, Al Kasha & Michael Omartian, *Ordinary Girl* – remains unreleased.

BLACK

Written by Gary William Friedman & Will Holt for the musical, *The Me Nobody Knows* – premiered at the Orpheum Theater, New York, on 18th May 1970.

Donna appeared – credited as Gayne Pierre – in the German production of the musical in 1970, titled *Ich Bin Ich*, and was part of the cast who performed this song on the English language version of the cast album.

See also: *Schwarz*.

BLACK LADY

Written by Donna with Pete Bellotte & Giorgio Moroder, and recorded by Donna for her 1977 album, *I REMEMBER YESTERDAY* – produced by Bellotte & Moroder.

B-side of *Love's Unkind* in Germany and the Netherlands.

BLACK POWER

Written by P. Thomas & G. Francropolus, and recorded by Donna in 1969 for the German TV mini-series, *11 Uhr 20*, which aired in January 1970 – in the show, Donna had a cameo role as a scantily-clad nightclub singer.

The track featured on Peter Thomas's album, *MOONFLOWERS & MINI-SKIRTS* – the album was reissued on CD in Germany in 1998 (Indigo 867 585-5).

BODY TALK

Written by Donna with Keith Diamond, Paul Chiten, Larry Henley & Anthony Smith, and recorded by Donna for her 1991 album, *MISTAKEN IDENTITY* – produced by Diamond.

BOOGIE OOGIE OOGIE

Written by Janice Johnson & Perry Kibble, and recorded by A Taste Of Honey for their self-titled 1978 album.

Performed by Donna on her Greatest Hits Tour in 2005.

A Taste Of Honey took the song to no.1 on the Hot 100 and R&B chart in the

States, and to no.3 in the UK. A remixed version achieved no.59 in the UK in 1985.

BORN TO DIE

Written by Giorgio Moroder & Pete Bellotte, and recorded by Donna for her 1974 album, *LADY OF THE NIGHT* – released in the Netherlands only.

Produced by Pete Bellotte.

BRAZIL

See: *Drivin' Down Brazil.*

BREAKAWAY

Written by Mike Stock, Matt Aitken & Pete Waterman, and recorded by Donna for her 1989 album, *ANOTHER PLACE AND TIME* – produced by Stock, Aitken & Waterman.

Belatedly remixed and released as a single in Europe, to promote Donna's 1990 compilation, *THE BEST OF* – the single charted at no.49 in the UK.

The single was also very popular in Latin America.

Official Versions:
Album Version.
Remix – Edit
Remix – Full Version
Power Radio Mix.
Extended Power Mix.
Instrumental Remix – Edit.

BREAKDOWN

Written by Pete Bellotte & Harold Faltermeyer, and recorded by Donna for her 1980 album, *THE WANDERER* – produced by Bellotte & Giorgio Moroder.

BREATH OF HEAVEN

Written by Amy Grant & Chris Eaton, and recorded by Grant – as *Breath Of Heaven (Mary's Song)* – for her 1992 album, *HOME FOR CHRISTMAS.*

Recorded by Donna for her 1994 album, *CHRISTMAS SPIRIT* – produced by Michael Omartian.

BRIDGE OVER TROUBLED WATER

Written by Paul Simon, and recorded by Simon & Garfunkel for their 1970 album with the same title.

Robert Guillaume sang the song to Donna in her *The Donna Summer Special* TV movie, which aired in the States on 27th January 1980 – Donna joined in with Guillaume, towards the end of the song.

Donna and Guillaume knew each other well, having previously worked together when they both appeared in the Viennese stage production of *Porgy And Bess*.

Hit Versions:
Simon & Garfunkel – no.1 on the Hot 100 in the States, and in the UK, in 1970.
Aretha Franklin – no.1 on the R&B chart, and no.6 on the Hot 100, in the States in 1970.

Linda Clifford – no.28 in the UK, and no.41 on the Hot 100 and no.49 on the R&B chart in the States, in 1979.

Dramatics – no.93 on the R&B chart in the States in 1989.

Hannah Jones – no.21 in the UK in 1991.

Mary J. Blige & Andrea Bocelli – no.75 on the Hot 100 in the States in 2010.

BRING DOWN THE REIGN

Written by Donna with Jamie Houston & Fred Kron, and recorded by Donna for her 2008 album, *CRAYONS* – produced by Gad.

BROOKLYN

Written by Donna with Pete Bellotte & Sylvester Levay, and recorded by Donna for her shelved 1981 album, *I'M A RAINBOW* – produced by Bellotte & Giorgio Moroder.

The album was finally released in 1996.

The song was written about, and dedicated to, Donna & Bruce Sudano's

first child, Brooklyn (Brook Lynne), who was born on 5th January 1980.

BURNING UP WITH FEVER

Written and recorded by Kiss's Gene Simmons, for his 1978 album: *KISS: GENE SIMMONS* – produced by Simmons & Sean Delaney, with backing vocals by Donna.

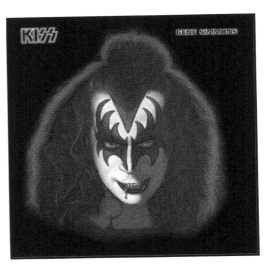

CAN'T GET TO SLEEP AT NIGHT

Written by Bruce Sudano & Bob Conti, and recorded by Donna for her 1979 album, *BAD GIRLS* – produced by Pete Bellotte & Giorgio Moroder.

CAN'T UNDERSTAND

Written by Donna & Hans Hammer-schmid, and recorded by Donna (as Donna Gaines) in 1972.

B-side of Donna's single, *If You Walkin' Alone*, released in Germany only in 1972. On the record label and sleeve Donna's surname was misspelled 'Gains'.

Donna revealed, in her autobiography *Ordinary Girl*, this was the first song she ever wrote. 'It's pretty simple,' she said. 'I was about fourteen. The first verse was, *Can't understand why this whole world keeps pulling me down to the ground / I walk two steps, they pull me back down / When will the world ever let me be*. What can I say? I was depressed. I actually started writing poetry, then music.'

The track was included on the 2011 German compilation, *FUNKY FRAULEINS VOL.2*.

CAN'T WE JUST SIT DOWN (AND TALK IT OVER)

Written by Tony Macaulay, and recorded by Donna for her 1977 album, *I REMEMBER YESTERDAY* – produced by Bellotte & Moroder.

Released as a single in select countries where the record company felt *I Feel Love* was a bit too radical – it achieved no.20 on the R&B chart in the States, but failed to enter the Hot 100.

Initially, where it was released, *I Feel Love* was the B-side – this track proved so popular, it was soon promoted to the A-side.

CARRIES ON

Song former model Twiggy recorded for her shelved 1979 album, *HEAVEN IN MY EYES* – produced by Donna & Juergen Koppers.

CARRY ON

Written by Giorgio Moroder & Marietta Waters, and recorded by Donna & Moroder for his 1992 album, *FOREVER DANCING* – released in Germany (Virgin Schallplatten 263 154).

The track featured Donna's daughters, Brooklyn & Amanda, among the backing vocalists.

Released as a single in Germany – the track was also featured on maxi 12" and CD singles issued in France in 1992.

Released as a single in the States in 1997, and in the UK the following year, for which numerous remixes were created.

The remix achieved no.25 on the Hot Dance Club Play chart in the States, but failed to enter the Hot 100 – in the UK, the single peaked at no.65.

Grammy Award:
Best Dance Recording.

Donna decided against attending the Grammy Awards ceremony, as she felt she had no chance of turning her nomination into a Grammy. 'To win a Grammy for dance after all these years seemed impossible,' she said. 'It really caught me off guard.'

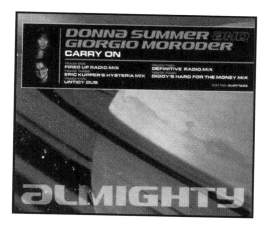

Official Versions:
Album Version.
Radio Version.
Extended Mix.
Instrumental.
Ace Down Under Mix.
Club Mix.
Definitive Mix.
Definitive Radio Mix.
Diddy's Hard For The Money Mix.
Euro Mix.
Fired Up Mix.
Fired Up Radio Mix.
Fired Up Dub.
Hot Tracks Mix.
Hysteria Mix.
Hysteria Radio.
Hysteriastrumental.
In-Sane Extended Version.
Outta Control Mix.
Outta Control Radio.
Outta Control Extended.
Slammin' Cox Mix.
Slammin' Cox Radio.
Untidy Dub.

CATS WITHOUT CLAWS

Written by Donna & Michael Omartian, and recorded by Donna for her 1984 album with the same title – produced by Omartian.

CELEBRATE ME HOME

Written by Kenny Loggins & Bob James, and recorded by Loggins for his 1976 album with the same title.

Donna performed the song on her All Systems Go Tour in 1987-88.

CHAIRMAN OF THE BOARD

Written by Donna with Bruce Sudano, Al Kasha & Michael Omartian, for the as yet unpublished play Donna worked on with Sudano, Kasha & Omartian, *Ordinary Girl* – remains unreleased.

CHRISTMAS IS HERE

Written by Donna with Michael & Stormie Omartian, and recorded by Donna for her 1994 album, *CHRISTMAS SPIRIT* – produced by Michael Omartian.

CHRISTMAS MEDLEY

This is a medley of three Christmas songs Donna performed when she appeared on *Bandstand* on 22nd December 1984.

Songs featured: *Silent Night, Hark! The Herald Angels Sing & O Come All Ye Faithful*.

See also: *Silent Night, Hark! The Herald Angels Sing & O Come All Ye Faithful*.

CHRISTMAS MEDLEY

This is a different medley of three festive songs recorded by Donna for her 1994 album, *CHRISTMAS SPIRIT* – produced by Michael Omartian.

Songs featured: *What Child Is This, Do You Hear What I Hear & Joy To The World*.

See also: *What Child Is This, Do You Hear What I Hear & Joy To The World*.

CHRISTMAS SONG, THE

Popular Christmas song written in 1944 by Mel Tormé & Bob Wells.

Recorded by Donna for her 1994 album, *CHRISTMAS SPIRIT* – produced by Michael Omartian.

Lead track on a *Christmas Spirit Sampler* promo CD single released in the States.

Hit Versions:
Nat 'King' Cole – no.80 in 1960, and no.65 in 1962, in the States; no.69 in the UK in 1991.
James Brown – no.12 on the Christmas Singles chart in the States in 1965.
Herb Alpert – no.1 on the Christmas Singles chart in the States in 1968.

Alexander O'Neal – no.30 in the UK in 1988.
Christina Aguilera – no.18 on the Hot 100 in the States in 2000.

Numerous other artists have recorded versions of the song, including Air Supply, Ray Charles, Bing Crosby & Frank Sinatra, John Denver, Celine Dion, Gloria Estefan, Ella Fitzgerald, Aretha Franklin, Judy Garland, Whitney Houston, the Jackson 5, Al Jarreau, Peggy Lee, Johnny Mathis, Kenny Rogers, Barbra Streisand, the Supremes, the Temptations, Andy Williams and Stevie Wonder.

CHRISTMAS SPIRIT

Written by Donna with Bruce Sudano & Michael Omartian, and recorded by Donna for her 1994 album, *CHRISTMAS SPIRIT* – produced by Omartian.

CHUCK E'S IN LOVE

Written and recorded by Rickie Lee Jones, for her self-titled 1979 album.

Donna performed the song, as part of a Grammy nominations medley, when she appeared at the Grammy Awards, staged at the Shrine Auditorium, Los Angeles, on 27th February 1980.

Rickie Lee Jones took the song to no.4 on the Hot 100 in the States, and to no.18 in the UK.

See also: *Grammy Nominations Medley*.

COLD LOVE

Written by Pete Bellotte, Harold Faltermeyer & Keith Forsey, and recorded by Donna for her 1980 album, *THE WANDERER* – produced by Bellotte & Giorgio Moroder.

This was the second single lifted from the album, after the title track – it achieved no.8 on the Hot Dance Club Play chart and no.33 on the Hot 100 in the States, no.29 in Canada, no.30 in Ireland and no.44 in the UK.

Grammy Award nomination:
Best Rock Vocal Performance, Female.

COME WITH ME

Written by Pete Bellotte & Giorgio Moroder, and recorded by Donna for her 1976 album, *A LOVE TRILOGY* – produced by Bellotte & Moroder.

B-side of *Spring Affair*.

Donna performed the song on the *Don Kirshner's Rock Concert* TV show in 1976.

COULD IT BE MAGIC

Written by Barry Manilow & Adrienne Anderson, and recorded by Manilow for his debut 1973 album, *BARRY MANILOW I*.

Recorded by Donna for her 1976 album, *A LOVE TRILOGY* – produced by Giorgio Moroder & Pete Bellotte.

Released as the follow-up to Donna's breakthrough single, *Love To Love You Baby*, the song achieved no.3 on the Hot Dance Club Play chart, no.21 on the R&B chart and no.52 on the Hot 100 in the States.

The single was also successful outside the States, charting at no.2 in the Netherlands, no.5 in Belgium, no.10 in South Africa, no.14 in Austria, no.23 in Germany, no.40 in the UK and no.45 in Canada.

B-side of *Walk Away* in the States.

Donna performed the song on numerous TV shows in 1976, including *Soul Train*, *Don Kirshner's Rock Concert*, *The Mike Douglas Show* and *Dick Clark's New Year's Rockin' Eve*.

Donna performed the song, with co-writer Barry Manilow, when she joined him on stage at Manhattan's Carnegie Hall on 8th March 1999.

Other Hit Versions:
Barry Manilow – no.6 on the Hot 100 in the States in 1975, and no.25 in the UK in 1978.
Take That – no.3 in the UK in 1992.
Barry Manilow (re-recording) – no.36 in the UK in 1993.

CRAYONS

Written by Donna with Ziggy Marley, Danielle Brisebois & Greg Kurstin, and recorded by Donna for her 2008 album, *CRAYONS* – produced by Kurstin.

Featured Ziggy Marley.

'He (Ziggy) was in L.A.,' said Donna, 'and I was in Florida, miles apart, but with today's technology, it made it possible for us to actually work together, and it's such an exciting thing.'

Donna felt the song encompassed a lot of what her album was about. 'Every song is a different colour,' she said. 'Since I'm also a visual artist, that title ties a lot of the loose ends of my life together.

'The song wrote itself pretty quickly. Taking it to the next level, we influence each other in life. You may have an Arab friend or an Israeli friend or an Indian friend, and so you go and eat a little Indian food, or have a little pita bread, or something you've never experienced, and as we immerse ourselves in each other's cultural experiences, it's like taking a crayon and colouring over the lines, and the lines become blurred between what's that and what's the other.'

CRAZY

Written by Seal & Guy Sigsworth, and recorded by Seal for his self-titled 1991 album.

Donna performed the song as a duet with Seal, as part of a medley, when she appeared at the *David Foster & Friends* concert, staged at the Mandalay Bay Events Center, Las Vegas, on 15th October 2010 – the medley also featured *Un-Break My Heart* and *On The Radio*.

The medley featured on the 2011 album, *HIT MAN RETURNS*, credited to David Foster & Friends. The release also

included a DVD and Blu-ray home video of the concert, and achieved no.108 in the States.

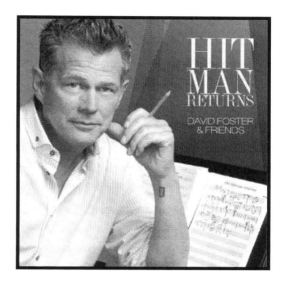

Hit Versions:
Seal – no.2 in the UK, and no.7 on the Hot 100 in the States, in 1991.
Alanis Morissette – no.65 in the UK, and no.6 on the 'bubbling under' section of the Hot 100 in the States, in 2005.

CRY OF A WAKING HEART

Written by Betsy Cook & Bruce Woolley, and recorded by Donna for her

1991 album, *MISTAKEN IDENTITY* – produced by Diamond.

DANCE INTO MY LIFE

Written by Donna with Giorgio Moroder & Pete Bellotte, and recorded by Donna for her 1977 album, *ONCE UPON A TIME* – produced by Moroder & Bellotte.

DANCING IN THE STREET

Written by Marvin Gaye & William Stevenson, and originally recorded by Martha & The Vandellas.

This is one of the songs the Crow, with Donna as lead singer, regularly included in their live set in 1965-66.

Hit Versions:
Martha & The Vandellas – no.2 on the Hot 100 and R&B chart in the States, and no.28 in the UK, in 1964.

Martha & The Vandellas (reissue) – no.4 in the UK in 1969.
Mamas & Papas – no.73 on the Hot 100 in 1967.
Ramsey Lewis – no.84 on the Hot 100 in 1967.
Donald Byrd – no.95 on the R&B chart in the States in 1977.
Hodges, James & Smith – no.85 on the R&B chart in 1979.
Van Halen – no.38 on the Hot 100 in 1982.
David Bowie & Mick Jagger – no.1 in the UK, and no.7 on the Hot 100 in the States, in 1985.

Other artists to have recorded the song include Atomic Kitten, Cilla Black, Carpenters, Grateful Dead, Dusty Springfield, the Kinks and the Who.

DANNY BOY

Song popular within Irish communities, with lyrics written by Frederick Weatherly to the tune of *Londonderry Air* – composed in 1855.

Donna revealed, in her autobiography *Ordinary Girl: The Journey*, this is one of the songs she often sang as a young girl – sometimes, for elderly people from the nursing home next to her home.

Hit Versions:
Don Byas Quartette – no.14 on the R&B chart in the States in 1948.
Al Hibbler – no.6 on the R&B chart in 1950.
Conway Twitty – no.10 on the Pop chart and no.18 on the R&B chart in the States in 1959.
Sil Austin – no.59 on the Hot 100 in 1959.

Andy Williams – no.64 on the Hot 100 in 1959.

Jackie Wilson – no.25 on the R&B chart and no.94 on the Hot 100 in 1965.

Patti LaBelle & Her Bluebells – no.76 on the R&B chart in 1965.

Ray Price – no.60 on the Hot 100 in 1967.

DAVID FOSTER & FRIENDS MEDLEY

This is a medley of three songs Donna performed with Seal, when she appeared at the *David Foster & Friends* concert, staged at the Mandalay Bay Events Center, Las Vegas, on 15th October 2010.

The three songs were Toni Braxton's *Un-Break My Heart*, Seal's *Crazy* and Donna's *On The Radio*.

DENVER DREAM

Written by Pete Bellotte, and recorded by Donna in 1974 – produced by Bellotte.

This was the first single credited to 'Donna Summer'.

'Donna means "lady" in Italian,' she said. 'I then married Helmuth Sommer, and I had it changed to the English version "Summer", so that I could kinda distance myself a little from my new married name, because I was already Sommer and I didn't want to throw people as I'd already become successful with that name. So, I thought if I could just change the spelling it would help me a little bit, and back then an astronomer told me that a "U" was better than an "O" in the name, anyway!'

Released as a single in Belgium and the Netherlands on Lark Records (INS 7510).

The single was listed on the *Tipparade* (chart breakers) section of the Dutch singles chart, but it failed to enter the Top 40.

'I don't think a lot of people understand where I am coming from musically,' stated Donna, around this time. 'I'm not an artist that's trying to establish a style. I'm an actress who sings, and that is kind of how I view myself. Whoever the character is in the song, that's who I try to become.'

DIM ALL THE LIGHTS

Written and recorded by Donna for her 1979 album, *BAD GIRLS* – produced by Bellotte & Giorgio Moroder.

'*Dim All The Lights* I wrote for my husband,' said Donna. 'I think I had had laryngitis, and I sounded like Rod Stewart. I figured I could give it to Rod Stewart to sing, you know. I ran into Rod at something we were doing, and I was so – petrified, that I just couldn't say it. So I wound up singing it myself ... obviously, it was a good thing that I kept it for myself, but I often wonder what would have happened had he recorded it.

The song, which featured the longest sustained note – about 16 seconds – sung by a female artist on a Top 40 hit, was the third single lifted from *BAD GIRLS*.

In the States, both *Dim All The Lights* and *No More Tears (Enough Is Enough)* occupied Top 3 positions on the Hot 100

at the same time – not a situation Donna was happy about, as Neil Bogart had promised he would wait a couple of weeks, before releasing her duet with Barbra Streisand. But, to Donna's annoyance, Bogart went ahead and released the duet immediately.

'Sure enough, *Enough Is Enough* knocked *Dim All The Lights* out of going to the number one spot,' wrote Donna, in her autobiography, *Ordinary Girl: The Journey*. 'It was the first song that I had written the words and music to alone. My personal goal of achieving a number one song as a singer-songwriter had been short-circuited.

'To me, my song was an accomplishment, but to Neil it seemed to be "product", and product only ... that did it for me. I wanted out – out of the company, out of my professional relationship with Neil, out of Beverly Hills.'

The single charted at no.2 on the Hot 100 and no.13 on the R&B chart in the States,

no.3 in Canada, no.14 in New Zealand, no.25 in Germany, no.29 in the UK, no.30 in Ireland and no.70 in Japan.

RIAA Award: Gold (December 1979) = 1 million.

Grammy Award nomination:
Best R&B Vocal Performance, Female.

The song featured in Donna's *The Donna Summer Special* TV movie, which aired in the States on 27th January 1980.

Official Versions:
Album Version.
7" / Single Edit.
12" Version.

1991 Remixes:
The 100 Watt Mix.
The 50 Watt Radio Edit.
The Kilowatt Radio Edit.
The 75 Watt Dub.

Laura Branigan recorded a cover version in 1995.

DINNER WITH GERSHWIN

Written by Brenda Russell, and recorded by Donna for her 1987 album, *ALL SYSTEMS GO* – produced by Richard Perry.

'I was working with Stanley Clark on my new album at the time,' said Brenda Russell. 'Stanley and I put the demo together for *Dinner With Gershwin*, and we sent the demo to David Geffen's publishing company. He was my publisher, actually. Geffen flipped out over it and said, "This song's got to go to Donna Summer." David has a way of making things happen.'

'I had the pleasure of working on the track,' said Russell. 'Richard Perry was the producer, and I got to hang around and put my two cents worth in. I guess you would have called me "Associate Producer". It was a great experience because I've always been a big fan of Donna's. She's an incredibly talented woman with just an amazing voice. I was very excited that she was going to sing the song … she did a fantastic job on that song. It was a real thrill for me to collaborate with her and put that thing together.'

Released as the lead single from the album – in the States, it achieved no.10 on the R&B chart, no.13 on the Hot Dance Club Play chart and no.48 on the Hot 100.

In the UK, Donna promoted the single with her first ever appearance on the popular music show, *Top Of The Pops* – the single peaked at no.13, giving Donna her biggest UK hit since 1979.

The single also charted at no.13 in Ireland, no.34 in the Netherlands and no.39 in Canada.

A 12" picture disc was issued in the UK.

Donna performed the song on several American TV shows in 1987, including *Solid Gold* and *The Tonight Show*.

Donna filmed two music videos to promote the song. In the first, high budget promo, she took a trip through time, meeting some of the people mentioned in the song – George Gershwin, Pablo Picasso, Mahalia Jackson. However, when Donna and Geffen executives viewed the final edit, they all agreed the promo looked amateurish – and scrapped it. A second, low budget, music video was quickly shot and released to promote the single.

Official Versions:
Album Version.
7" / Single Edit.
Extended Version.
Instrumental.

Writer Brenda Russell recorded her own version of the song for her 1990 album, *KISS ME WITH THE WIND*.

DIVA MEGAMIX, THE

Megamix featured on the various artists compilation, *PURE DISCO 2*, released in the UK in 1997 (Polydor 555 263-2).

Songs featured: *Reach Out I'll Be There* (Gloria Gaynor), *Hot Stuff*, *I Found Love (Now That I Found You)* (Love & Kisses), *I Will Survive* (Gloria Gaynor), *I Feel Love* & *Last Dance*.

DO WHAT MOTHER DO

Written by Veit Marvos & Richard Palmer-James, and recorded by the Veit Marvos Red Point Orchestra for a similarly titled album, released in Germany circa 1972-73.

Donna, at this time, was a member of the Veit Marvos Red Point Orchestra.

See also: *Back Off Boogaloo*.

DO YOU HEAR WHAT I HEAR

Festive song written by Noel Regney & Gloria Shayne Baker in 1962 – first recorded by the Harry Simeone Chorale.

Recorded by Donna, as part of *Christmas Medley*, for her 1994 album, *CHRISTMAS SPIRIT* – produced by Michael Omartian.

The medley also featured *What Child Is This* & *Joy To The World*.

Other artists to have recorded versions of the song include Bing Crosby, Glen Campbell, Carpenters, Perry Como, Destiny's Child, Celine Dion, Bob Dylan, Kenny G, Whitney Houston, Mahalia Jackson, Gladys Knight, Johnny Mathis, Andy Williams and Vanessa Williams.

DO YOU WANNA DANCE?

Written and originally recorded, as *Do You Want To Dance?*, by Bobby Freeman in 1958.

Donna performed the song at selected concerts between 1990 and 1992.

Hit Versions:
Beach Boys – no.12 on the Hot 100 in the States in 1965.
Barry Blue – no.7 in the UK in 1973.
Bette Midler – no.17 on the Hot 100 in the States in 1973.

Other artists to have recorded the song include Eddie Cochran, John Lennon, the Ramones, Cliff Richard, Del Shannon, Ray Stevens and T. Rex.

DOES HE LOVE YOU

Written by Sandy Know & Billy Stritch, and recorded by Reba McEntire & Linda Davis for McEntire's 1993 compilation album, *GREATEST HITS VOLUME TWO*.

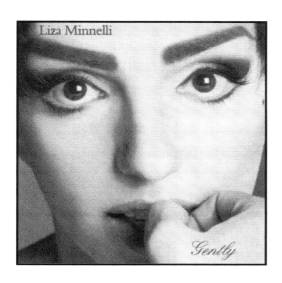

Recorded by Donna, as a duet with Liza Minnelli, for Minnelli's 1996 album, *GENTLY* – produced by Brooks Arthur.

'Liza was very friendly, she was really sweet,' said Donna. 'We had a great, really intimate time. As crazy as we can get, it is nice to know that people can have that level of intimacy with other people. I am that kind of person. I am not very public in a lot of ways. I try to keep it that way. I do press when I have to do it, otherwise I stay out of the press if I can.'

Reba McEntire & Linda Davis took the song to no.1 on the Country chart in the States in 1993, and to no.62 in the UK six years later.

DOMINO

Written by Pete Bellotte, and recorded by Donna for her 1974 album, *LADY OF THE NIGHT* – released in the Netherlands only.

Produced by Pete Bellotte.

DONNA SUMMER 'ETERNITY' MEGAMIX, THE

This 3:41 minute megamix featured on the 2004 various artists compilation, *DISCOMANIA* (Mercury 9821319).

Songs featured: *Hot Stuff*, *I Feel Love* and *Bad Girls* – the latter also featured elements of *Love To Love You Baby*.

DONNA SUMMER MEDLEY

This medley of Donna's hits was recorded by Unlimited Beat in 1997.

The medley featured: *I Feel Love, Love To Love You Baby, Could It Be Magic, Hot Stuff, This Time I Know It's For Real, Love's Unkind, Bad Girls, Try Me, I Know We Can Make It* and *I Don't Wanna Get Hurt*.

Official Versions:
Radio Medley (5:33 minutes).
Extended Medley (10:25 minutes).

DON'T CRY FOR ME ARGENTINA

Written by Andrew Lloyd-Webber & Tim Rice, for the 1978 musical, *Evita* – originally performed by Julie Covington.

Recorded by Donna for her shelved 1981 album, *I'M A RAINBOW* – produced by Pete Bellotte & Giorgio Moroder. The album was finally released in 1996.

Performed by Donna on the TV special, *A 70s Celebration: The Beat Is Back* in 1993 – however, time constraints meant the song was edited out of the final broadcast. The same year, she also performed the song when she appeared as a guest on *Live With Regis & Kathie Lee*.

Released as a promo CD single in the States.

'It's like the song belongs to me now,' said Donna. 'It's almost like it's my song. I know it may sound presumptuous, but I don't mean it to. I just feel such a connection to that song. I feel like so many things have transpired in my life and my career, and I wind back up with the audience, where it all begins.'

Hit Versions:
Julie Covington – no.1 in the UK in 1976.
Shadows (instrumental) – no.5 in the UK in 1978.
Festival – no.72 on the Hot 100 in the States in 1980.
Sinead O'Connor – no.53 in the UK in 1992.
Madonna – no.3 in the UK, and no.17 on the Hot 100 in the States, in 1996.
Mike Flowers Pops – no.30 in the UK in 1996.
Glee Cast – no.67 in the UK in 2011.

Other artists who have recorded the song include Tina Arena, Joan Baez, Shirley Bassey, Cilla Black, the Carpenters, Petula Clark, Judy Collins, Barbara Dickson, Tom Jones, Olivia Newton-John and Elaine Paige.

DON'T RAIN ON MY PARADE

Written by Bob Merrill & Jule Styne for the 1964 musical, *Funny Girl* – performed by Barbra Streisand.

Donna added the song to the set list for her Eyelash Tour in 2010.

DON'T WANNA WORK

See: *I Don't Wanna Work That Hard.*

DOROTHY

Written by H. Prestwood, and recorded by former model Twiggy for her shelved 1979 album, *HEAVEN IN MY EYES* – produced by Donna & Juergen Koppers.

DOWN, DEEP INSIDE
(THEME FROM 'THE DEEP')

Written by Donna (lyrics) & John Barry (music), and recorded by Donna as the theme song for the 1977 film, *The Deep*.

The film, based on Peter Benchley's novel of the same title, was directed by Peter Yates, and starred Robert Shaw, Jacqueline Bisset & Nick Nolte.

The album also featured *Theme From 'The Deep' (Down, Deep Inside) (A Love Song)* and an instrumental version of the song.

Released as a single in most countries, but excluding the USA – it did, however, achieve no.3 on the Hot Dance Club Play chart.

The single charted at no.5 in Belgium & the UK, no.6 in the Netherlands, no.10 in

Ireland, no.16 in South Africa, no.25 in Germany and no.70 in Australia.

BPI Award: Silver (October 1977) = 250,000.

B-side of the *I Feel Love* 12" single in the States

Golden Globe nomination:
   Best Original Song.

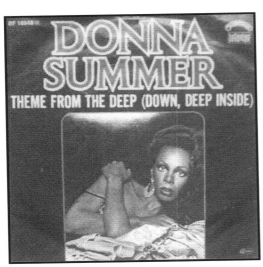

An extended, 6:11 minute version of the song was included on the CD reissue of Donna's album, *LIVE AND MORE*, replacing *MacArthur Park Suite*, which was too long to be included on a single CD reissue.

Official Versions:
Album Version.
Album Version (A Love Song).
Instrumental.
Extended Version.

DREAM-A-LOT'S THEME
(I WILL LIVE FOR LOVE)

Written by Donna & Nathan DiGesare, and recorded by Donna for the 2003 compilation, *THE JOURNEY – THE BEST OF* – produced by Moroder.

Released as a promo 12" single in the States – it achieved no.20 on Billboard's Hot Dance Club Play chart.

The song is registered with the American Society of Composers, Authors & Publishers (ASCAP) under the title 'Dreamway Express'.

DREAMCATCHER

Written by Donna & M. Hanna, and recorded by Donna for the 2000 soundtrack album, *NATURALLY NATIVE* – produced by James Marienthal.

DRIVIN' DOWN BRAZIL

Written by Donna with Danielle Brisebois & Greg Kurstin, and recorded by Donna for her 2008 album, *CRAYONS* – produced by Kurstin.

Donna wrote the song after seeing a man getting into a low-ride Bonneville on Brazil Street, Miami. 'I just made up this story,' she said. 'He's on Brazil Street and he's headed straight down to the actual country from there. It's Friday night and he's going to see his girlfriend.

He's envisioning her and he's got this long drive ahead of him.'

The song is also registered with the American Society of Composers, Authors & Publishers (ASCAP) under the title 'Brazil'.

DU BIST DAS LICHT DER WELT (LIGHT OF THE WORLD)

Written by Stephen Schwartz & John-Michael Tebelak for the musical, *Godspell* – premiered in New York City on 24th February 1971.

Donna appeared – credited as Donna Gaines – in the Austrian production of the musical in 1971, and was part of the cast who performed this song, in German, on stage and on the cast album.

ELIZABETH RECITATIVE

Written by Michael & Stormie Omartian, and recorded by Donna – playing the part of Elizabeth – for the 2000 cast album, *CHILD OF THE PROMISE*.

The album, which was sub-titled 'A Musical Story Celebrating the Birth of Jesus', was produced by Michael Omartian.

END OF THE WEEK

Written by Pete Bellotte & Sylvester Levay, and recorded by Donna for her shelved 1981 album, *I'M A RAINBOW* – produced by Bellotte & Giorgio Moroder.

The album was finally released in 1996.

ENDLESS SUMMER MEDLEY

Medley of *Dim All The Lights*, *Hot Stuff*, *Bad Girls* & *Last Dance* – featured on the B-side of Donna's 1994 single, *Any Way At All*.

A music video, aimed at promoting Donna's *ENDLESS SUMMER* compilation, featured a montage of clips from other music videos, concert performances and the film, *Thank God It's Friday*.

EYES

Written by Donna & Michael Omartian, and recorded by Donna for her 1984 album, *CATS WITHOUT CLAWS* – produced by Omartian.

Released as a single in select countries – it registered at no.97 in the UK, but failed to chart anywhere else.

FACE THE MUSIC

Written by Donna with Bruce Sudano & Michael Omartian, and recorded by Donna during the sessions for her 1984 album, *CATS WITHOUT CLAWS* – produced by Omartian.

The song failed to make the final track listing for the album, but was released as the B-side of *Supernatural Love* in the States.

Featured as a bonus track on the remastered released of the album *CATS WITHOUT CLAWS*, as part of *THE CD COLLECTION* box-set, in 2014.

FAIRY TALE HIGH

Written by Donna with Giorgio Moroder & Pete Bellotte, and recorded by Donna for her 1977 album, *ONCE UPON A*

TIME – produced by Moroder & Bellotte.

Released as the album's lead single in Germany – failed to chart.

A live version, recorded at the Universal Amphitheatre, Los Angeles, featured on Donna's 1978 album, *LIVE AND MORE*.

FAME (THE GAME)

Written by Donna & Toby Gad, and recorded by Donna for her 2008 album, *CRAYONS* – produced by Gad.

'It's critical, but in a funny way,' stated Donna. 'There's a certain amount of tongue-in-cheekiness about it … the song isn't negatively critical, it's meant to shine the light on what it is and just question, "Is this what we should all be struggling to have?" Well, no.'

The single gave Donna her third no.1 from her *CRAYONS* album, and her 15th in total, on Billboard's Hot Dance Club Play chart.

Official Versions:
Album Version.
Dave Aude Radio.
Dave Aude Club.
Dave Aude Dub.
Dave Aude Dub Instrumental.
Dave Chase Radio.
Dave Chase Full Vocal.
Dave Chase Dub.
Dave Chase Instrumental.
Extended Ultimix Album Version.
Ralphi Rosario Radio.
Ralphi Rosario Club.
Ralphi Rosario Dub.
Ralphi Radio.

FAMILY, THE

Written by Giorgio Moroder & Pete Bellotte, and recorded by Roberta Kelly for her 1976 album, *TROUBLE MAKER* – produced by Moroder & Bellotte, with backing vocals by Donna.

FASCINATION

Written by David Tyson & Eddie Schwartz, and recorded by Donna for her

1987 album, *ALL SYSTEMS GO* – produced by Harold Faltermeyer.

Released as a promo 7" single in Canada, with *All Systems Go* on the B-side.

FASTER AND FASTER TO NOWHERE

Written by Donna with Giorgio Moroder & Pete Bellotte, and recorded by Donna for her 1977 album, *ONCE UPON A TIME* – produced by Moroder & Bellotte.

A live version, recorded at the Universal Amphitheatre, Los Angeles, featured on Donna's 1978 album, *LIVE AND MORE*.

FINALE (WE STARVE LOOK / FLESH FAILURES)

Written James Rado & Gerome Ragni (book and lyrics) & Galt MacDermot (music) for the controversial 'tribal love-rock' musical, *Hair*.

Donna appeared in the German production of the musical in 1968, titled *Haare*, and was part of the cast who performed this song on stage and on the German cast album.

FORGIVE ME

Written by Dony McGuire & Reba Rambo, and recorded by Donna for her 1984 album, *CATS WITHOUT CLAWS* – produced by Michael Omartian.

Grammy Award:
Best Inspirational Performance.

FRED ASTAIRE

Written by Donna with Keith Diamond, Anthony Smith & Donna Wyant, and recorded by Donna for her 1991 album, *MISTAKEN IDENTITY* – produced by Diamond.

FREEZE

Written by Donna with Bruce Sudano & Anthony Smith – registered with the American Society of Composers, Authors & Publishers (ASCAP), but never released.

FRIENDS

Written by Giorgio Moroder & Pete Bellotte, and recorded by Donna for her 1974 album, *LADY OF THE NIGHT* – released in the Netherlands only.

Produced by Pete Bellotte.

FRIENDS UNKNOWN

Written by Donna with Keith Diamond, Anthony Smith & Vanessa Smith, and recorded by Donna for her 1991 album, *MISTAKEN IDENTITY* – produced by Diamond.

Tom Bradley, L.A.'s Mayor, declared 18th March 1992 as 'Donna Summer Day' in Los Angeles, as she was honoured with a star on Hollywood's famous 'Walk of Fame'. After singing *Friends Unknown* for over 600 fans at the event, Donna stated: 'I wrote it for the fans as a thank you.'

FROM A DISTANCE

Written by Julie Gold, and recorded by Nanci Griffith for her 1987 album, *LONE STAR STATE OF MIND*.

Recorded by Donna, with Nanci Griffith & Raul Malo, for the official 1996 German Olympic album, *ONE VOICE*

(MCA MCAD 11403) – produced by Michael Omartian.

Hit Versions:
Bette Midler – no.2 on the Hot 100 in the States in 1990, and no.6 in the UK in 1991.
Cliff Richard – no.11 in the UK in 1990.

FUGE / FUGUE

Written by Gary William Friedman & Will Holt for the musical, *The Me Nobody Knows* – premiered at the Orpheum Theater, New York, on 18th May 1970.

Donna appeared – credited as Gayne Pierre – in the German production of the musical in 1970, titled *Ich Bin Ich*, and was part of the cast who performed this song on stage and on the German cast album.

Donna was also part of the cast who performed the song on the English language version of the cast album.

Original song title: *Fugue For Four Girls*.

FULL OF EMPTINESS

Written by Giorgio Moroder & Pete Bellotte, and recorded by Donna for her 1974 album, *LADY OF THE NIGHT* – released in the Netherlands only.

Produced by Pete Bellotte.

The track also featured on Donna's second album, *LOVE TO LOVE YOU BABY* – side 2 of the album opened with the song, and closed with a reprise.

Omitted from the CD issue of the *LADY OF THE NIGHT* album, as it was available on *LOVE TO LOVE YOU BABY*.

B-side of *The Hostage* in Germany.

FUN STREET

Written by Veit Marvos & Richard Palmer-James, and recorded by the Veit Marvos Red Point Orchestra for a similarly titled album, released in Germany circa 1972-73.

Donna, at this time, was a member of the Veit Marvos Red Point Orchestra.

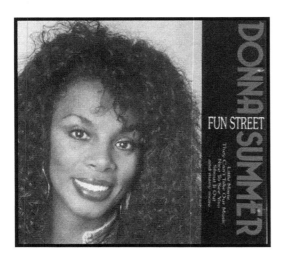

See also: *Back Off Boogaloo*.

GEORGIA ON MY MIND

Written by Hoagy Carmichael & Stuart Gorrell, and originally recorded by Hoagy Carmichael & His Orchestra in 1930 – best known for the Ray Charles version.

Prompted by the 2004 biopic, *Ray*, which starred Jamie Foxx as Ray Charles, Donna performed the song at many of her concerts in late 2004 and early 2005.

Hit Versions:
Ray Charles – no.1 on the Hot 100 and no.3 on the R&B chart in the States, and no.24 in the UK, in 1960.
Willie Nelson – no.1 on the Country chart and no.84 on the Hot 100 in the States in 1978.

Other artists to have recorded the song include Louis Armstrong, Michael Bolton, James Brown, Coldplay, Ella Fitzgerald, Billie Holiday, Tom Jones, Gladys Knight, Jerry Lee Lewis, Dean Martin, Glenn Miller, Van Morrison, Jo Stafford, the Stylistics, Usher, Fats Waller and Grover Washington, Jr..

GET ETHNIC

Written by Donna with Keith Diamond, Paul Chiten, Larry Henley & Anthony Smith, and recorded by Donna for her

1991 album, *MISTAKEN IDENTITY* – produced by Diamond.

GIRL FROM IPANEMA, THE

Bossa nova song written by Antonio Carlos Jobim & Vinicius de Moraes, with English lyrics by Norman Gimbel – first recorded by Pery Ribeiro in 1962.

Donna performed the song at some of her concerts between 1990 and 1992, including dates in Brazil (Ipanema being a region of Rio de Janeiro).
Stan Getz, with Astrud & João Gilberto, took the song to no.5 on the Hot 100 in the States, and to no.29 in the UK, in 1964.

GIVE ME MUSIC

Written by Donna with Michael Omartian & Jay Graydon – registered with the American Society of Composers, Authors & Publishers (ASCAP), but never released.

GOD BLESS AMERICA

Patriotic American song written by Irving Berlin in 1918 – revised twenty years later.

As a tribute to John F. Kennedy, his wife Carolyn and his sister-in-law Lauren Bessette, who all died in a plane crash on 16th July 1999, Donna performed the song during her concert at New York's Jones Beach seven days later.

Donna performed the song during the Major League Baseball's World Series Game 2, held on 24th October 2004.

GOD BLESS THE CHILD

Written by Billie Holiday & Arthur Herzog, Jr. in 1939, and originally recorded by Holiday.

Donna performed the song on her Silver Girl Tour in 1986.

Numerous artists have recorded the song, including Tony Bennett, Blood, Sweat & Tears, Eva Cassidy, Billy Eckstine & Linda Ronstadt, Ella Fitzgerald, Aretha Franklin, Crystal Gayle, Gladys Knight, Frankie Laine, Lou Rawls, Liza Minnelli, Diana Ross, the Simpsons, Barbra Streisand and Stevie Wonder.

GOOD LOVIN'

Written by Rudy Clark & Arthur Resnick, and originally recorded by the Olympics in 1965.

Donna & Brooklyn Dreams performed the song as part of a 1960s medley, when Donna hosted *The Midnight Special* TV show – aired in the States on 26th May 1978.

Other songs in the medley: *So Fine, Maybe*, *My Girl*, *My Guy*, The *Way You Do The Things You Do*, *I Heard It Through The Grapevine* and *Heat Wave*.

Donna performed the same medley on her Bad Girls tour in 1979.

Hit Versions:
Olympics – no.81 on the Hot 100 in the States in 1965.
Young Rascals – no.1 on the Hot 100 in the States in 1966.

Other artists to have recorded the song include Tommy James & The Shondells, Herbie Mann, Bobby McFerrin and the Who.

GOTCHA ON LOVE

Written by Donna & Bruce Roberts.

Donna mentioned the song, when she appeared on *Larry King Live* on 7th December 2003. 'We have actually just wrote another song called *Gotcha On Love*,' she revealed, 'and I think it's going to be on my next album.'

Remains unreleased.

GOTTA HAVE A DRESS

Written by Donna with Bruce Sudano, Al Kasha & Michael Omartian, for the as yet unpublished play Donna worked on with Sudano, Kasha & Omartian, *Ordinary Girl* – remains unreleased.

GRAMMY NOMINATIONS MEDLEY

This medley of Grammy nominated songs was performed by Donna, with Kenny Rogers, when they appeared at the Grammy Awards, staged at the Shrine Auditorium, Los Angeles, on 27th February 1980.

The medley featured: *Reunited* (Donna & Kenny), *Honesty* (Kenny), *I Will Survive* (Donna), *Chuck E's In Love* (Donna), *Minute By Minute* (Donna & Kenny), *After The Love Has Gone* (Donna & Kenny), *She Believes In Me* (Kenny) & *What A Fool Believes* (Donna & Kenny).

GRAND ILLUSION

Written by Donna & Giorgio Moroder, and recorded by Donna for her 1980 album, *THE WANDERER* – produced by Moroder & Pete Bellotte.

B-side of *Cold Love*.

GREATEST LOVE OF ALL

Written by Michael Masser & Linda Creed, for the 1977 film *The Greatest*, a film biography of the heavyweight boxer, Mohammed Ali – at the time, Linda Creed was battling breast cancer, and her lyrics describe her emotions, on being a young mother fighting a terminal illness (she died in 1986, aged 36). The song was originally recorded by George Benson.

Donna performed the song in concert at select dates during her 2004-05 dates.

On 2nd April 2005, Donna attended *Celebrity Fight Night* – she performed *Greatest Love Of All* and dedicated it to Mohammad Ali.

Hit Versions:
George Benson – no.2 on the R&B chart and no.24 on the Hot 100 in the States, and no.27 in the UK, in 1977.
Whitney Houston – no.1 on the Hot 100 and no.3 on the R&B chart in the States, and no.8 in the UK, in 1986.

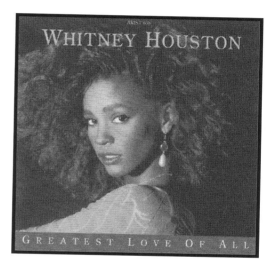

GUILTY

Written by Donna with Michael Omartian & Jay Graydon – registered with the American Society of Composers, Authors & Publishers (ASCAP), but never released.

HAPPILY EVER AFTER

Written by Donna with Giorgio Moroder & Pete Bellotte, and recorded by Donna for her 1977 album, *ONCE UPON A TIME* – produced by Moroder & Bellotte.

HAPPINESS IN THE WORLD

Written and recorded by Tom Winter for his 1976 album, *WINTERFERENCE* – produced by Alf Schwegler, with backing vocals by Donna.

HARK! THE HERALD ANGELS SING

This is a popular Christian hymn written by Charles Wesley – it was first published in *Hymns And Sacred Poems* in 1739.

Performed by Donna, as a medley with *Silent Night* and *O Come All Ye Faithful*, when she appeared on *Bandstand* on 22nd December 1984.

Numerous artists have recorded the song, including Mariah Carey, Johnny Cash, Nat King Cole, Neil Diamond, Amy Grant, Mahalia Jackson, Frank Sinatra and Andy Williams.

HÄTT ICH EINE MILLION DOLLARS (IF I HAD A MILLION DOLLARS)

Written by Gary William Friedman & Will Holt for the musical, *The Me Nobody Knows* – premiered at the Orpheum Theater, New York, on 18th May 1970.

Donna appeared – credited as Gayne Pierre – in the German production of the musical in 1970, titled *Ich Bin Ich*, and was part of the cast who performed this song on stage and on the German cast album.

See also: *If I Had A Million Dollars*.

HEAL THEM

Donna sang this Christian hymn at an Easter Telethon Benefit concert in the early 1980s.

HEAVEN IN MY EYES

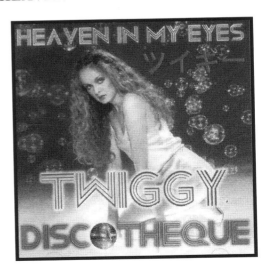

Song former model Twiggy recorded for her shelved 1979 album with the same title – produced by Donna & Juergen Koppers.

The album was finally released in 2007, and also included an up-dated remix of the title track by OUTpsiDER.

HE IS YOUR BROTHER

Written by Benny Andersson & Björn Ulvæus, and recorded by Björn & Benny, Agnetha & Anni-Frid/Frida (*aka* ABBA), for their 1973 album, *RING RING*.

Donna, along with other participating artists, backed ABBA as they sang the song at the opening of *The Music For UNICEF Concert: A Gift Of Song*, staged at the United Nations Assembly, New York, on 9th January 1979 – the concert was televised the following day.

Other featured artists at the charity concert were the Bee Gees, Rita Coolidge, John Denver, Earth, Wind & Fire, Andy Gibb, Kris Kristofferson, Olivia Newton-John and Rod Stewart.

See also: *Mimi's Song*, *Put A Little Love In Your Heart*.

HEAT WAVE

Written by Brian Holland, Lamont Dozier & Edward Holland, and recorded by Martha & the Vandellas for their 1963 album with the same title.

The song is also known by the title, *(Love Is Like A) Heat Wave*.

Donna & Brooklyn Dreams performed the song as part of a 1960s medley, when Donna hosted *The Midnight Special* TV show – aired in the States on 26th May 1978.

Other songs in the medley: *So Fine*, *Maybe*, *My Girl*, *My Guy*, The *Way You Do The Things You Do*, *Good Lovin'* and *I Heard It Through The Grapevine*.

Donna performed the same medley on her Bad Girls tour in 1979.

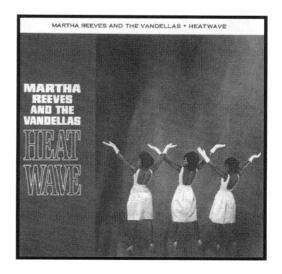

Hit Versions:

Martha & the Vandellas – no.1 on the R&B chart and no.4 on the Hot 100 in the States in 1963.

Linda Ronstadt – no.5 on the Hot 100 in the States in 1975.

HEAVEN KNOWS

Written by Donna with Giorgio Moroder & Pete Bellotte, and recorded by Donna – as part of *MacArthur Park Suite* – for her 1978 album, *LIVE AND MORE* – produced by Moroder & Bellotte.

Featured Brooklyn Dreams – the lead male vocals were by the trio's Joe Esposito.

The song also featured on Brooklyn Dreams' 1979 album, *SLEEPLESS NIGHTS* – however, on this version Donna and Joe Esposito sang each other's lines, as compared with the version on Donna's album.

As part of *MacArthur Park Suite*, the song went to no.1 on the Hot Dance Club Play chart in the States. As a stand alone

single, it achieved no.4 on the Hot and no.10 on the R&B chart.

Outside the USA, the single charted at no.2 in Canada, no.14 in New Zealand, no.15 in Australia and no.34 in the UK.

Donna, with Brooklyn Dreams, performed the song when she appeared on *The Midnight Special* TV show in 1979.

RIAA Award: Gold (March 1979) = 1 million.
Official Versions:
Album Version.
Album Version (Brooklyn Dreams).
7" / Single Edit.
12" Extended Version.

HEAVEN'S JUST A WHISPER AWAY

Written by Keith Diamond, Larry Henley & Anthony Smith, and recorded by Donna for her 1991 album, *MISTAKEN IDENTITY* – produced by Diamond.

Donna performed the song on the *Showtime At The Apollo* TV show in 1991.

HE'S A REBEL

Written by Donna with Michael Omartian & Jay Graydon, and recorded by Donna for her 1983 album, *SHE WORKS HARD FOR THE MONEY* – produced by Omartian.

Released as a single in Spain.

Grammy Award:
Best Inspirational Performance.

HIGHWAY RUNNER

Written by Donna & Giorgio Moroder, and recorded by Donna for her shelved 1981 album, *I'M A RAINBOW* – produced by Moroder & Pete Bellotte.

The album was finally released in 1996.

Featured on the 1982 soundtrack album, *FAST TIMES AT RIDGEMOUNT HIGH*.

HOSTAGE, THE

Written by Giorgio Moroder & Pete Bellotte, and recorded by Donna for her 1974 album, *LADY OF THE NIGHT* – released in the Netherlands only.

Produced by Pete Bellotte.

Moroder & Bellotte placed the song with Global Records in Munich, Germany. 'Giorgio Moroder had offered the production to virtually every other record company and couldn't get a deal,' said Peter Kirsten, Global's owner. 'It was later I found out that we really were their last chance. However, I immediately believed in the recording, and we made a deal for three singles, with additional album options.

'I signed Donna Summer because I was genuinely optimistic about her prospects, and reckoned I could almost smell success for this particular single. You don't always sense these things right away, but this time everything worked out. I had this feeling of excitement and those butterflies in the stomach, like when you meet a beautiful woman for the first time.'

Released as a single in Belgium, France, Germany and the Netherlands, where it took off first – it rose to no.2 on the Belgian and Dutch singles charts.

The single looked like taking off in Germany as well, before Palestinian terrorists took 11 Israeli athletes hostage at the Summer Olympics, which were being staged in Munich.

Tragically, all 11 athletes were killed – so, because of its title, Donna's single was immediately removed from playlists at German radio stations, and planned TV appearances were cancelled. Unsurprisingly, with no promotion whatsoever, the single failed to chart.

A demo 7" single was released in the UK.

Donna performed the song on two episodes of the Dutch musical comedy show, *Van Oekel's Discohoek* (*Van Oekel's Disco Corner*), hosted by Dolf Brouwers as Sjef van Oekel. The two episodes – 4 and 5 – aired on Dutch TV on 1st & 22nd August 1974.

Donna's performance of the song was also featured in the Dutch TV film, *Van Oekel Blikt Terug* (*Van Oekel Looks Back*), which aired on Dutch TV on 31st December 1974.

For all its success, in a 1995 interview Donna said, '*The Hostage* was an awful song. It was one of my first Giorgio Moroder productions. I'd have to sue

somebody if they ever released it in America!'

HOT STUFF

Written by Pete Bellotte, Harold Faltermeyer & Keith Forsey, and recorded by Donna for her 1979 album, *BAD GIRLS* – produced by Bellotte & Giorgio Moroder.

Featured a guitar solo by Jeff 'Skunk' Baxter, formerly of the Doobie Brothers and Steely Dan.

Lead single from the album – it gave Donna her second no.1 on the Hot 100 in the States, rising to the top when her *BAD GIRLS* album was atop the albums chart.

With *Bad Girls*, the single also gave Donna her eighth no.1 on the Hot Dance Club Play chart, and peaked at no.3 on the R&B chart.

Outside the USA, the single achieved no.1 in Australia, Canada & Switzerland, no.2 in Norway & Sweden, no.3 in Austria & New Zealand, no.4 in Ireland, no.5 in Germany, no.7 in Belgium & Japan, no.11 in the UK, no.14 in the Netherlands and no.18 in Zimbabwe.

The single was released as a 12" single in France on translucent blue, green, orange, red and yellow vinyl.

RIAA Award: Platinum (August 1979) = 2 million.

No.9 best-selling single of 1979 in the USA.

Grammy Award:
Best Rock Vocal Performance, Female.

Donna was the first woman and the first African-American artist to win a Grammy in the 'Rock' category.

The song featured in Donna's *The Donna Summer Special* TV movie, which aired in the States on 27th January 1980.

A live version, recorded at the Hammerstein Ballroom, New York, in February 1999, was included on the 1999 album, *LIVE & MORE ENCORE!*

Ranked at no.67 on *Billboard*'s 'Greatest Songs Of All-Time' listing.

Ranked at no.104 on *Rolling Stone* magazine's '500 Greatest Songs Of All-Time'.

Official Versions:
Album Version.
7" / Single Edit.
Live Version.

The song was used in an advertising campaign for Burger King in the early 1990s, and was featured in the popular 1997 film, *The Full Monty*.

Arsenal Football Club recorded a version of the song, sampling the original and changing some lyrics, in the lead up to

the FA Cup Final in 1998 – the single achieved no.9 in the UK.

HOW GREAT THOU ART

Christian hymn based on a Swedish poem written by Carl Gustav Boberg in 1885 – it was translated into English by a British missionary, Stuart K. Hine.

Performed by Donna, with *A Song For You*, on the first leg of her Once Upon A Time Tour in 1977-78.

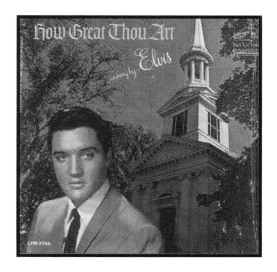

Donna also performed the song, as a medley with *Amazing Grace* and

Operator, on her Rainbow Tour in 1984 and her Silver Girl Tour in 1986.

Artists to have recorded the song include Susan Boyle, Charlie Daniels, Tennessee Ernie Ford, Elvis Presley, Roy Rogers, and Carrie Underwood.

HOW I FEEL

Written by Gary William Friedman & Will Holt for the musical, *The Me Nobody Knows* – premiered at the Orpheum Theater, New York, on 18th May 1970.

Donna appeared – credited as Gayne Pierre – in the German production of the musical in 1970, titled *Ich Bin Ich*, and was part of the cast who performed this song on the English language version of the cast album.

I BELIEVE IN JESUS

Written and recorded by Donna for her 1980 album, *THE WANDERER* – produced by Giorgio Moroder & Pete Bellotte.

Grammy Award nomination:
Best Inspirational Performance.

I BELIEVE (IN YOU)

Written by Harold Faltermeyer & Keith Forsey, and recorded by Donna as a duet with Joe 'Bean' Esposito for her shelved 1981 album, *I'M A RAINBOW* – produced by Giorgio Moroder & Pete Bellotte.

The album was finally released in 1996.

I CANNOT BE SILENT

Written by Michael & Stormie Omartian, and recorded by Donna with Crystal Lewis (as Elizabeth & Mary, respectively) for the 2000 original cast album, *CHILD OF THE PROMISE* – produced by Michael Omartian.

I CAN'T STOP LOVING YOU

Written and originally recorded by Don Gibson in 1957, but best known for the version recorded by Ray Charles in 1962.

Donna performed the song, with the host, as part of a country medley, when she appeared as a guest on the *Eddie Rabbit Special* in 1982 – she also sang *Stand By Your Man,* plus *Oh Lonesome Me* with Eddie Rabbit.

Ray Charles took the song to no.1 on the Hot 100 and R&B chart in the States, and to no.1 in the UK.

Other artists to have recorded the song include Ella Fitzgerald, Connie Francis,

Jerry Lee Lewis, Van Morrison, Ricky Nelson, Elvis Presley and Frank Sinatra.

I DO BELIEVE (I FELL IN LOVE)

Written and recorded by Donna for her 1983 album, *SHE WORKS HARD FOR THE MONEY* – produced by Michael Omartian.

B-side of *She Works Hard For The Money*.

I DON'T WANNA GET HURT

Written by Mike Stock, Matt Aitken & Pete Waterman, and recorded by Donna for her 1989 album, *ANOTHER PLACE AND TIME* – produced by Stock, Aitken & Waterman.

Donna admitted the song wasn't one of her favourites. 'It's not that I didn't like the song, it was a cute song – I just didn't think that it was mature enough for me,' she explained. 'I just felt like this is a song for a little kid to sing, and I felt kind of awkward doing it. There's no real lyric to the song. I mean there is, but not really, so I had a hard time promoting that song because I felt like it was just not right for me. But it did okay.'

The song wasn't released as a single in the States, but gave Donna another Top 10 hit in the UK, where it achieved no.7. The single also charted at no.6 in Belgium, no.25 in Germany and no.30 in the Netherlands.

Official Versions:
Album Version.
7" Remix.
Pete Hammond Original 12" Version.
Phil Harding 12" Version.
Instrumental.

I DON'T WANNA WORK THAT HARD

Written by Donna – she revealed, on her 1999 home video *Live & More Encore!*, she wrote the song on the road in Brazil.

Donna performed the song on her Mid Summer Nights Dream Tour in 1996-97, and at select dates on more recent tours.

Featured on Donna's 1999 home video, *Live & More Encore!* – recorded at Manhattan's Hammerstein Ballroom on 28th February 1999, on which it was listed as simply *Don't Wanna Work*.

I FEEL LOVE

Written by Donna with Pete Bellotte & Giorgio Moroder, and recorded by Donna for her 1977 album, *I REMEMBER YESTERDAY* – produced by Bellotte & Moroder.

'In 1977,' said Donna, 'the songwriter and producer Pete Bellotte and I were working at my house in California. We wrote an entire song – the lyrics to which I don't have anymore – and sang it to the melody of *I Feel Love*. But I thought, "No, the song is too crowded. The song is like a chant – we need to let it breathe." So we started removing elements, then stripped the lyrics back to one line – *I Feel Love* – and it took off.'

'Each song on Donna's *I REMEMBER YESTERDAY*,' said Moroder, 'featured an old sound from the forties, fifties, sixties and seventies. I wanted to end the album with a track that sounded like it was from the future …

'It was never my intention for Donna to sing *I Feel Love* the way she ultimately did. In the studio, she started to fool around and sing it in that high voice, and it turned out to be just the perfect thing for the song.'

Initially, in the States, the song was released as the B-side of *Can't We Just Sit Down (And Talk It Over)*, as the record company felt it was 'too techno'. However, it was agreed if the A-side didn't take off – which it didn't – the two songs would be flipped.

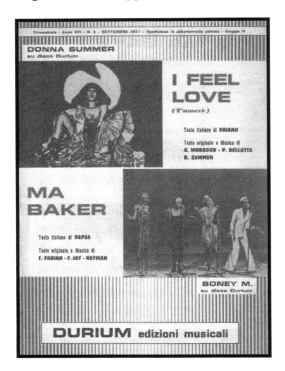

In the States, the single gave Donna her fourth no.1 on the Hot Dance Club Play chart, and achieved no.6 on the Hot 100 and no.9 on the R&B chart.

The single hit no.1 in Australia, Austria, Belgium, Ireland, the Netherlands & the UK, no.2 on Canada, New Zealand & Switzerland, no.3 in Germany, no.5 in Sweden, no.6 in South Africa, no.8 in Norway, no9 in Zimbabwe and no.33 in France.

'I was ecstatic when it got to no.1 (in the UK),' said Donna, speaking in 2008, 'not least because the song was so unusual and, although it sounds very simple, I had put a lot of work into it. I still love it now and my dancers and backing singers, who are pretty young, are hearing it for the first time – and they're digging it.'

RIAA Award: Gold (November 1977) = 1 million.

BPI Award: Gold (August 1977) = 500,000.

No.7 best-selling single of 1977 in the UK.

A live version, recorded at the Universal Amphitheatre, Los Angeles, featured on Donna's 1978 album, *LIVE AND MORE*.

A second live version, recorded at the Hammerstein Ballroom, New York, in February 1999, was included on the 1999 album, *LIVE & MORE ENCORE!*

Official Versions:
Album Version.
7" / Single Edit.
12" Mix.
Live Version (1978).
Live Version (1999).

7" / Single Edit (different – as featured on several compilations, including *ENDLESS SUMMER & THE JOURNEY: THE BEST OF DONNA SUMMER*).

The single was remixed in 1978 by Patrick Cowley – he created a 15:45 minute remix that, initially, was only available as an acetate.

In 1980, Cowley's remix was released as a promo 12" single, serviced to DJs who were members of Disconet only, titled: *I*

Feel Love / I Feel Megalove: The Patrick Cowley Mega Mix.

Demand for Cowley's remix was so high, in 1982 a decision was finally taken to make it available commercially – it charted at no.18 in Ireland and no.21 in the UK.

Official 1982 Remixes:
Mega Mix (15:45 minutes).
Mega Edit (8:50 minutes).
7" Edit Part 1.
7" Edit Part 2.

The song was re-recorded / remixed again in 1995. Eddie Gordon, of Manifesto Records, had to persuade Donna to re-record her vocals for these remixes, as the original master tapes had been lost in a fire at Casablanca Records. Donna eventually agreed, but only after Gordon agreed she and her husband Bruce Sudano could approve the new recordings.

'I remember hearing *I Feel Love* for the first time when I was seventeen, in a disco,' said Gordon. 'The power of it blew me away then.'

The 1995 version took the song into the UK's Top 10 for a second time, when it rose to no.8 – the single also charted at no.16 in Finland, no.24 in Ireland and no.28 in the Netherlands.

Official 1995 Remixes:
12" Masters At Work Mix.
Masters At Work 86th St. Mix.
Masters At Work Hard Dub.
Rollo & Sister Bliss Monster Mix.
Rollo & Sister Bliss Monster Mix –
  Radio Edit.
Rollo & Sister Bliss Tuff Dub.
Summer '77 Re-EQ '95.

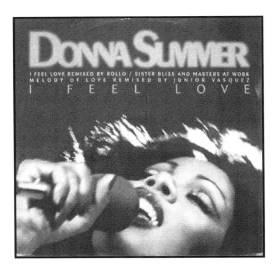

Ranked no.76 on VH1's '100 Greatest Dance Songs' listing in October 2000.

The song was inducted into the Dance Music Hall Of Fame on 20th September 2004. Donna was also inducted, as an artist, but she was unable to attend the ceremony – she was represented by her youngest daughter, Amanda.

Bronski Beat & Marc Almond recorded a cover version, as a medley with John Leyton's hit, *Johnny Remember Me*, in 1985 – the single, which also featured elements of *Love To Love You Baby*, charted at no.3 in the UK.

Numerous artists have sampled the song over the years, including Madonna on *Future Lovers*, from her 2005 album, *CONFESSIONS ON A DANCE FLOOR*.

I FOUND A STAR

Written by Donna with Bruce Sudano, Al Kasha & Michael Omartian, for the as yet unpublished play Donna worked on with Sudano, Kasha & Omartian, *Ordinary Girl* – remains unreleased.

I FOUND THE ANSWER

Christian gospel song written by Johnny Lange in 1957 – originally recorded by George Beverly Shea.

This is the first song Donna ever performed in public, when she was just 10 years old – she sang it at the Grant A.M.E. Church in Boston, Massachusetts, when her mother volunteered her to take the place of the choir's soloist, who was ill.

'I opened my mouth to sing and this voice came rushing out,' Donna recalled. 'It sort of knocked everyone out of the pews. When I looked up, everyone in the whole church was crying.'

Donna performed the song, backed by a gospel choir, on her *Donna Summer Special* TV show, which aired on ABC TV in the States on 27th January 1980.

I GOT IT BAD (AND THAT AIN'T GOOD)

Written by Duke Ellington & Paul Francis Webster, and recorded live by Donna at the Universal Amphitheatre,

Los Angeles, as part of her *My Man Medley* – featured on her 1978 album, *LIVE AND MORE*.

The medley also featured *The Man I Love* and *Some Of These Days*.

Other artists to have recorded the song include Louis Armstrong, Count Basie, Tony Bennett, Cher, Nat King Cole, Doris Day, Ella Fitzgerald, Carly Simon, Nina Simone and Frank Sinatra.

I GOT YOUR LOVE

Written by Donna & Bruce Roberts, and recorded by Donna in 2003 – produced by Peter Stengaard.

The song was first heard playing in the background of the TV show, *Sex And The City*. It featured in Season 6, Episode 7, titled *The Post-It Always Strikes Twice* – the episode aired on 3rd August 2003 in the States.

Released as a single in the States in 2005, and featured on Donna's 2007

compilation, *THE BEST OF – THE MILLENNIUM COLLECTION VOLUME 2*.

The single achieved no.4 on Billboard's Hot Dance Club Play chart in the States, but it failed to enter the Hot 100 or R&B chart.

Official Versions:
Original Radio Edit.
Eddie Baez Extended Vocal.
Eddie Baez Vocal Anthem Mix.
Eddie Baez Dub/Instrumental.
L.E.X. Club.
L.E.X. Radio Edit.
Ralphi Rosario Extended Vocal.
Ralphi Rosario Dub.

I HEARD IT THROUGH THE GRAPEVINE

Written by Norman Whitfield & Barrett Strong, and originally recorded by Smokey Robinson & The Miracles for their 1968 album, *SPECIAL OCCASION*.

Donna & Brooklyn Dreams performed the song as part of a 1960s medley, when Donna hosted *The Midnight Special* TV show – aired in the States on 26th May 1978.

Other songs in the medley: *So Fine, Maybe, My Girl, My Guy,* The *Way You Do The Things You Do, Good Lovin'* and *Heat Wave.*

Donna performed the same medley on her Bad Girls tour in 1979.

Hit Versions:

Gladys Knight & the Pips – no.1 on the R&B chart and no.2 on the Hot 100 in the States, and no.47 in the UK, in 1967.

Marvin Gaye – no.1 on the Hot 100 and R&B chart in the States in 1968, and no.1 in the UK in 1969.

Slits – no.60 in the UK in 1979.

Roger – no.1 on the R&B chart and no.79 on the Hot 100 in the States in 1981.

Marvin Gaye (reissue) – no.8 in the UK in 1986.

I LOVE YOU

Written by Donna with Giorgio Moroder & Pete Bellotte, and recorded by Donna for her 1977 album, *ONCE UPON A TIME* – produced by Moroder & Bellotte.

With *Rumour Has It*, the song gave Donna her fifth no.1 on the Hot Dance Club Play chart in the States, where it also charted at no.28 on the R&B chart and no.37 on the Hot 100.

Outside the USA, the single charted at no.10 in Norway & the UK, no.16 in Ireland, no.32 in Canada and no.47 in Australia.

A live version, recorded at the Universal Amphitheatre, Los Angeles, featured on Donna's 1978 album, *LIVE AND MORE*.

Official Versions:
Album Version.
7" / Single Edit.
Live Version.

I NEED TIME

Written by Donna with Pete Bellotte &
Giorgio Moroder, and recorded by
Donna for her shelved 1981 album, *I'M
A RAINBOW* – produced by Bellotte &
Giorgio Moroder.

The album was finally released in 1996.

I REMEMBER YESTERDAY

Written by Donna with Pete Bellotte &
Giorgio Moroder, and recorded by
Donna for her similarly titled 1977
album – produced by Bellotte &
Moroder.

On the album, which also featured *I
Remember Yesterday (Reprise)*, this song
represented the 1940s.

As the lead single from the album in
some countries, excluding the USA, it
achieved no.14 in the UK and no.24 in
Austria & the Netherlands.

A live version, recorded at the Universal
Amphitheatre, Los Angeles, featured on
Donna's 1978 album, *LIVE AND MORE*.

I WILL ALWAYS LOVE YOU

Written and recorded by Dolly Parton,
for her 1974 album, *JOLENE* – however,
the best known and most successful
version was recorded by Whitney

Houston, for her 1992 film, *The Bodyguard*.

In 1983, when she was asked, "What do you sing in the shower?" Donna answered: 'Whitney Houston's *I Will Always Love You* – a great warm-up song to exercise the voice to!'

Hit Versions:
Dolly Parton – no.1 on the Country chart in the States in 1974.
Dolly Parton (re-recording) – no.1 on the Country chart, and no.53 on the Hot 100, in the States in 1982.
Whitney Houston – no.1 on the Hot 100 and R&B chart in the States, and no.1 in the UK, in 1992.

I WILL GO WITH YOU (CON TE PARTIRÓ)

Written by Francesco Sartori & Lucio Quarantotto, and recorded in Italian by Andrea Bocelli for his 1995 album, *BOCELLI*.

Two years later, Bocelli recorded an English version of the song as a duet with Sarah Brightman, titled *Time To Say Goodbye*.

'I told Bruce (Sudano),' said Donna, 'that I wanted to do the consummate dance recording of the century. While we were taking, Andrea's version of the song was playing in the background. All of a sudden, Bruce said, "Turn it off – that's the song!" So, since no official English lyrics existed, I decided to reinterpret it.'

Donna re-wrote the English lyrics and re-titled the song *I Will Go With You*, which is a more literal translation of the Italian title. She recorded the song for her 1999 album, *LIVE & MORE ENCORE!* – produced by Hex Hector.

'I've worked with all kinds of pop stars – Madonna, Jennifer Lopez, Jessica Simpson, Ricky Martin,' said Hex Hector. 'Donna Summer was the only person who I was completely star struck with. The reason for that is because

Donna was such an important part of my childhood.

'Epic hand-picked me to produce this record, which was a trip. It was like my childhood and my career coming full circle. Once she started, I got goose-bumps, because it was Donna Summer. She sounded just as powerful as when she was younger. Her voice was so powerful that she had to stand about ten feet away from the mic! As amazing a singer as Donna was, this was probably the hardest vocal I've ever done, and the reason for that is – and it's no fault to Donna – translating an opera song on to a dance track is no easy feat. It took awhile just to get it right, but it was unbelievable.'

The single gave Donna her 11th no.1 on the Hot Dance Club Play chart in the States, and charted at no.79 on the Hot 100 – and is Donna's most recent entry on that chart.

The single achieved no.35 in Canada, no.44 in the UK and no.59 in the Netherlands.

Grammy nomination:
Best Dance Recording.

Donna performed the song on several TV shows1999, including:

- *Rosie O'Donnell Show* on 8th June.
- *The Today Show* on 2nd July.
- *The Oprah Winfrey Show* on 18th July.

Official Versions:
Album Version.
Radio Edit.
Club 69 Future Mix.
Club 69 Radio Mix.
Club 69 Trippy Dub.
Club 69 Underground Anthem.
Club 69 Underground Dub.
Groovy G Club Mix.
Groovy G Radio Edit.
Hex Hector Extended Vocal Mix.
Italian Uptempo Version.
Johnny Newman Drifting Mix.
Richie Santana Virus Dub.
Rosabel Attitude Vox.
Rosabel Dark Dub.
Rosabel Main Vox.
Rosabel Radio Remix.
Messy Boys Jazz Dub.

Skill Masters Remix.
Trouser Enthusiasts Twisted Kiss Mix.
Trouser Enthusiasts Sudden Death Dub.
Warren Rigg Summer Dub.
Warren Rigg Radio Edit – Cold End.
Welcome Downtempo Extended Remix.
Welcome Downtempo Radio Mix.
Welcome Summertime Fun Extended
  Mix.
Welcome Summertime Fun 7" Remix.

A live recording of the song was included on *THE BEST OF THE SUMMER CONCERT SERIES VOLUME ONE*, a various artist 'Today Presents' compilation issued in 2000.

I WILL SURVIVE

Written by Dino Fekaris & Freddie Perren, and recorded by Gloria Gaynor for her 1978 album, *LOVE TRACKS*.

Donna performed the song, as part of a Grammy nominations medley, when she appeared at the Grammy Awards, staged at the Shrine Auditorium, Los Angeles, on 27th February 1980.

Gloria Gaynor took the song to no.1 on the Hot 100 and no.5 on the R&B chart in the States, and to no.1 in the UK.

See also: *Grammy Nominations Medley*.

I WON'T LET GO

Song recorded by Brooklyn Dreams for their 1980 album, *WON'T LET GO* – backing vocals by Donna.

IF I COULD LIVE OUR LOVE AGAIN

This is a song Donna is known to have recorded for her 1991 album, *MISTAKEN IDENTITY*, however, it failed to make the final track listing and remains unreleased.

IF I HAD A MILLION DOLLARS

Written by Gary William Friedman & Will Holt for the musical, *The Me Nobody Knows* – premiered at the Orpheum Theater, New York, on 18th May 1970.

Donna appeared – credited as Gayne Pierre – in the German production of the musical in 1970, titled *Ich Bin Ich*, and was part of the cast who performed this song on the English language version of the cast album.

See also: *Hätt Ich Eine Million Dollars*.

(IF IT) HURTS JUST A LITTLE

Written by David Batteau, Dan & Michael Sembello, and recorded by Donna for her self-titled 1982 album – produced by Quincy Jones.

IF IT MAKES YOU FEEL GOOD

Written by Mike Stock, Matt Aitken & Pete Waterman, and recorded by Donna for her 1989 album, *ANOTHER PLACE AND TIME* – produced by Stock, Aitken & Waterman.

IF THERE IS MUSIC THERE

Written by Donna & Michael Omartian, for the as yet unpublished play Donna worked on with Bruce Sudano, Al Kasha & Michael Omartian, *Ordinary Girl* – remains unreleased.

Performed by Donna on her Live & More Encore Tour in 1999 – however, the song wasn't included on Donna's *Live & More Encore!* album, but it did feature on the accompanying home video.

IF YOU GOT IT FLAUNT IT

Written by Donna with Giorgio Moroder & Pete Bellotte, and recorded by Donna for her 1977 album, *ONCE UPON A TIME* – produced by Moroder & Bellotte.

IF YOU WALKIN' ALONE

Written by Donna & Hans Hammerschmid, and recorded by Donna (as Donna Gaines) in late 1969.

The song featured, as background music, in the German TV mini-series, *11 Uhr 20*, which aired in three parts in January 1970.

The track was released as a single in Germany in 1972, b/w *Can't Understand* (Philips 388 419 PF) – on the record label and sleeve, Donna's surname was misspelled 'Gains'.

I'LL BE HOME FOR CHRISTMAS

Christmas song written in 1943 by Kim Gannon, Buck Ram & Walter Kent – first recorded by Bing Crosby.

Recorded by Donna for her 1994 album, *CHRISTMAS SPIRIT* – produced by Michael Omartian.

Hit Version:
Josh Groban – no.95 on the Hot 100 in the States in 2006.

Recorded by numerous other artists, including the Beach Boys, Tony Bennett, Pat Boone, Peabo Bryson & Roberta Flack, Carpenters, Johnny Cash, Perry Como, Doris Day, Neil Diamond, Fats Domino, Gloria Estefan, Connie Francis, Amy Grant, Al Green, Whitney Houston, Dean Martin, Johnny Mathis, the Osmonds, Elvis Presley, Frank Sinatra and Barbra Streisand.

I'M A FIRE

Written by Donna with Al Kasha & Sebastian Arocha Morton, and recorded by Donna for her 2008 album, *CRAYONS* – produced by Morton.

Lead single from the album – it gave Donna her 13th no.1 on Billboard's Hot Dance Club Play chart.

Official Versions:
Album Version.
Original Version.

Radio Edit.
Baggi Begovic & Soul Conspiracy Original Mix.
Baggi Begovic & Soul Conspiracy Mixshow.
Baggi Begovic & Soul Conspiracy Dub.
BBW Solitaire Edit.
BBW Red Top Electro Edit.
Craig C Mixshow.
Craig C Burnin' Club Mix.
Craig C Burnin' Radio Mix.
Craig C Burnin' Vocal Mastermix.
Craig C Dub.
Lost Daze Remix.
Lost Daze Dub.
Matty's Soulflower Club Mix.
Matty's Soulflower Reprise.
Matty's Soulflower Beats.
Matty's Soulflower Acapella.
Redtop Dub.
Redtop Extended Mix.
Redtop Burnin' Extended Vocal Mix.
Roca Sound Original Album Mix.
Rod Carrillo Groove Dub.
Rod Carrillo Leave It On The Floor Mix.
Seamus Haji Mix.
Seamus Haji Dub.
Sebastian Arocha Norton's Original Version.
Solitaire Radio Edit.
Solitaire Club Mix.
Solitaire Club Mix W/Spanish.
Solitaire Dub Mix.
Solitaire Instrumental.

I'M A RAINBOW

Written by Bruce Sudano, and recorded by Donna for her shelved 1981 album with the same title – produced by Pete Bellotte & Giorgio Moroder.

The album was finally released in 1996.

I'M EVERY WOMAN

Written by Nickolas Ashford & Valerie Simpson, and recorded by Chaka Khan for her 1978 album, *CHAKA* – backing vocals by Whitney & Cissy Houston.

Performed by Donna, with Chaka Khan & Gloria Estefan, at their 'Three Divas On Broadway' benefit concert, staged at Manhattan's Lunt-Fontanne Theater on 11th December 1996.

Donna, on the evening, was under doctor's orders with 'flu symptoms, so her vocal participation in the concert was minimal. 'I guess three years of constant touring has finally caught up with me,' said Donna, 'but it feels good to still be wanted and appreciated after all these years.'

Donna, with Chaka & Gloria, also sang *Turn The Beat Around*.

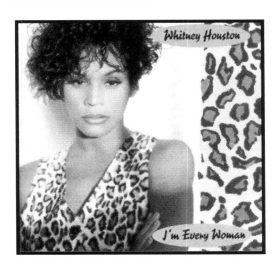

Hit Versions:
Chaka Khan: no.1 on the R&B chart and no.21 on the Hot 100, and no.11 in the UK, in 1978.

Chaka Khan (remix) – no.8 in the UK in 1989.
Whitney Houston – no.4 on the Hot 100 and no.5 on the R&B chart, and no.4 in the UK, in 1993.

I'M FREE

Written by Donna with Bruce Sudano & Michael Omartian, and recorded by Donna for her 1984 album, *CATS WITHOUT CLAWS* – produced by Omartian.

An extended mix of the song was included on Donna's 12" single, *Eyes*.

Donna performed the song when she appeared, as the guest host, on Dick Clark's *Bandstand Christmas Special*, which aired in the States on 22nd December 1984.

(I'M IN LOVE WITH) DONNA SUMMER

Written and recorded by Andrew Johnson, for his 2009 album, *NOW THEN*.

'It's really just a bit of fluff that popped in my head while I was driving one day,' said Johnson. 'I forget the original inspiration, but I think the chorus melody came first, and then I wrote a load of verses, a few of which made it in to the finished song. I write and record very fast, so it didn't take very long for me to get to the finished version. It was purely by chance that I released it as a single.'

I'M THE ONE

Written by V. Hicks, G. Bernard & J. Mumford, and recorded by Sunshine for their cancelled 1978 album, *WATCHIN' DADDY DANCE* – produced by Donna & Juergen Koppers.

Remains unreleased.

IMPOSSIBLE DREAM, THE

Written by Mitch Leigh & Joe Darion for the 1965 musical, *Man Of La Mancha*.

Donna performed the song on her All Systems Go Tour in 1987-88, and on select tour dates between 1990 and 1992.

Artists to have recorded the song include Shirley Bassey, Glen Campbell, the Carpenters, Cher, Roberta Flack, Lesley Garrett, Tom Jones, Johnny Mathis, Matt Monro, Eddie Murphy, Elvis Presley, Diana Ross & the Supremes, the Temptations, Luther Vandross and Andy Williams.

IN ANOTHER PLACE AND TIME

Written by Mike Stock, Matt Aitken & Pete Waterman, and recorded by Donna for her 1989 album, *ANOTHER PLACE AND TIME* – produced by Stock, Aitken & Waterman.

Released as a single in Australia and Japan.

INCOMMUNICADO

Written by Bruce Sudano, Carlotta McKee & Gordon Grote, and recorded by Musical Youth for their 1983 album, *DIFFERENT STYLE* – produced by Peter Collins, with backing vocals by Donna.

INTRO: PRELUDE TO LOVE

Written by Donna with Pete Bellotte & Giorgio Moroder, and recorded by Donna for her 1976 album, *A LOVE TRILOGY* – produced by Bellotte & Moroder.

ISN'T SHE LOVELY

Written and recorded by Stevie Wonder, to celebrate the birth of his daughter, Aisha – featured on his 1976 album, *SONGS IN THE KEY OF LIFE*.

As part of a tribute to Stevie, Donna joined Ella Fitzgerald, Lionel Richie, Tina Arena, Ray Parker, Jr., Quincy Jones, Sheena Easton & Glen Campbell, to sing the song – as *Isn't He Lovely* – at the American Music Awards on 25th January 1982. Donna and the other artists, before they were joined by Ella Fitzgerald, also performed Stevie's *You Are The Sunshine Of My Life*.

Stevie refused to allow Motown to release the song as a single, however, a cover version by David Parton did chart at no.4 in the UK in 1977.

IT'S NOT THE WAY

Written by Donna & Michael Omartian, and recorded by Donna for her 1984 album, *CATS WITHOUT CLAWS* – produced by Omartian.

B-side of *Eyes*.

IT'S ONLY LOVE

Written by Donna with Al Kasha & Sebastian Arocha Morton, and recorded by Donna for her 2008 album, *CRAYONS* – produced by Morton.

This track wasn't included on the USA edition of the album, but was released as a digital single on iTunes.

The track achieved no.14 on Billboard's Hot Dance Club Play chart.

Official Versions:
Album Version.
Original Version.
Lost Daze Remix.
Lost Daze Dub.
Soulcast Icon Mix.
Soulcast Radio Edit.

IT'S OVER

Written by Donna, and recorded by Sunshine for their cancelled 1978 album, *WATCHIN' DADDY DANCE* – produced by Donna & Juergen Koppers.

Remains unreleased.

Donna later recorded the song herself, as *Maybe It's Over*, for her 1984 album, *CATS WITHOUT CLAWS*.

See also: *Maybe It's Over*.

JE T'AIME… MOI NON PLUS

Written and originally recorded, as a duet with Brigitte Bardot, by Serge Gainsbourg in 1967 – however, this version wasn't released until 1986.

English translation: 'I love you… me neither'.

This was the song that inspired Donna to write *Love To Love You Baby*.

15:45 minute version recorded by Donna & Giorgio Moroder for the 1978 soundtrack album, *THANK GOD IT'S FRIDAY* – produced by Moroder & Pete Bellotte.

Released as a promo 12" single in the States.

Hit Versions:
Serge Gainsbourg & Jane Birkin – no.1 in the UK, and no.69 on the Hot 100 in the States, in 1968.
Judge Dread – no.9 in the UK in 1975.
René & Yvette (from the TV series, 'Allo 'Allo) – no.57 in the UK in 1986.

Gainsbourg & Birkin's single was banned by the BBC in the UK, and in several other countries, due to its overtly sexual content.

See also: *Love To Love You / Love To Love You Baby*.

JEANNIE

Written by Tom Chapin, Veit Marvos & Richard Palmer-James, and recorded by the Veit Marvos Red Point Orchestra for a similarly titled album, released in Germany circa 1972-73.

Donna, at this time, was a member of the Veit Marvos Red Point Orchestra.

See also: *Back Off Boogaloo*.

JEREMY

Written by Donna with Pit Floss, Andy Slovic & Harold Faltermeyer, and recorded by Donna for her 1987 album, *ALL SYSTEMS GO* – produced by Faltermeyer.

JESUS, NAME ABOVE ALL NAMES

This is a song Donna recorded circa 1980-81, during either *THE WANDERER* or *I'M A RAINBOW* sessions – it failed to make either album and remains unreleased.

JOURNEY: THE DONNA SUMMER MEGAMIX, THE

32:33 minute megamix by Paul 'DJ Pauly' Yates, released as a promo CDr in the States, to promote Donna's 2003 compilation, *THE JOURNEY – THE BEST OF*.

Featured songs: *Love To Love You Baby, This Time I Know It's For Real, Walk Away, Hot Stuff, Bad Girls, I Feel Love, Last Dance, You're So Beautiful, Dream-A-Lot's Theme (I Will Live For Love), Love Is In Control (Finger On The Trigger), She Works Hard For The Money* and *No More Tears (Enough Is Enough)*.

The Baaad Donna Summer Ohio Players

Dionne Warwick
Anita Ward
Gene Chandler

JOURNEY TO THE CENTRE OF YOUR HEART

Written by Pete Bellotte & Giorgio Moroder, and recorded by Donna for her 1979 album, *BAD GIRLS* – produced by Bellotte & Moroder.

B-side of *Hot Stuff*.

JOY TO THE WORLD

Traditional hymn written by Isaac Watts, and first published in 1719 in *The Psalms Of David: Imitated In The Language Of The New Testament* – the melody was composed by Lowell Mason in 1839.

Recorded by Donna, as part of *Christmas Medley*, for her 1994 album, *CHRISTMAS SPIRIT* – produced by Michael Omartian.

The medley also featured *What Child Is This* & *Do You Hear What I Hear*.

Three Dog Night took the song no.1 on the Hot 100 in the States, and to no.24 in the UK, in 1971.

L.A. IS MY LADY

Written by Alan & Marilyn Bergman, Quincy & Peggy Lipton Jones, and recorded by Frank Sinatra for his 1984 album with the same title.

Donna, along with Eddie Van Halen and David Lee Roth, made a cameo appearance in the video – in a parody of her *She Works Hard For The Money*, she played a waitress who, after serving someone, wipes her brow.

LA DOLCE VITA

This is a song Donna had worked on with Giorgio Moroder before her passing – features vocals by Moroder.

'The song was begun a few years ago in Nashville with Nathan DiGesare,' said Bruce Sudano, Donna's widower, 'and then tweaked over time when we went back to Nashville to visit.'

The track featured on the posthumous remix album, *LOVE TO LOVE YOU DONNA*, released in 2013.

'I wanted a new song on the CD,' said Sudano, 'but couldn't get approval of the demo until Giorgio came on and reworked the track and added his touch. The vocal used is actually one from early on in the writing process.'

LA VIE EN ROSE

Written by Edith Piaf & Louis 'Louiguy' Gugliemi, and originally performed by Piaf – in French – in 1946. The English lyrics were written at a later date by Mack David.

English translation: 'Life In Pink'.

Donna recorded a version of the song for the 1993 various artist tribute album, released as *EDITH PIAF TRIBUTE* in France and *TRIBUTE TO EDITH PIAF* in the States – produced by Jacques Arnoul.

The two albums released in France and the States featured a slightly different mix of Donna's recording.

Released as a single in France and the States, and as a promo CD single in the UK – however, the single failed to chart.

Official Versions:
Album Version – France.
Album Version – USA.
Radio Mix.
12" Mix.
Extended Soul Mix.
Full Bass Mix.
Stringapella Mix.
Techno Mix.
US Radio Mix.

Grace Jones took the song to no.12 in the UK in 1985.

Other artists to have performed or recorded the song include Louis Armstrong, Shirley Bassey, Tony Bennett & k.d. lang, Petula Clark, Bing Crosby, Celine Dion, Ella Fitzgerald, Aretha Franklin, Julio Iglasias, B.B. King, Brenda Lee, Dean Martin, Bette Midler, Liza Minnelli and Elaine Paige.

LADY OF THE NIGHT

Written by Giorgio Moroder & Pete Bellotte, and recorded by Donna for her 1974 album with the same title – released in the Netherlands only.

Produced by Pete Bellotte.

Released as a single in Belgium and the Netherlands in 1974, and in Germany the following year.

The single achieved no.3 in Belgium, no.4 in the Netherlands and no.7 in Germany.

Donna performed the song, with *The Hostage*, in the Dutch TV film, *Van Oekel Blikt Terug* (*Van Oekel Looks Back*), which aired on Dutch TV on 31st December 1974.

LAMB OF GOD

Written by & Michael Omartian, and recorded by Donna for her 1994 album, *CHRISTMAS SPIRIT* – produced by Omartian.

A promo CD single was released in the States.

LAST DANCE

Written by Paul Jabara, and recorded by Donna for the 1978 soundtrack album, *THANK GOD IT'S FRIDAY* – produced by Giorgio Moroder & Bob Esty.

The album also featured *Last Dance (Reprise)*.

Donna, in the studio, sang the song just twice, from which the final version was mixed. She recorded the song in the summer of 1977, a year before it was released.

'I knew it was a winner the first time I heard it,' she said. 'When I sang it, I fell under a spell. Usually, I don't listen to any of my tapes after I record them. But *Last Dance*, I listened to that for a very long time. I used to put it on in my car and drive down Mulholland Drive, blaring it and singing. I could just sense that the song was going to be a big hit.'

In the film, Donna had a small role as an aspiring singer, Nicole Sims – she gets her chance, and sings *Last Dance* towards the end of the film.

As a single, the song gave Donna her sixth no.1 on the Hot Dance Club Play chart in the States, where it also achieved no.3 on the Hot 100 and no.5 on the R&B chart.

The single peaked at no.3 in Canada & New Zealand, no.8 in Belgium & the Netherlands, no.16 in Sweden, no.51 in the UK and no.69 in Australia.

Donna performed the song on *The Midnight Special*, *Dick Clark's Live Wednesday* and *American Bandstand* TV shows in 1978.

RIAA Award: Gold (July 1978) = 1 million.

Academy Award: Song Of The Year.

Golden Globe: Best Original Song.

Grammy Award:
Best R&B Vocal Performance, Female.

Donna performed the song at the 51st Academy Awards ceremony, staged at the Dorothy Chandler Pavilion, Los Angeles, on 9th April 1979.

A live version, recorded at the Universal Amphitheatre, Los Angeles, featured on Donna's 1978 album, *LIVE AND MORE.*

A second live version, recorded at the Hammerstein Ballroom, New York, in February 1999, was included on the 1999 album, *LIVE & MORE ENCORE!*

Donna performed the song at a Karaoke Night, when she appeared as Aunt Oona in Season 5, Episode 23 of the American sitcom, *Family Matters*, which aired on 6th May 1994.

Official Versions:
Soundtrack Album Version.
7" / Single Edit.
12" Edit.
Live Version (1978).
Live Version (1999).

Edit (as featured on Donna's 1979 compilation, *ON THE RADIO: GREATEST HITS VOLUMES I & II*).

'Of all the songs from those days,' said Donna, speaking in 1998, 'I probably still feel most connected to *Last Dance*. Sing it and it brings tears to my eyes. For me, it's become a poignant song. There were a lot of people in my life who are not with us anymore. It's like I'm singing to the memory of people who were special to me.'

The song was reissued as a single in some countries in 1999, but it failed to chart.

Ranked no.6 on VH1's '100 Greatest Dance Songs' listing in October 2000.

The song featured in the *Today, I Am A Clown* episode of *The Simpsons* – the episode aired in the States on 8th February 2004.

Performed by Donna, backed by the top six female contestants, on the Season 7 finale of *American Idol* in 2008 – she also performed *Stamp Your Feet*.

Performed by Donna when she appeared at the Nobel Peace Prize Concert, staged in Oslo, Norway, on 11th December 2009.

Performed by Donna as the finale, when she was inducted into the Hollywood Bowl's Hall of Fame on 18th June 2010.

Performed by Donna, with *No More Tears (Enough Is Enough)*, with contestant Prince Poppycock on the *America's Got Talent* finale, staged on 15th September 2010.

Two days later, the song was played on the final episode of the American soap opera, *As The World Turns*, which first aired on 2nd April 1956 and ran for 13,858 episodes.

Donna performed the song, as the finale, when she appeared at the *David Foster & Friends* concert, staged at the Mandalay Bay Events Center, Las Vegas, on 15th October 2010 – at the end of the song, she was joined on stage by David Foster and his friends, including Michael Bolton, Charice, Natalie Cole, Kenny Loggins, Ne-Yo and Seal. The performance was featured on the 2011 home DVD and Blu-ray release, *HIT MAN RETURNS*, credited to David Foster & Friends, but was omitted from the accompanying CD.

LEAN ON ME

Written and recorded by Bill Withers for his 1972 album, *STILL BILL*.

Performed by Donna, with a host of other celebrities including Stevie Wonder, John Travolta, Nelly Furtado and Brian McKnight, when she appeared at the Race Against MS (Multiple Sclerosis) dinner, staged at Century City's Century Plaza on 18th May 2001.

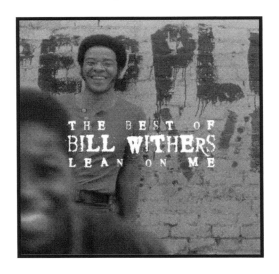

Hit Versions:
Bill Withers – no.1 on the Hot 100 and R&B chart in the States, and no.18 in the UK, in 1972.

Mud – no.7 in the UK in 1976.

Club Nouveau – no.1 on the Hot 100 and no.2 on the R&B chart in the States, and no.3 in the UK, in 1987.

Thelma Houston & the Winans – no.73 on the R&B chart in the States in 1989.

Michael Bolton – no.14 in the UK in 1994.

LEAVE ME ALONE

Written by Harold Faltermeyer & Keith Forsey, and recorded by Donna for her shelved 1981 album, *I'M A RAINBOW* – produced by Pete Bellotte & Giorgio Moroder.

The album was finally released in 1996.

Had the album been issued in 1981, as planned, it is likely this track would have been the lead single.

LET IT BE

Written by Paul McCartney (but credited to John Lennon & Paul McCartney), and recorded by the Beatles for their 1970 album with the same title.

Performed by Donna, with Jools Holland on piano, when she appeared as a guest on *Later With Jools Holland* in the UK – aired on 11th June 2004.

'I really fought to do that,' said Donna, 'because everybody wanted me to do one of my old songs, and I thought, "This is an intimate moment, so let's do something special here." Actually, when we came to rehearsal we were doing *On The Radio*, but it wasn't working in the key we were in so I suggested *Let It Be*, and Jools liked it and it worked great.'

Hit Versions:

Beatles – no.1 in the USA and no.2 in the UK in 1970.

Ferry Aid – no.1 in the UK in 1987.

Boys On The Block – no.76 on the R&B chart in the States in 1987.

Kris Allen – no.63 on the Hot 100 in the States in 2010.

Jennifer Hudson ft. the Roots – no.98 on the Hot 100 in the States in 2010.

LET THERE BE HAPPINESS IN THE WORLD

Written and recorded by Tom Winter in 1976 – background vocals by Donna & Roberta Kelly.

LET THERE BE PEACE

Written by Donna & Keith Diamond, and recorded by Donna for her 1991 album, *MISTAKEN IDENTITY* – produced by Diamond.

LET'S DANCE

Written by V. Hicks, G. Bernard & J. Mumford, and recorded by Sunshine for their cancelled 1978 album, *WATCHIN' DADDY DANCE* – produced by Donna & Juergen Koppers.

Remains unreleased.

LET'S WORK TOGETHER NOW

Written by Pete Bellotte, and recorded by Donna for her 1974 album, *LADY OF THE NIGHT* – released in the Netherlands only.

Produced by Pete Bellotte.

B-side of *The Hostage* in the Netherlands.

LICHT SINGT (LIGHT SINGS)

Written by Gary William Friedman & Will Holt for the musical, *The Me Nobody Knows* – premiered at the Orpheum Theater, New York, on 18th May 1970.

Donna appeared – credited as Gayne Pierre – in the German production of the musical in 1970, titled *Ich Bin Ich*, and was part of the cast who performed this song on stage and on the German cast album.

Donna was also part of the cast who performed the song on the English language version of the cast album.

LIPSTICK ON YOUR COLLAR

Written by Edna Lewis & George Geohring, and recorded by Connie Francis in April 1959.

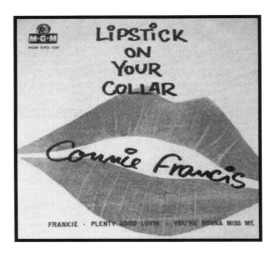

Donna revealed, in her autobiography *Ordinary Girl: The Journey*, this was one of her favourite songs to sing when she was a young girl.
Connie Francis took the song to no.5 on the Hot 100 in the States, and to no.3 in the UK.

LITTLE MARIE

Written and recorded by Chuck Berry for his 1964 album, *ST. LOUIS TO LIVERPOOL*.

Recorded by the Veit Marvos Red Point Orchestra for a similarly titled album, released in Germany circa 1972-73 – Donna, at this time, was a member of the Veit Marvos Red Point Orchestra.

Chuck Berry took the song to no.54 on the R&B chart in the States.

See also: *Back Off Boogaloo*.

LITTLE MISS FIT

Written by Giorgio Moroder & Pete Bellotte, and recorded by Donna for her 1974 album, *LADY OF THE NIGHT* – released in the Netherlands only.

Produced by Pete Bellotte.

LIVIN' IN AMERICA

Written by Donna with Davis Foster, Quincy Jones, Rod Temperton & Steve Lukather, and recorded by Donna for her self-titled 1982 album – produced by Quincy Jones.

'*Livin' In America* is just about my favourite cut (on the album),' said Donna. 'It's really how I feel about this country – the land of the free, one nation under God, indivisible. It may sound corny, but to me it's about believing and being positive about what you believe.'

B-side of *The Woman In Me*.

Performed by Donna at *The 50th Presidential Inauguration Gala*, for the inauguration of President Ronald Reagan, staged at the Capitol's Rotunda on 21st January 1985.

LOOKING UP

Written by Donna with Pete Bellotte & Giorgio Moroder, and recorded by Donna for her 1980 album, *THE WANDERER* – produced by Moroder & Bellotte.

LOVE HAS A MIND OF ITS OWN

Written by Donna with Michael Omartian & Bruce Sudano, and recorded by Donna as a duet with Matthew Ward for her 1983 album, *SHE WORKS HARD FOR THE MONEY* – produced by Omartian.

Michael Ward wasn't credited on the sleeve, when the song was issued as a single, which charted at no.35 on the R&B chart and no.70 on the Hot 100 in the States, and no.44 in Canada.

LOVE IS HERE TO STAY

Jazz standard written by George & Ira Gershwin for the 1938 film, *The Goldwyn Follies*.

Donna performed the song, as part of a medley with *There's No Business Like Show Business* and *The Man I Love*, on The Rainbow Tour in 1984.

Numerous artists have recorded the song, including Ray Charles, Ella Fitzgerald & Louis Armstrong, Billie Holiday, Jack Jones, Gene Kelly, Barry Manilow, Oscar Peterson, Frank Sinatra, Lisa Stansfield and Dinah Washington.

LOVE IS IN CONTROL
(FINGER ON THE TRIGGER)

Written by Quincy Jones, Rod Temperton & Merria Ross, and recorded by Donna for her self-titled 1982 album – produced by Jones.

Released as the lead single from the album – in the States, it charted at no.3 on the Hot Dance Club Play chart, no.4 on the R&B chart and no.10 on the Hot 100.

Outside the USA, the single achieved no.3 in Norway, no.5 in Spain & Switzerland, no.6 in the Netherlands, no.7 in South Africa, no.10 in Canada, no.13 in Sweden, no.14 in Belgium & Ireland, no.17 in Australia, no.18 in Italy & the UK, no.40 in New Zealand, no.48 in France and no.71 in Japan.

Grammy Award nomination:
Best R&B Vocal Performance, Female.

Official Versions:
Album Version.
7" / Single Edit.
12" Extended Version.
Instrumental.
Dance Remix.

Sheena Easton recorded a cover version of the song for her 2001 album, *FABULOUS*.

LOVE IS JUST A BREATH AWAY

Written by Donna with David Foster & Rod Temperton, and recorded by Donna for her self-titled 1982 album – produced by Quincy Jones.

B-side of *State Of Independence*.

Sampled by Cassius on the *Cassius 99* remixes in 1999.

LOVE IS THE HEALER

Written by Donna & Nathan DiGesare, and recorded by Donna for her 1999 album, *LIVE & MORE ENCORE!* – produced by DiGesare & Thunderpuss.

Released as a single in the States, plus select European countries, including Germany and Italy (but not the UK).

The single gave Donna her 12th no.1 on the Hot Dance Club Play chart in the States.

Donna performed the song on *The View* and *The Queen Latifah Show* in 1999.

Official Versions:
Album Version.
Eric Kupper's I Feel Healed 7" Mix).
Eric Kupper's I Feel Healed 12" Mix).
Future Primitive Tribal Tech Mix.
J.P.'s Sound Factory Mix.
Sussex House Club Vocal.
Thunderpuss 2000 Club Mix.
Thunderpuss 2000 Radio Mix.
Thunder Drum-A-Pella.
Tim Rex Lunar Vocal Mix.

Performed by Donna on *VH1 Divas 2000: A Tribute To Diana Ross, An Honors Concert For VH1's Save The Music*, staged at New York's Madison Square Garden on 9th April 2000 and aired two days later.

LOVE ON & ON

Written by Michael O'Hara, Denise Rich & George Lyter, and recorded by Donna in 1999 – produced by Hex Hector.

Featured on some formats of Donna's 1999 single, *I Will Go With You (Con Te Partiró)*.

LOVE SHOCK

Written by Donna with Bruce Sudano & Harold Faltermeyer, and recorded by Donna for her 1987 album, *ALL SYSTEMS GO* – produced by Faltermeyer.

B-side of *Only The Fool Survives*.

LOVE TO LOVE YOU / LOVE TO LOVE YOU BABY

Written by Donna with Pete Bellotte & Giorgio Moroder – produced by Bellotte.

The song that was destined to put Donna on the international map was inspired by *Je T'Aime... Moi Non Plus*, which Moroder happened to mention was doing well in England – in fact, originally, it was suggested Donna record a cover version of the French smash.

'I didn't want to do somebody else's song,' said Donna, 'so I came up with the idea of doing a similar thing myself, but with my own song.'

But, initially, Moroder and Bellotte both told her: no way! That simply wasn't her image. Moroder did, however, like the line "I'd love to love you" that Donna came up with – so much so, he called

Donna into the studio the following morning, to work on turning it into a song.

'I told Giorgio that I had an idea for a song,' said Donna, 'and I sang the melody to him, and he put down a track. I came into the studio the next day and he wanted me to put down my vocal, but I wasn't really prepared, so I ad-libbed – and that was left on the song. I was goofing around. I was lying on the floor, moaning, and we were all hysterical. It was just too funny!'

'We really just thought of *Love To Love You Baby* as a bit of fun,' said Moroder. 'One afternoon Donna came to the office and said she'd come up with the title *Love To Love You Baby*. That sounded good to me.

'Back then, I had a studio in the basement of my Munich apartment building, called Music Land – which later became famous when such acts as the Rolling Stones, Led Zeppelin and Elton John used it – and it happened to be empty that afternoon, so I went straight down there and composed the song. Then, a day or two later, Donna came in and we did a very rough demo.'

'I came up with an image of Marilyn Monroe singing the song in that light and fluffy but highly sensual voice of hers,' said Donna, 'and hers was the image I used when I laid down the first vocal track for the song. That would be the only track we did that day. *'Perfetto!'* Giorgio cried when I finished. Before noon, we had the vocal for the record down cold.'

Moroder took the demo to the MIDEM international music festival in January 1975, where he met the founder and owner of Casablanca Records, Neil Bogart – who liked the demo enough to take it home with him, and play it at a party he was having. He noticed how the song instantly changed the mood of the party, and in response to repeated requests, the demo was played over and over again.

Bogart knew he was on to something, but something niggled him … he sat on the demo for a while, until it suddenly struck him: the demo was too short. He phoned Moroder – at 3:00 in the morning – and asked for an extended, twenty minute version of the song.

Moroder, and Donna when he told her of the request, thought Bogart was crazy, and Moroder further pointed out he would need to find the right singer for the actual record. 'No, no, no!' Bogart reacted. 'Whoever is on that demo is the only person who can sing that song. It's the voice you want to take home and make love to.'

So, with the studio lights dimmed and candles lit, the demo was extended to 16:50 minutes. 'I'd only intended to give Giorgio my idea for the song,' said Donna. 'When it came to expanding it to seventeen minutes, Giorgio left all those oohs and aahs in because the song didn't have any more words!'

'I wasn't really singing on that record,' admitted Donna, 'but you never do know. I'm sure that when Madonna started, people thought she was going to be a one hit wonder, too.'

The original three minute version of *Love To Love You* was even more explicit than the extended version that followed. It was released as a single in Germany (Atlantic ATL 10625) and the Netherlands on (Groovy GR 1211) in 1975 – it achieved no. 17 in the Netherlands.

Donna performed the song on the final episode, episode 12, of the Dutch musical comedy show, *Van Oekel's Discohoek* (*Van Oekel's Disco Corner*), hosted by Dolf Brouwers as Sjef van Oekel. The episode, which saw Donna thanking van Oekel for making her successful (*The Hostage* having been a big hit in the Netherlands), aired on Dutch TV on 29th April 1975.

Before it was released internationally, the song was re-titled *Love To Love You Baby*.

'They didn't know it was me,' admitted Donna, when she was asked about her parents' reaction to the song. 'They heard *Love To Love You Baby*, but they just didn't know who it was. They were used to me belting. They really hadn't heard me sing that way, and the way the song was produced, I really kind of created the voice for that song.

'The song had been on the radio, and people would call my Mom and go, "You know – that's Donna's song" and she would say, "That's not my daughter, she doesn't sing like that!" I called her one day from Europe and asked her if she'd heard my song, and she said, "What is it?" and I told her it was that song, and she said "I have been telling everyone that is not your song". Anyway, it was pretty funny. She got used to the idea. I mean, they were liberal church people … they knew that I was young and out of their control at some point.'

The song was banned by the BBC in the UK, due to its 'orgasmic moans', and by numerous radio stations across the States – none of which stopped it from breaking Donna internationally.

In the States, the single gave Donna her first no.1 on the Hot Dance Club Play chart – more importantly, it also achieved no.2 on the Hot 100 and no.3 on the R&B chart, and became Donna's first million seller.

Outside the USA, the single charted at no.2 in Norway, no.4 in Australia & the UK, no.5 in Sweden, no.6 in Germany & Switzerland, no.8 in New Zealand, no.9 in Austria, and no.11 in Ireland & Italy.

RIAA Award: Gold (February 1976) = 1 million.

Donna performed the song on numerous TV shows in 1976, including *Soul Train*, *American Bandstand*, *The Mike Douglas Show* and *Dick Clark's New Year's Rockin' Eve*.

The song was dubbed 'orgasmic rock', and it led to Donna being labelled 'the first lady of love' – an image Donna was never comfortable with. 'It was never me,' she admits, 'but I still got tired of living up to it. I didn't see myself as pretty or glamorous, but I knew I had a voice and that I was intelligent. Neil (Bogart) helped me see myself differently.'

With the single's success, Donna returned to the States for the first time in seven years, in November 1975 – a move, initially, she viewed as a step backward. She found her sudden stardom fun, but a bit terrifying, too.

'The first time I saw the movie, *The Bodyguard*,' she said, 'with Whitney Houston, I thought I was watching a documentary of my own life, with all the tension and difficulties of putting on that kind of show.'

A live version, recorded at the Universal Amphitheatre, Los Angeles, featured on Donna's 1978 album, *LIVE AND MORE*.

Ranked no.63 on VH1's '100 Greatest Dance Songs' listing in October 2000.

For many years, Donna refused to perform the song in any of her concerts, and admitted she 'just hates it'. However, she did eventually start performing the song again, albeit with a different, less erotic arrangement.

'Casablanca worked very hard at creating that ('sex-goddess') image around me,' said Donna, 'but I was never comfortable with that image, because that is not me. I wanted to be taken seriously.'

The song has been sampled by numerous artists over the years, including:

- Digital Underground on *Freaks Of The Industry*, from their 1990 album, *SEX PACKETS*.

- TLC on *I'm Good At Being Bad*, on initial pressings of their 1999 album, *FANMAIL*. However, due to the song's explicit nature, Donna requested the sample be removed from all future pressings of the album.

- Beyoncé on *Naughty Girl*, which featured on her 2003 album, *DANGEROUSLY IN LOVE* – as a single, it achieved no.3 on the Hot 100 and no.8 on the R&B chart in the States, and no.10 in the UK.

'What she (Beyoncé) used of the song,' said Donna, 'she used in good context to her own music. I'm always happy when someone uses the songs I wrote because I get publishing. I was saying, "Go Beyoncé! Go Beyoncé!" I don't have to work for it – it's like sending out your elf to bring back money!'

In 2000, the song was used in an advertising campaign for Mercedes Benz cars.

LOVE WILL ALWAYS FIND YOU

Written by Pete Bellotte & Giorgio Moroder, and recorded by Donna for her 1979 album, *BAD GIRLS* – produced by Bellotte & Moroder.

LOVER BOY

Written by Bruce Sudano, and recorded by former model Twiggy for her shelved 1979 album, *HEAVEN IN MY EYES* – produced by Donna & Juergen Koppers.

LOVE'S ABOUT TO CHANGE MY HEART

Written by Mike Stock, Matt Aitken & Pete Waterman, and recorded by Donna for her 1989 album, *ANOTHER PLACE AND TIME* – produced by Stock, Aitken & Waterman.

Released as a single, the song achieved no.3 on the Hot Dance Club Play chart and no.85 on the Hot 100 in the States, no.11 in Ireland, no.20 in the UK and no.83 in Australia.

Donna performed the song on *The Arsenio Hall Show* in the States in 1989.

Official Versions:
Album Version.
Extended Remix.
Instrumental.
Dub.
Dub 2 / Love Dub.
Clivilles & Cole 7" Mix.
Clivilles & Cole 12" Mix.
PWL 7" Mix.
PWL 12" Mix.
Loveland's Full-On 7" Radio Edit.

LOVE'S UNKIND

Written by Donna with Pete Bellotte & Giorgio Moroder, and recorded by Donna for her 1977 album, *I REMEMBER YESTERDAY* – produced by Bellotte & Moroder.

On the album, this song represented the 1950s.

As a single, the song achieved no.2 in Ireland, no.3 in the UK, no.13 in Zimbabwe, no.18 in Austria, Belgium & Germany and no.32 in the Netherlands.

BPI Award: Gold (January 1978) = 500,000.

A live version, recorded at the Universal Amphitheatre, Los Angeles, featured on Donna's 1978 album, *LIVE AND MORE*.

LOVIN' YOU

Song Rafaella Carrà recorded for her 1988 album, *RAFAELLA*.

Donna sang the song, as a duet with her, when she appeared as a guest on Carrà's Italian TV show, *Il Principe Azzurro* (*The Blue Prince*) in 1989.

LUCKY

Written by Donna with Bruce Sudano, Joe Esposito, Eddie Hokenson & Giorgio Moroder, and recorded by Donna for her 1979 album, *BAD GIRLS* – produced by Moroder & Pete Bellotte.

LUFT (AIR)

Written James Rado & Gerome Ragni (book and lyrics) & Galt MacDermot (music) for the controversial 'tribal love-rock' musical, *Hair*.

Donna appeared in the German production of the musical in 1968, titled *Haare*, and was part of the cast who performed this song on stage and on the cast album.

LUSH LIFE

Jazz standard written by Billy Strayhorn between 1933-38 – first performed in public by Kay Davis with the Duke Ellington Orchestra in 1948, at the Carnegie Hall, New York.

Recorded by Donna for her self-titled 1982 album – produced by Quincy Jones.

'It was one of the hardest songs I've ever sung,' admitted Donna. 'Quincy insisted I do it, and I'm glad he did … usually, I record very quickly – I study the song and make a character for myself, and once I know who she is in the song, then I nail it. I don't like singing songs hundreds of times, I think you lose something in the spontaneity of the song.'

Numerous artists have recorded the song, including Nat King Cole, Natalie Cole, Sammy Davis, Jr., Billy Eckstine, Johnny Hartman, Jack Jones, Johnny Mathis & Linda Ronstadt.

MacARTHUR PARK

Written by Jimmy Webb, and originally recorded by Richard Harris for his 1968 album, *A TRAMP SHINING*.

Recorded by Donna, as part of *MacArthur Park Suite*, for her 1978 album, *LIVE AND MORE* – produced by Giorgio Moroder & Pete Bellotte.

The album also featured *MacArthur Park (Reprise)* – again, as part of *MacArthur Park Suite*.

'I had been sitting on the idea of re-doing *MacArthur Park* for many years,' said Moroder. 'Pete also liked the song, so we thought, "Why don't we just do it with Donna?" Even though it's a song that's not mine, it is probably my best work with Donna. I think the arrangement, the vocals, the mixes, are all top of the line.'

Donna has revealed she recorded her version of the song in one take. 'I went into the studio one day,' she said, 'and Giorgio had done this sort of up-tempo version of it. I had no idea he had done it. He just said, "Let me work on some different cuts, and we're going to put this together, and we're going to do this," etc., and I'm like, okay – whatever.

'When I get to the studio, he plays the first track, about twenty seconds of it. I tell him to stop the track. I get up. I walk into the studio. I get on the microphone. I said play it, because I know the words. I said play the song – start all over, and they started at that point. I recorded the song the way you hear it.

'There was one tiny mistake at some point. I don't know if I was off-mic, or whatever it was that needed to be fixed. Then, they had me sing a safety tape, which they didn't use. But the take that's on there is the one I did out of the excitement of the moment. It was a great track, and I was so happy with it that I didn't want to change it.'

Jimmy Webb, who wrote the song, is on record as saying: 'Donna Summer's vocal performance of *MacArthur Park* is nothing short of astounding.'

Promo 12" singles, featuring *MacArthur Park Suite*, were released in the UK & USA.

A yellow vinyl 12" was issued in Germany.

This song gave Donna her first no.1 on the Hot 100 in the States, and *MacArthur Park Suite* topped the Hot Dance Club Play chart.

The single topped the Hot 100 the same week *LIVE AND MORE* was no.1 on the Billboard 200 album chart – thus Donna became the first female artist to achieve to conquer both charts simultaneously.

The single also hit no.1 in Canada, no.4 in New Zealand, no.5 in the UK, no.7 in Ireland, no.8 in Australia & on the R&B chart in the States, no.9 in the Netherlands, no.11 in Belgium, no.16 in Sweden and no.39 in Germany.

RIAA Award: Gold (October 1978) = 1 million.

BPI Award: Silver (October 1978) = 250,000.

Grammy Award nomination:
Best Pop Vocal Performance, Female.

Performed by Donna on *Dick Clark's Live Wednesday* TV show on 19th October 1978 in the States.

Official versions:
Album Version.
Album Version (Reprise).
7" / Single Edit.
12" Edit.

A live version by Donna, recorded at the Hammerstein Ballroom, New York, in February 1999, featured on her 1999 album, *LIVE & MORE ENCORE!*

A second live version was included on the 2005 album, *NIGHT OF THE PROMS* – this was a live compilation from the Belgian part of the *Night Of The Proms* music festival.

Ranked no.89 on VH1's '100 Greatest Dance Songs' listing in October 2000.

Performed by Donna when she appeared at the Nobel Peace Prize Concert, staged in Oslo, Norway, on 11th December 2009.

Performed by Donna when she was inducted into the Hollywood Bowl's Hall of Fame on 18th June 2010.

The Laidback Luke Remix, included on the posthumous remix album *LOVE TO LOVE YOU DONNA* in 2013, gave Donna her 17th no.1 on Billboard's Dance Club Play chart.

Other Hit Versions:

Richard Harris – no.2 on the Hot 100 in the States, and no.4 in the UK, in 1968.

Waylon Jennings & The Kimberlys – no.93 on the Hot 100 in 1969.

Four Tops – no.27 on the R&B chart and no.38 on the Hot 100 in the States in 1971.

Richard Harris (reissue) – no.38 in the UK in 1972.

Numerous other artists have recorded the song, including Glen Campbell, Sammy Davis, Jr., Percy Faith, Liza Minnelli, Elaine Paige, Diana Ross & The Supremes, Frank Sinatra, the Three Degrees and Andy Williams.

MacARTHUR PARK SUITE

17:47 minute suite of songs Donna recorded for her 1978 album, *LIVE AND MORE*. The suite comprised:

- *MacArthur Park.*
- *One Of A Kind.*
- *Heaven Knows.*
- *MacArthur Park (Reprise).*

Released as a 12" single, the suite gave Donna her seventh no.1 on Billboard's Hot Dance Club Play chart in the States.

The suite, due to its length, was replaced on the single disc CD issue of *LIVE AND MORE* by an extended version of *Down, Deep Inside (Theme From The Deep)*.

The suite was released on CD, in its entirety, on Donna's 1987 compilation, *THE DANCE COLLECTION*.

See also: *MacArthur Park*, *One Of A Kind* & *Heaven Knows*.

MAN I LOVE, THE

Written by George & Ira Gershwin, and recorded live by Donna at the Universal Amphitheatre, Los Angeles, as part of her *My Man Medley* – featured on her 1978 album, *LIVE AND MORE*.

The medley also featured *I Got It Bad (And That Ain't Good)* and *Some Of These Days*.

Donna also performed the song, as part of a medley with *There's No Business Like Show Business* and *Love Is Here To Stay*, on The Rainbow Tour in 1984.

MAN IN THE MIRROR

Written by Siedah Garrett & Glen Ballard, and recorded by Michael Jackson for his 1987 album, *BAD*.

Donna performed the song, as part of an all-star ensemble, as the finale of the Nobel Peace Prize Concert, staged in

Oslo, Norway, on 11th December 2009. Among the artists joining Donna on stage were Will Smith and his wife Jada, plus their children Jaden & Willow, Natasha Bedingfield, Wyclef Jean, Toby Keith and Westlife.

Michael Jackson took the song to no.1 on the Hot 100 and R&B chart in the States, and to no.21 in the UK, in 1988. Following Michael's passing in June 2009, the song re-entered the UK chart, and rose to no.2.

MARY AND ELIZABETH RECITATIVE

Written by Michael & Stormie Omartian, and recorded by Donna with Crystal Lewis (as Elizabeth & Mary, respectively) for the 2000 soundtrack album, *CHILD OF THE PROMISE* – produced by Michael Omartian.

MAYBE

Written by Richard Barrett, and originally recorded by the Chantels in October 1957.

Donna & Brooklyn Dreams performed the song as part of a 1960s medley, when Donna hosted *The Midnight Special* TV show – aired in the States on 26th May 1978.

Other songs in the medley: *So Fine, My Girl, My Guy, The Way You Do The Things You Do, Good Lovin', I Heard It Through The Grapevine* and *Heat Wave*.

Donna performed the same medley on her Bad Girls tour in 1979.

Hit Versions:
Chantels – no.2 on the R&B chart and no.15 on the Hot 100 in the States in 1958.
Three Degrees – no.4 on the R&B chart and no.29 on the Hot 100 in 1070.

MAYBE IT'S OVER

Written and recorded by Donna for her 1984 album, *CATS WITHOUT CLAWS* – produced by Omartian.

B-side of *There Goes My Baby*.

See also: *It's Over*.

MELANIE

Written by Donna & Giorgio Moroder, and recorded by Donna for her shelved 1981 album, *I'M A RAINBOW* – produced by Moroder & Pete Bellotte.

The album was finally released in 1996.

MELODY OF LOVE
(WANNA BE LOVED)

Written by Donna with Joe Carrano, Robert Clivilles & David Cole, and recorded by Donna for her 1994 compilation album, *ENDLESS SUMMER* – produced by Donna & Welcome Productions.

Released as a single, the song gave Donna her 10th no.1 on the Hot Dance Club Play chart in the States, but it failed to enter the Hot 100 or the R&B chart.

The single peaked at no.21 in the UK, where Donna promoted the song with her third appearance of *Top Of The Pops* – the show aired on 9th March 1989.

Donna performed the song when she appeared on *The Late Show With David Letterman* in 1995.

Official Versions:
Album Version.
Boss Mix.
Classic Club Mix.
D'Tribe.
Epris Mix.
Epris Radio Mix.
Mijangos Powertools Trip #1.
AJ & Humpty's Anthem Mix.
Stomp Mix.
West End 7" Radio Mix.
West End Edit.

MIDNIGHT SPECIAL MEDLEY

Donna performed this 10 minute medley of hits with Brooklyn Dreams, when she hosted *The Midnight Special* TV show – the episode aired in the States on 26th May 1978.

Donna & Brooklyn Dreams sang the following songs: *So Fine, Maybe, My Girl, My Guy, The Way You Do The Things You Do, Good Lovin', I Heard It Through The Grapevine* and *Heat Wave*.

See also: individual songs in the medley.

MIMI'S SONG

Written by Donna with Virgil Weber, for her eldest daughter, Mimi, whose father is Donna's first husband, Helmuth Sommer.

Recorded live by Donna at the Universal Amphitheatre, Los Angeles, and featured on her 1978 album, *LIVE AND MORE*.

'Having Mimi changed my whole life,' said Donna, in a 1977 interview. 'As soon as she was born, I realised that – wow! Suddenly, someone else has become a real part of your life, someone you're responsible for, someone you have to care for and give understanding and love. I know that every mother will understand when I say that it made my own life richer in every way.'

Donna performed the song at *The Music For UNICEF Concert: A Gift For Song*,

staged at the United Nations General Assembly, New York, on 9th January 1979 – aired the following day in many countries. Before singing the song, from her and her daughter, Donna dedicated the song to all the children of the world, and at the end of the song she was joined onstage by Mimi, who wished everyone 'Goodnight'.

The aim of the concert was to raise money for UNICEF's world hunger programs, and to mark the start of the International Year Of The Child.

Donna also donated her song, for inclusion on the accompanying charity album, *MUSIC FOR UNICEF: A GIFT OF SONG*. She did offer an alternate recording of the song for the album, but the same live recording featured on her *LIVE AND MORE* album was used.

See also: *He Is Your Brother*, *Put A Little Love In Your Heart* and *You've Got A Friend*.

MINUTE BY MINUTE

Written by Michael McDonald & Lester Abrams, and recorded by the Doobie Brothers for their 1978 album with the same title.

Donna performed the song, with Kenny Rogers, as part of a Grammy nominations medley, when she appeared at the Grammy Awards, staged at the Shrine Auditorium, Los Angeles, on 27th February 1980.

The Doobie Brothers took the song to no.14 on the Hot 100 and no.74 on the R&B chart in the States, and to no.47 in the UK.

See also: *Grammy Nominations Medley*.

MISTAKEN IDENTITY

Written by Donna with Keith Diamond, Anthony Smith & Donna Wyant, and recorded by Donna for her 1991 album with the same title – produced by Diamond.

Donna has revealed the song was inspired by the police beating of a black motorist, Rodney King, in Los Angeles in March 1991.

'I felt I had to make a comment about that,' said Donna. 'I distanced the song from the actual events by putting myself in Rodney King's place.'

The acquittal of the four police officers who allegedly beat King in April 1992 sparked riots across Los Angeles, in which 53 people lost their lives.

MODERN AGE LOVE AFFAIR

Written and recorded by Bruce Sudano, for his 1981 album, *FUGITIVE KIND* – backing vocals by Donna (credited as Donna Sudano).

MOTHER

This is one of the original songs written by members of the Crow, possibly including Donna, which the group regularly performed live in 1965-66 – the song was influenced by Frank Zappa's *Mothers Of Invention*.

MR MUSIC

Written by Donna with Evan Bogart, Meredith Wilson & J. R. Rotem, and recorded by Donna for her 2008 album, *CRAYONS* – produced by Rotem.

'Mr Music,' said Donna, 'he's like any DJ, the guy on the radio station, the guy in the DJ booth, the guy that's changing your moods, the guy that keeps you going, the guy that's on the radio in the morning when you're driving. He's everything you need him to be. Music fast forwards you from one place to another because it takes you away from where you are in a strange way and elevates your mood. When I play *Mr Music*, it's euphoric – it's very happy.'

MY BABY DON'T CALL ME BABY

Written by Pete Bellotte & T. Baldursson, and recorded by former model Twiggy for her shelved 1979 album, *HEAVEN IN MY EYES* – produced by Donna & Juergen Koppers.

The album was finally released in 2007, and also included an up-dated remix by OUTpsiDER.

MY BABY UNDERSTANDS

Written and recorded by Donna for her 1979 album, *BAD GIRLS* – produced by Pete Bellotte & Giorgio Moroder.

B-side of *No More Tears (Enough Is Enough)* (7" single) in the UK.

Sampled by Ne-Yo & Jamie Foxx in 2008, on *She Got Her Own (Miss Independent Part 2)*, a remix of Ne-Yo's *Miss Independent*.

MY DREAM IS FOR YOU

Written by Donna & Michael Omartian, for the as yet unpublished play Donna worked on with Bruce Sudano, Al Kasha & Michael Omartian, *Ordinary Girl* – remains unreleased.

MY GIRL

Written by Smokey Robinson & Ronald White, and recorded by the Temptations for their 1965 album, *THE TEMPTATIONS SING SMOKEY*.

Donna & Brooklyn Dreams performed the song as part of a 1960s medley, when Donna hosted *The Midnight Special* TV show – aired in the States on 26th May 1978.

Other songs in the medley: *So Fine, Maybe, My Guy, The Way You Do The Things You Do, Good Lovin', I Heard It Through The Grapevine* and *Heat Wave*.

Donna performed the same medley on her Bad Girls tour in 1979.

Hit Versions:
Temptations – no.1 on the Hot 100 and R&B chart in the States, and no.43 in the UK, in 1965.
Otis Redding – no.11 in the UK in 1965, and no.36 in the UK in 1968.
Eddie Floyd – no.43 on the R&B chart in the States in 1970.
Amii Stewart & Johnny Bristol (medley) – no.39 in the UK, and no.63 on the Hot 100 and no.76 on the R&B chart in the States, in 1980.
Whispers – no.26 in the UK in 1980.
Daryl Hall, John Oates with David Ruffin & Eddie Kendrick (medley) – no.20 on the Hot 100 and no.40 on the R&B chart in the States in 1985.
Amii Stewart & Deon Estus (medley) – no.63 in the UK in 1986.
Suave – no.3 on the R&B chart and no.20 on the Hot 100 in the States in 1988.
Temptations (reissue) – no.2 in the UK in 1992.

MY GUY

Written by Smokey Robinson, and recorded by Mary Wells for her 1964 album, *MARY WELLS SINGS MY GUY*.

Donna & Brooklyn Dreams performed the song as part of a 1960s medley, when Donna hosted *The Midnight Special* TV show – aired in the States on 26th May 1978.

Other songs in the medley: *So Fine, Maybe*, *My Girl*, *The Way You Do The Things You Do*, *Good Lovin'*, *I Heard It Through The Grapevine* and *Heat Wave*.

Donna performed the same medley on her Bad Girls tour in 1979.

Hit Versions:
Mary Wells – no.1 on the Hot 100 in the States, and no.5 in the UK, in 1964.
Mary Wells (reissue) – no.14 in the UK in 1972.
Amii Stewart & Johnny Bristol (medley) – no.39 in the UK, and no.63 on the Hot 100 and no.76 on the R&B chart in

the States, in 1980.

Sister Sledge – no.14 on the R&B chart and no.23 on the Hot 100 in the States in 1982.

Amii Stewart & Deon Estus (medley) – no.63 in the UK in 1986.

MY LIFE

Written by Donna with Pete Waterman, P. Berry & G. Miller, for the as yet unpublished play Donna worked on with Bruce Sudano, Al Kasha & Michael Omartian, *Ordinary Girl* – remains unreleased.

This was one of three songs Donna recorded at PWL Studios in early 1996, and it's known she later re-recorded it – however, neither studio version has ever been released.

A snippet of Donna in the studio, recording the song, featured in VH1's *Behind The Music* special.

Donna performed the song on her Live & More Encore Tour in 1999 – her performance at Manhattan's Hammerstein Ballroom on 4th February featured on her live album, *LIVE & MORE ENCORE!* and the similarly titled home video.

MY MAN MEDLEY

Medley of three songs: *The Man I Love, I Got It Bad (And That Ain't Good)* and *Some Of These Days*.

Donna performed the medley on the *Don Kirshner's Rock Concert* TV show in 1976.

A live version of the medley, recorded at the Universal Amphitheatre, Los Angeles, featured on Donna's 1978 album, *LIVE AND MORE*.

See also: *The Man I Love, I Got It Bad (And That Ain't Good) & Some Of These Days*.

MY PRAYER FOR YOU

Written by Donna & Nathan DiGesare, and recorded by Donna for the 1999 children's album, *SING ME TO SLEEP, MOMMY* – produced by DiGesare.

The album was sub-titled 'A Collection Of Original Ballads & Lullabies'.

MYSTERY OF LOVE

Written by John Lang, Bill Meyers & Richard Page, and recorded by Donna for her self-titled 1982 album – produced by Quincy Jones.

NA NA HEY HEY KISS HIM GOODBYE

Written by Paul Leka, Dale Frashuer & Gary DeCarlo, and originally recorded by the trio in 1969 as Steam.

Recorded by the Veit Marvos Red Point Orchestra for a similarly titled album, released in Germany circa 1972-73 – Donna, at this time, was a member of the Orchestra.

Hit Versions:
Steam – no.1 on the Hot 100 in the States, and no.9 in the UK, in 1969-70.
Bananarama – no.5 in the UK, and no.1 on the Bubbling Under section of the Hot 100 in the States, in 1983.
Nylons (as *Kiss Him Goodbye*) – no.12 on the Hot 100 in the States in 1987.

See also: *Back Off Boogaloo*.

NATURE BOY

Written by Eden Ahbez and first published in 1947 – the following year, Nat 'King' Cole had a major hit with his recording.

Performed by Donna when she was inducted into the Hollywood Bowl's Hall of Fame on 18th June 2010.

'It was a great moment for me,' said Donna, when she was interviewed after her induction, 'to be able to do something different.' Donna went on to reveal, 'I will begin work on a standards album. I will probably do an all-out dance album and a standards album. I'm gonna do both, and we will release them however we're gonna release them – we are not sure which is going first.'

Hit Versions:
Nat 'King' Cole – no.1 on the Pop chart and no.2 on the R&B chart in the States in 1948.

Bobby Darin – no.24 in the UK and no.40 on the Hot 100 in the States in 1961.

George Benson – no.26 in the UK in 1977.

Central Line – no.21 in the UK in 1983.

Numerous other artists have recorded the song, including Philip Bailey, David Bowie, Natalie Cole, Harry Connick, Jr., Celine Dion, Ella Fitzgerald & Joe Pass, Marvin Gaye, Engelbert Humperdinck, Aaron Neville, Sarah Vaughan and Grover Washington.

NEED-A-MAN BLUES

Written by Pete Bellotte & Giorgio Moroder, and recorded by Donna for her 1975 album, *LOVE TO LOVE YOU BABY* – produced by Bellotte.

B-side on *Love To Love You* – released in the Netherlands in 1975, and of *Love To Love You Baby*.

NEVER LOSE YOUR SENSE OF HUMOUR

Written by Donna with Paul Jabara & Greg Mathieson, and recorded by Jabara – as a duet with Donna – for his 1979 album, *THE THIRD ALBUM* – produced by Jabara.

Released as a single around the same time as *No More Tears (Enough Is Enough)*, which completely overshadowed it.

NEW YORK MINUTE

Written by Don Henley, Danny Kortchmar & Jai Winding, and recorded by Henley for his 1989 album, *THE END OF THE INNOCENCE*.

Donna performed the song on her Endless Summer Tour in 1995.

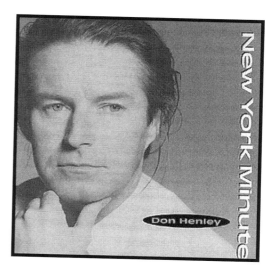

Don Henley took the song to no.48 on the Hot 100 in the States.

NICE TO SEE YOU

Written by Veit Marvos & Richard Palmer-James, and recorded by the Veit Marvos Red Point Orchestra for a similarly titled album, released in Germany circa 1972-73.

Donna, at this time, was a member of the Veit Marvos Red Point Orchestra.

Released as a single in the Netherlands.

See also: *Back Off Boogaloo*.

NICKEL-BAG ANNIE

This is a song Donna revealed she wrote, in her autobiography *Ordinary Girl: The Journey*, inspired by her maternal grandmother, Annie Glouster – who, when she visited the family, brought a handkerchief stuffed full of nickels, and gave one each to Donna and her siblings.

NIGHTLIFE

Written by Pete Bellotte & Giorgio Moroder, and recorded by Donna for her 1980 album, *THE WANDERER* – produced by Moroder & Bellotte.

NIGHTS IN WHITE SATIN

Written by Justin Hayward, and recorded by the Moody Blues for their 1967 album, *DAYS OF FUTURE PASSED*.

Donna performed the song on her Greatest Hits Tour in 2005, and occasionally at some of her more recent concerts.

The Moody Blues took the song to no.2 on the Hot 100 in the States and no.19 in the UK; the single was reissued in the UK in 1972 and charted at no.9.

NO MORE TEARS (ENOUGH IS ENOUGH)

Written by Paul Jabara & Bruce Roberts, and recorded by Donna as a duet with Barbra Streisand – produced by Giorgio Moroder & Gary Klein.

Recorded at Village Recorder Studios, Los Angeles, between the 14th and 28th August 1979.

A 11:46 minutes version featured on Donna's 1979 compilation, *ON THE RADIO: GREATEST HITS VOLUMES I & II*, and a shorter 8:24 minutes edit was included on Streisand's 1979 album, *WET*.

Original title: *Enough Is Enough*.

Paul Jabara was instrumental in making the duet happen. 'I asked Donna if she wanted to come with me to Barbra's for lunch,' recalled Jabara. 'She immediately said, "I'd love to!" When I called Barbra, her son Jason answered. I told him to ask his mother about bringing Donna to lunch with me. He screamed, "Donna Summer!" It turns out Jason's the biggest Donna fan in the world. So I owed it all to him.'

'Barbra and Donna were both intimidated by each other,' said Jabara, 'and couldn't

understand why the other person should be intimidated – it was crazy'.

'They were nervous,' confirmed Charles Koppelman, executive producer for the collaboration. 'They had a lot of compromising to do. They would wonder, "Is her line better than my line?" … they were not temperamental at all, they would never have been able to compromise enough to make the duet come off as fairly as it does. But it did get a little tense at times.'

Initially, the Streisand's producers didn't want to include the track on her new album, as it didn't fit in with the album's 'wet' theme. Streisand, on the other hand, did want the track on her album. The problem was solved by adding a ballad introduction, starting with the lyrics, 'It's raining, it's pouring, my love life is boring me to tears after all these years …'

At the same time, the song's title was changed to, *No More Tears (Enough Is Enough)*.

Bob Esty, an arranger/producer who worked on the record, has admitted the first recording session didn't go well. 'She (Barbra Streisand) freaked out,' he revealed. 'Her initial session with Donna was a disaster. She thought Donna sang rings around her – that disco was Donna's thing, and she didn't stand a chance. When I walked into that recording session, you could have cut the air with a knife.'

'It was fun,' said Donna, on working with Barbra Streisand. 'She's a funny girl. She did a lot of funny things. There was a lot of comedy going back and forth between us. I had just finished eight nights at the Universal Amphitheatre. The next day, we had this recording session. Barbra and I were in the studio and we were holding the high note on *Enough Is Enough*, and I didn't breathe right. I just held the note too long – and I fell off my stool!

'Barbra kept holding her note, and then at the end of the note, she said, "Are you all right?" It was hysterical, because by the time she asked me, I was coming to. I hit the floor and it jolted me. She didn't stop holding her note. It was the height of professionalism. She thought I was playing around.'

'I enjoyed working with Donna,' said Streisand, 'discount any of the stories that say otherwise … working with

Donna was the least painful of all the duets I've done. Maybe because we were so intimidated by each other, we were on our best behaviour! I liked the result, which was sort of the other side of a love song.'

In the States, the 7" single was released on Streisand's record label (Columbia), and the 12" single on Donna's label (Casablanca) – the reverse was the case in the UK, with the 12" being issued by Streisand's label (CBS).

A translucent red vinyl 12" singles was released in Mexico.

The duet gave Donna her fourth no.1 on the Hot 100 in just over a year in the States, and her ninth no.1 on the Hot Dance Club Play chart.

The duet charted at no.1 in Canada & Sweden, no.3 in Norway & the UK, no.4 in Switzerland, no.7 in Ireland & New Zealand, no.8 in Australia, no.16 in Austria, no.17 in Zimbabwe, no.20 in the Netherlands & on the R&B chart in the

States, no.31 in Germany and no.59 in Japan.

RIAA Award (7"): Gold (February 1980) = 1 million.

RIAA Award (12"): Gold (February 1980) = 1 million.

Performed by Donna, with the show's host, when she appeared on *The Rosie O'Donnell Show* on 24th June 1999.

Official Versions:
Album Version (*ON THE RADIO*).
Album Version (*WET*).
7"/ Single Edit (Casablanca).
7" / Single Edit (Columbia).

A live version, by Donna & Tina Arena, featured on Donna's *LIVE & MORE ENCORE!* album, released in 1999. The duet was recorded at Donna's concert staged at the Hammerstein Ballroom, New York, on 4th February 1999.

On 19th June 2004 Donna appeared on the ITV special, *Disco Mania*, in the UK – she performed the song with Irish boy band, Westlife. This version subsequently featured on the various artist compilation, *DISCOMANIA* (Mercury 9821319), and was produced by Bill Padley & Jem Godfrey.

'I never normally do retro shows,' said Donna, about *Disco Mania*, 'because I want to stay away from all that. I figure I did it once, I don't really need to re-live it all the time, but when they came over to America and explained the whole show, I liked the idea of it.'

Performed by Donna when she appeared at the Nobel Peace Prize Concert, staged in Oslo, Norway, on 11th December 2009.

Performed by Donna when she was inducted into the Hollywood Bowl's Hall of Fame on 18th June 2010.

Performed by Donna, with *Last Dance*, with contestant Prince Poppycock on the *America's Got Talent* finale, staged on 15th September 2010.

A cover version by Kym Mazelle & Jocelyn Brown charted at no.13 in the UK in 1994.

NO ORDINARY LOVE SONG

Written by Donna & Michael Omartian, for the as yet unpublished play Donna worked on with Bruce Sudano, Al Kasha & Michael Omartian, *Ordinary Girl* – remains unreleased.

Donna performed the song on her Mid Summer Nights Dream Tour in 1996-97.

NOBODY

Written by Donna & Michael Collin Hanna – registered with the American Society of Composers, Authors & Publishers (ASCAP).

Donna never released the song on any of her albums, but she did perform it in concert. A live version, filmed at the Hammerstein Ballroom, New York, on 4th January 1999, featured on Donna's 1999 home video, *Live & More Encore!*

NOW I NEED YOU

Written by Donna with Giorgio Moroder & Pete Bellotte, and recorded by Donna for her 1977 album, *ONCE UPON A TIME* – produced by Moroder & Bellotte.

O COME ALL YE FAITHFUL

Traditional hymn, originally titled *Adeste Fideles*, generally attributed to John Francis Wade – it was translated into English by a Roman Catholic priest, Frederick Oakeley.

Performed by Donna, as a duet with co-host Marilyn McCoo, on the *Solid Gold Christmas Special*, which aired in the States on 10th December 1982.

Performed by Donna, as a medley with *Silent Night* and *Hark! The Herald Angels Sing*, when she appeared on *Bandstand* on 22nd December 1984.

Recorded by Donna for her 1994 album, *CHRISTMAS SPIRIT* – produced by Michael Omartian.

Other artists to have recorded the hymn include Andrea Bocelli, Harry Connick, Jr., Bing Crosby, Celine Dion, Bob Dylan, Faith Hill, Frank Sinatra, Luther Vandross and Andy Williams.

O HOLY NIGHT

Popular Christmas carol composed in 1847 by Adolphe Adam, with lyrics from Placide Cappeau's French poem, *Minuit, Chrétiens* ('Midnight, Christians'). The singing version, also known by the title *Cantique De Noël*, was created by John Sullivan Dwight, a Unitarian minister.

Performed by Donna on the *Solid Gold Christmas Special*, which aired in the States on 10th December 1982.

Recorded by Donna for her 1994 album, *CHRISTMAS SPIRIT* – produced by Michael Omartian.

Hit Version:
Josh Groban – no.9 on the 'bubbling Under' section of the Hot 100 in the States in 2003, and no.9 on the Hot Holiday Songs chart in 2008.

OH BILLY PLEASE

Written by Donna & Michael Omartian, and recorded by Donna for her 1984 album, *CATS WITHOUT CLAWS* – produced by Omartian.

OH LONESOME ME

Written and originally recorded by Don Gibson in 1958.

Donna performed the song, with the host, as part of a country medley, when she appeared as a guest on the *Eddie Rabbit Special* in 1982 – she also sang *Stand By Your Man,* plus *I Can't Stop Loving You* with Eddie Rabbit.

Hit Versions:
Don Gibson – no.1 on the Country chart and no.7 on the Hot 100 in the States in 1958.
Johnny Cash – no.13 on the Country chart in 1961.
Craig Douglas – no.11 in the UK in 1962.
Stonewall Jackson – no.63 on the Country chart in 1970.
Loggins & Messina – no.92 on the Country chart in 1975.
Kentucky Headhunters – no.8 on the Country chart in 1990.

OH, SEGNE GOTT MEIN SEEL (O BLESS THE LORD)

Written by Stephen Schwartz & John-Michael Tebelak for the musical, *Godspell* – premiered in New York City on 24th February 1971.

Donna appeared – credited as Donna Gaines – in the Austrian production of the musical in 1971, and was part of the cast who performed this song, in German, on stage and on the cast album.

OLD FASHIONED GIRL

Written by Bruce Sudano & Albano, and recorded by Brooklyn Dreams for their self-titled 1977 album – produced by Skip Konte, with backing vocals by Donna.

ON MY HONOR

Written by Donna with Bruce Sudano & Harold Faltermeyer, and recorded by Donna for her 1979 album, *BAD GIRLS* – produced by Pete Bellotte & Giorgio Moroder.

Released as a promo 7" single in the UK.

B-side of *Bad Girls*.

ON THE RADIO

Written by Donna & Giorgio Moroder, and recorded by Donna for the 1979

soundtrack album, *FOXES* – produced by Moroder.

The song was also released on Donna's 1979 compilation, *ON THE RADIO: GREATEST HITS VOLUMES I & II*.

The album featured two versions of the song, the opening 4:00 minute version and the closing 5:50 'Long Version'.

At 7:34 minutes, the version featured on the *FOXES* soundtrack was even longer –

this version was included on the 2003 Deluxe Edition of Donna's *BAD GIRLS* album.

Released as a single, the song charted at no.4 in Canada, no.5 on the Hot 100 and no.6 in Norway, no.9 on the R&B chart in the States, no.16 in Belgium, no.18 in Ireland, no.20 in the Netherlands, no.32 in New Zealand & the UK, no.34 in Germany, no.36 in Australia and no.58 in Japan.

Donna performed the song on several TV shows in 1980, including *The Tonight Show*, *The Dinah Shore Show* and *The Tomorrow Show*.

Performed by Donna when she was inducted into the Hollywood Bowl's Hall of Fame on 18th June 2010.

RIAA Award: Gold (March 1980) = 1 million.

Grammy Award nomination:
Best Pop Vocal Performance, Female.

Official Versions:
Soundtrack Version (7:34) / 12" Version.
Album Version (4:00) / Single Version.
Album Version (5:50).
Instrumental.

Donna performed the song as a duet with Seal, as part of a medley, when she appeared at the *David Foster & Friends* concert, staged at the Mandalay Bay Events Center, Las Vegas, on 15th October 2010 – the medley also featured *Un-Break My Heart* and *Crazy*. The medley featured on the 2011 album, *HIT MAN RETURNS*, credited to David

Foster & Friends. The release also included a DVD and Blu-ray home video of the concert.

A cover version recorded by Martine McCutcheon charted at no.7 in the UK in 2001.

ONCE UPON A TIME

Written by Donna with Giorgio Moroder & Pete Bellotte, and recorded by Donna for her 1977 album with the same title – produced by Moroder & Bellotte.

The double album also featured *(Theme) Once Upon A Time*, on Side 3 and again on Side 4 – this was much slower than the opening version of the song.

Released as a single in Japan.

B-side of *I Love You, Rumour Has It & MacArthur Park*.

Donna performed the song when she appeared on the TV show, *The Midnight Special*, in 1978.

A live version, recorded at the Universal Amphitheatre, Los Angeles, featured on Donna's 1978 album, *LIVE AND MORE*.

The song featured in Donna's *The Donna Summer Special* TV movie, which aired in the States on 27th January 1980.

ONE NIGHT IN A LIFETIME

Written by Pete Bellotte & Harold Faltermeyer, and recorded by Donna for her 1979 album, *BAD GIRLS* – produced by Bellotte & Giorgio Moroder.

ONE OF A KIND

Written by Donna with Giorgio Moroder & Pete Bellotte, and recorded by Donna – as part of *MacArthur Park Suite* – for her 1978 album, *LIVE AND MORE* – produced by Moroder & Bellotte.

ONE WORD

Written by Paul Jabara for Donna – the song has been cited as something of an apology from Donna, to the gay community, for comments she has always denied making.

'She did a demo for it,' revealed Bob Esty. 'It was a song about coming to terms with knowledge – that we're going to fight this thing (AIDS) and we're going to win. The song had a few personal references about friends dying and a feeling of helplessness to change the situation.

'Paul (Jabara) tried, even while he himself was struggling with AIDS, to get Donna back with her gay fans. He thought the whole gay controversy thing had been blown out of proportion.'

Sadly, Paul Jabara died of an AIDS-related illness on 29th September 1992.

ONLY ONE, THE

Written by Mike Stock, Matt Aitken & Pete Waterman, and recorded by Donna for her 1989 album, *ANOTHER PLACE AND TIME* – produced by Stock, Aitken & Waterman.

ONLY ONE MAN

Written by Donna with Bob Conti & Virgil Weber.

A live version, recorded at the Universal Amphitheatre, Los Angeles, featured on Donna's 1978 album, *LIVE AND MORE*.

B-side of *Heaven Knows*.

ONLY THE FOOL SURVIVES

Written by Donna with Bruce Sudano, John Bettis, Virgil Weber & Michael

Omartian, and recorded by Donna as a duet with Mickey Thomas for her 1987 album, *ALL SYSTEMS GO* – produced by Harold Faltermeyer.

Mickey Thomas was the lead singer of Starship in the 1980s, and still tours with a band called 'Starship featuring Mickey Thomas'.

Released as a single in Canada and Japan.

The song was planned as the second single from the album in the States, but its release was cancelled, and only a promo 7" single was issued.

The single charted at no.40 in Canada.

ONLY WORDS

One of three unreleased songs Donna mentioned she had written, for a new album scheduled for July 2002, in her 2001 holiday message to fans – the other two songs were *Rain On My Shoulders* and *Work It*.

OPERATOR

Written by William Spivery, and recorded by the Manhattan Transfer for their self-titled 1975 album.

Donna performed the song, as a medley with *Amazing Grace* and *How Great Thou Art*, on her Rainbow Tour in 1984 and her Silver Girl Tour in 1986.

Manhattan Transfer took the song to no.22 on the Hot 100 in the States.

ORDINARY MIRACLE

This is a song Donna recorded for the shelved 1995 soundtrack album, *LET IT BE ME* – produced by Narada Michael Walden.

The film was released as a home video in 1998, and the song could be heard playing over the end credits – this is the only official release of the song.

OUR LOVE

Written by Donna & Giorgio Moroder, and recorded by Donna for her 1979 album, *BAD GIRLS* – produced by Moroder & Pete Bellotte.

Released as a single in Spain.

B-side of *Sunset People* in the UK.

OVER THE RAINBOW

Written by Harold Arlen & E.Y. Harburg, and first sung by Judy Garland in the 1939 film, *The Wizard Of Oz*.

Performed in concert by Donna during her Rainbow Tour in 1984.

Hit Versions:
Demensions – no.16 on the Hot 100 in the States in 1960.
Matchbox (medley) – no.15 in the UK in 1980.

Sam Harris – no.67 in the UK in 1985.
Eva Cassidy – no.42 in the UK in 2001.
Israel Kamukawiwo'ole – no.46 in the UK in 2007-08.
Danielle Hope – no.29 in the UK in 2010.

PANDORA'S BOX

Written by Pete Bellotte & Giorgio Moroder, and recorded by Donna for her 1975 album, *LOVE TO LOVE YOU BABY* – produced by Bellotte.

B-side of *Virgin Mary* – released in the Netherlands only.

PAPA, CAN YOU HEAR ME?

Written by Michel Legrand, Alan & Marilyn Bergman, and recorded by Barbra Streisand for the 1983 film, *Yentl*.

Performed by Donna, as one of the songs nominated for Best Original Song, at the 56th Academy Awards ceremony, staged at the Dorothy Chandler Pavilion, Los Angeles, on 9th April 1984.

Ironically, the song that picked up the Oscar in the Best Original Song category was one Donna had been offered but rejected: *Flashdance… What A Feeling*.

PART OF YOUR WORLD

Written by Alan Menken & Howard Ashman for the 1989 Disney film, *The Little Mermaid*.

Donna performed this song, with her daughters Brooklyn & Amanda, on her Mid Summer Nights Dream Tour in 1996-97.

PEARLS

Written by Sade Adu & Andrew Hale, and recorded by Sade for their 1992 album, *LOVE DELUXE*.

Donna performed the song on her Greatest Hits Tour in 2005, and at select dates on more recent tours.

PEOPLE, PEOPLE

Written by Donna with Michael Omartian & Bruce Sudano, and recorded by Donna for her 1983 album, *SHE WORKS HARD FOR THE MONEY* – produced by Omartian.

Released as a single in the Netherlands.

B-side of *Love Has A Mind Of Its Own* in most other countries.

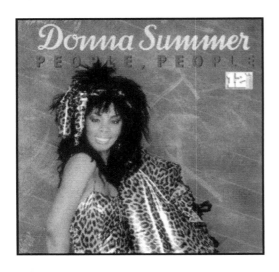

PEOPLE TALK

Written by Donna & Giorgio Moroder, and recorded by Donna for her shelved 1981 album, *I'M A RAINBOW* – produced by Moroder & Pete Bellotte.

The album was finally released in 1996.

PLANET IS ALIVE, THE

Written and recorded by Donna, as the theme song for the documentary, *The Power Of Faith – The Planet Is Alive: A Portrait Of Pope John Paul II*.

The documentary featured a music video of Donna singing the song with a choir of children – this was included on the home video (VHS), released in the States in 1987, to coincide with the Papal visit to the USA and Canada in September.

The documentary was released on DVD in 2005.

POWER OF LOVE

Written by Luther Vandross & Marcus Miller, and recorded by Vandross for his 1991 album with the same title.

Recorded by Donna for the 2005 tribute album, *SO AMAZING: ALL ALL-STAR TRIBUTE TO LUTHER VANDROSS* – produced by Hani (Albader).

Released as a promo 12" and CD single in the States.

Official Versions:
Album Mix.
Single Mix.
Radio Mix.
Hani's Extended Mix.

Hani Mixshow Edit.
Hani Mixshow Instrumental.
Power Keys.

POWER OF ONE, THE

Written by Mark Chait & Mervyn Warren, and recorded by Donna for the 2000 soundtrack album, *POKÉMON 2000: THE POWER OF ONE* – produced by David Foster, Bruce Sudano & Nathan DiGesare.

Released as a single in Japan and the States.

The single achieved no.2 on the Hot Dance Club Play chart in the States.

Official Versions:
Soundtrack Album Version.
Jonathan Peters Club Mix.
Jonathan Peters Radio Mix.
Jonathan Peters Drum-A-Pella.
Jonathan Peters Sound Factory Mix.
Jonathan Peters Sound Factory Dub.
Tommy Musto Vocal Mix.
Tommy Musto Gel Dub.
Musto Beats.

of the song – Springsteen contributed the guitar solo and backing vocals.

PRETENDERS

Written by Bruce Sudano, Joe Esposito & B. Incorvaia, and recorded by Sudano for his 1981 album, *FUGITIVE KIND* – backing vocals by Donna (credited as Donna Sudano).

PROTECTION

Written by Bruce Springsteen, and recorded by Donna for her self-titled 1982 album – produced by Quincy Jones.

Springsteen wrote the song for Donna, after David Geffen – founder of Geffen Records – approached Springsteen's producer and manager, Jon Landau. Originally, Springsteen wrote *Cover Me* for Donna, but after he was persuaded to keep that song for himself, he wrote *Protection*.

Springsteen, with the E Street Band, recorded a version of the track in early 1982 – then, in March, he and Ray Bittan travelled to Los Angeles, to work with Donna and Quincy Jones, on her version

'When Bruce brought me the song originally,' said Donna, 'we tried doing it as a duo. It was a great idea, but it really didn't work out.

'The tune just wasn't written that way and eventually I did it myself. But, it's funny – I heard him doing it so much in the studio, that to me, I sound just like him on the track.'

Released as a single in Belgium, the Netherlands and Japan.

Grammy nomination:
Best Rock Vocal Performance, Female.

PUT A LITTLE LOVE IN YOUR HEART

Written by Jackie DeShannon, Randy Myers & Jimmy Holiday, and recorded by DeShannon for her 1969 album with the same title.

Donna, along with other participating artists, sang the song at the close of *The Music For UNICEF Concert: A Gift Of Song*, staged at the United Nations Assembly, New York, on 9th January 1979 – the concert was televised the following day.

Other featured artists at the charity concert were ABBA, the Bee Gees, Rita Coolidge, John Denver, Earth, Wind & Fire, Andy Gibb, Kris Kristofferson, Olivia Newton-John and Rod Stewart.

Hit Versions:
Jackie DeShannon – no.4 on the Hot 100 in the States in 1969.
Annie Lennox & Al Green – no.9 on the Hot 100 in the States, and no.28 in the UK, in 1988.

See also: *Mimi's Song*, *He Is Your Brother*.

QUEEN FOR A DAY

Written by Donna with Giorgio Moroder & Pete Bellotte, and recorded by Donna for her 1977 album, *ONCE UPON A TIME* – produced by Moroder & Bellotte.

QUEEN IS BACK, THE

Written by Donna with Evan Bogart & J. R. Rotem, and recorded by Donna for her 2008 album, *CRAYONS* – produced by Rotem.

Sampled *Lose Control* by Kevin Federline.

'It isn't so much about reclaiming a title,' said Donna. 'I'm just saying I'm back on track, making music, back here for my peeps!'

'I'm making fun of myself,' she admitted. 'There's irony, it's poking fun at the idea of being called a Queen. That's a title that has followed me, followed me, and followed me.

'We were sitting and writing, and that title kept popping up in my mind and I'm thinking, "Am I supposed to write this? Is this too arrogant to write?" But people call me "the Queen", so I guess it's OK to refer to myself as what everybody else refers to me as. We started writing the song, and thought it was kind of cute and funny.'

RAIN ON MY SHOULDERS

This was one of three unreleased songs Donna mentioned she had written, for a new album scheduled for July 2002, in her 2001 holiday message to fans – the other two songs were *Only Words* and *Work It*.

Donna mentioned the song again, in another message to fans in July 2002, along with a further two unreleased songs, *Tearing Down The Berlin Wall* and *Till You Get It*.

RAIN, RAIN

Written by Donna & Michael Omartian, for the as yet unpublished play Donna worked on with Bruce Sudano, Al Kasha & Michael Omartian, *Ordinary Girl* – remains unreleased.

REACH OUT AND TOUCH
(SOMEBODY'S HAND)

Written by Nickolas Ashford & Valerie Simpson, and recorded by Diana Ross for her self-titled 1970 album.

Donna first met Diana Ross when she attended one of her concerts, in Munich, Germany, when she was only 21-22.

'When she used to sing *Reach Out And Touch*,' Donna recalled, 'she would give the microphone out to people in the audience. My sister grabbed the microphone and handed it to me, and I started singing – I knew every word of those songs, I was such a fan. She (Diana Ross) said, "Gimme that mic, girl – you sound too good!" or something, and she moved on. It was really cute.'

Diana Ross took the song to no.7 on the R&B chart and no.20 on the Hot 100 in the States, and to no.33 in the UK.

REFLECTIONS

Written by Brian Holland, Lamont Dozier & Edward Holland, Jr., and recorded by Diana Ross & The Supremes for their 1968 album with the same title.

Performed by Donna on *VH1 Divas 2000: A Tribute To Diana Ross, An Honors Concert For VH1's Save The Music*, staged at New York's Madison Square Garden on 9th April 2000 and aired two days later.

Diana Ross & The Supremes took the song to no.2 on the Hot 100 and no.4 on the R&B chart in the States, and to no.5 in the UK.

REJOICE!

This is a Christian hymn Donna, as the character Aunt Oona, performed when she fronted a church choir in Season 8, Episode 22 – *Pound Foolish* – of the American sitcom, *Family Matters*. The episode aired on 25th April 1997.

RESPECT

Written and recorded by Otis Redding, for his 1965 album, *OTIS BLUE*.

Donna revealed, in her autobiography *Ordinary Girl: The Journey*, this was one of the songs she sang when, aged 17, she auditioned to join a rock group.

Donna was drawn into a club where six white college guys were rehearsing by the music but, asked if she had come for the audition, she answered, 'Yeah'. The guys were actually looking for a male lead vocalist but, after singing a few songs, Donna was offered the job and happily accepted. The band agreed to call themselves 'The Crow' in Donna's honour, as she stood out as the only black member of the band.

Hit Versions:
Otis Redding – no.4 on the R&B and no35 on the Hot 100 in the States in 1965.
Aretha Franklin – no.1 on both American charts, and no.10 in the UK, in 1967.
Real Roxanne – no.71 in the UK in 1988.

Adeva – no.17 in the UK, and no.84 on the R&B chart in the States, in 1989; a remix charted at no.65 in the UK in 1993.

REUNITED

Written by Dino Fekaris & Freddie Perren, and recorded by Peaches & Herb for their 1978 album, *2 HOT*.

This was the opening song Donna performed with Kenny Rogers, as part of a Grammy nominations medley, when she appeared at the Grammy Awards, staged at the Shrine Auditorium, Los Angeles, on 27th February 1980.

Hit Versions:
Peaches & Herb – no.1 on the Hot 100 and R&B chart in the States, and no.4 in the UK, in 1978.
Louise Mandrell & R.C. Bannon – no.13 on the Country chart in the States in 1979.

Peaches & Herb were succeeded at no.1 on the Hot 100 by Donna's *Hot Stuff*.

See also: *Grammy Nominations Medley*.

RIDING THROUGH THE STORM

Written by V.M. McKay, and recorded –
as *Through The Storm* – by Yolanda
Adams, for her 1991 album with the
same title.

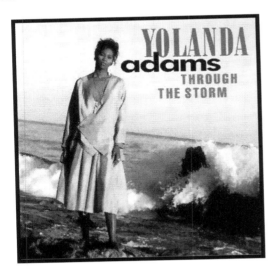

Donna performed the song on her Mid
Summer Nights Dream Tour in 1996-97,
and sometimes included the song on
subsequent dates – initially, Donna was
inspired to sing the song by the passing
of her mother and sister.

A live performance of the song featured
on Donna's 1999 home video, *Live &
More Encore!* – recorded at Manhattan's
Hammerstein Ballroom on 4th February
1999.

ROMEO

Written by Pete Bellotte & Sylvester
Levay, and recorded by Donna for her
shelved 1981 album, *I'M A RAINBOW* –
produced by Bellotte & Giorgio
Moroder.

The album was finally released in 1996.

Featured on the 1983 soundtrack album,
FLASHDANCE – Donna was offered, but
turned down, the film's title song,
Flashdance… What A Feeling, which
Irene Cara did record. The song went on
to win a Golden Globe Award and
Academy Award.

ROSIE CHRISTMAS

Written by Donna with D. Rich & G. Lorenzo, and recorded by Donna for the 2000 festive album, *ANOTHER ROSIE CHRISTMAS* – produced by Ric Wake.

RUMOUR HAS IT

Written by Donna with Giorgio Moroder & Pete Bellotte, and recorded by Donna for her 1977 album, *ONCE UPON A TIME* – produced by Moroder & Bellotte.

With *I Love You*, the song gave Donna her fifth no.1 on the Hot Dance Club Play chart in the States, where it also charted at no.21 on the R&B chart and no.53 on the Hot 100.

Elsewhere, the single achieved no.19 in the UK, no.21 in Germany, no.22 in the Netherlands and no.37 in Canada.

Official Versions:
Album Version.
7"/ Single Edit.
Live Version.

A live version, recorded at the Universal Amphitheatre, Los Angeles, featured on Donna's 1978 album, *LIVE AND MORE*.

RUNNER WITH THE PACK

Written by Pete Bellotte, and recorded by Donna for her shelved 1981 album, *I'M A RAINBOW* – produced by Bellotte & Giorgio Moroder.

The album was finally released in 1996.

RUNNING FOR COVER

Written and recorded by Donna for her 1980 album, *THE WANDERER* – produced by Giorgio Moroder & Pete Bellotte.

B-side of *Who Do You Think You're Foolin'*.

SAVING MY LOVE FOR YOU

Written by Donna & R. Gaines, and recorded by Sunshine for their cancelled 1978 album, *WATCHIN' DADDY DANCE* – produced by Donna & Juergen Koppers.

Remains unreleased.

SALLY GO 'ROUND THE ROSES

Written by Zell Sanders & Lona Stevens, and recorded by the Jaynetts for their 1963 album with the same title.

Donna (as Donna Gaines) recorded the song in 1971 – produced by Vince Melouney. Her version was released as a single in some European countries, including the Netherlands – it was her first solo single and, today, it is one of Donna's rarest records.

'Vince Melouney, who used to be the drummer of the Bee Gees,' revealed Donna, in an interview in 2004, 'recorded that song with me in London … I bet you that song's somewhere in London, in one of the studios, just sitting on someone's shelf – and they didn't even know they've got it.'

The Jaynetts took the song to no.2 on the Hot 100 and no.4 on the R&B chart in the States.

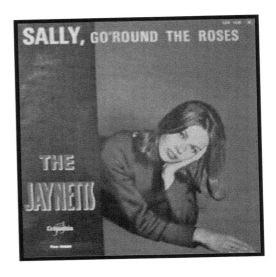

SAND ON MY FEET

Written by Donna & Toby Gad, and recorded by Donna for her 2008 album, *CRAYONS* – produced by Gad.

Donna wrote the song as a love song to her husband, Bruce Sudano. '*Sand On My Feet* is one of the few times I've written from my own point of view,' she said. 'I'm almost always writing from a man's point of view or another person's point of view.'

SAY A LITTLE PRAYER

Written by Donna with Keith Diamond, Anthony Smith & Donna Wyant, and recorded by Donna for her 1991 album, *MISTAKEN IDENTITY* – produced by Diamond.

SAY SOMETHING NICE

Written by Donna with Giorgio Moroder & Pete Bellotte, and recorded by Donna for her 1977 album, *ONCE UPON A TIME* – produced by Moroder & Bellotte.

SCHALL (SOUNDS)

Written by Gary William Friedman & Will Holt for the musical, *The Me Nobody Knows* – premiered at the Orpheum Theater, New York, on 18th May 1970.

Donna appeared – credited as Gayne Pierre – in the German production of the musical in 1970, titled *Ich Bin Ich*, and was part of the cast who performed this song on stage and on the German cast album.

The album also featured *Schall (Reprise)*.

See also: *Sounds*.

SCHWARZ (BLACK)

Written by Gary William Friedman & Will Holt for the musical, *The Me Nobody Knows* – premiered at the Orpheum Theater, New York, on 18th May 1970.

Donna appeared – credited as Gayne Pierre – in the German production of the musical in 1970, titled *Ich Bin Ich*, and was part of the cast who performed this song on stage and on the German cast album.

See also: *Black*.

SCHWEBEN IM RAUM
(WALKING IN SPACE)

Written James Rado & Gerome Ragni (book and lyrics) & Galt MacDermot (music) for the controversial 'tribal love-rock' musical, *Hair*.

Donna appeared in the German production of the musical in 1968, titled *Haare*, and was part of the cast who performed this song on stage and on the cast album.

SCIENCE OF LOVE

Written by Donna & Toby Gad, and recorded by Donna for her 2008 album, *CRAYONS* – produced by Gad.

SEND IN THE CLOWNS

Written by Stephen Sondheim for the 1973 musical, *A Little Night Music* – originally sang by Glynis Johns.
Donna performed the song at some of her concert dates in the early 1990s.

Judy Collins took the song to no.6 in the UK, and to no.36 on the Hot 100 in the States, in 1975. A couple of years later, the song re-entered the Hot 100, and rose to a new peak of no.19.

SENTIMENTAL

Written by Donna with Mike Stock, Matt Aitken & Pete Waterman, and recorded by Donna for her 1989 album, *ANOTHER PLACE AND TIME* – produced by Stock, Aitken & Waterman.

SHE WORKS HARD FOR THE
MONEY

Written by Donna & Michael Omartian, and recorded by Donna for her 1983 album with the same title – produced by Omartian.

Donna was on her way to a Grammy after-party, and she had to go to the ladies' room as soon as she arrived at Chasen's Restaurant, in Beverly Hills. 'When I got to the rest room,' she said, 'I saw an attractive attendant sitting by a small television set, fast asleep. This poor woman had to have been cooped up in the bathroom all night long. I blurted out, "she works hard for the money".'

Donna instantly felt a strange excitement race through her, and she asked her manager Susan (Munao) to get her a piece of paper – toilet paper, anything! 'I had to write the words,' she said, 'to what clearly was becoming a song.'

Donna discovered the rest room attendant was called Onetta – as well as name-checking her in the song, Donna had her photograph taken with Onetta Johnson, which featured on the back cover of her album sleeve.

'When I recorded it,' said Donna, 'I recorded it to be an anthem. Working people, period – not just women but working people – need an anthem. They need something to go, "You know what – somebody gets it!"'

'I work hard. When I'm working, it ain't easy – it's not easy being onstage in 100 degree weather, with more lights on you and the sun shining in the day-time, when you do one of these outdoor gigs. There have been days where I've felt like I was going to die on stage – literally die – where I didn't know if I inhaled one more breath that it would dry my entire lungs out, and I would just collapse.'

The song was released as the lead single from the album of the same name, and gave Donna only her second no.1 (after *Bad Girls*) on the R&B chart in the States, where it also achieved no.3 on the Hot 100.

Outside the USA, the single charted at no.2 in Canada, no.4 in Australia, no.11 in Germany & South Africa, no.16 in Belgium, no.17 in the Netherlands, no.23 in New Zealand, no.25 in the UK, no.26 in Ireland and no.52 in Japan.

Donna performed the song on *The Tonight Show* in 1983.

Grammy nomination:
Best Pop Vocal Performance, Female.

Donna performed the song, as the coveted opening number, when she attended the Grammy Awards ceremony, staged at the Shrine Auditorium, Los Angeles, on 28th February 1984. Her performance later featured on the 1994 album, *GRAMMY'S GREATEST MOMENTS VOLUME I.*

The music video, which explored the song's theme, was the first by a female African-American artist to enjoy 'heavy rotation' on MTV.

Donna performed the song when she appeared on Disneyland's *30th Anniversary Celebration*, which aired in the States on 18th February 1985 – on this occasion, the women working hard for their money were Cinderella and Snow White.

Official Versions:
Album Version.
7" / Single Edit.
12" Extended Mix.
Instrumental.

Donna, as the character Aunt Oona, performed the opening lines of the song, when she appeared in Season 8, Episode 22 – *Pound Foolish* – of the American sitcom, *Family Matters*. The episode aired on 25th April 1997.

In the early 1990s the song was used in an advertising campaign for Burger King, and in the mid-1990s, the song featured in an advertising campaign for Zellers, a Canadian department store.

In early 1999, Donna re-recorded the song for a McDonald's commercial – the chorus was changed to: 'You get more for your money, 'cause McDonald's treats you right.'

Performed by Donna when she appeared at the Nobel Peace Prize Concert, staged in Oslo, Norway, on 11th December 2009.

SHOUT IT OUT

Written by Veit Marvos & Richard Palmer-James, and recorded by the Veit Marvos Red Point Orchestra for a similarly titled album, released in Germany circa 1972-73.

Donna, at this time, was a member of the Veit Marvos Red Point Orchestra.

B-side of *Do It Yourself*, a Veit Marvos Red Point Orchestra single which didn't feature Donna.

See also: *Back Off Boogaloo*.

SHUT OUT

Song recorded by Paul Jabara, as a medley with *Heaven Is A Disco*, for his 1977 album with the same title – produced by Arthur G. Wright & Marc Paul Simon.

Donna sang backing vocals on *Shut Out*, but not on *Heaven Is A Disco*.

Released as a single in Italy.

SILENT NIGHT

This popular Christmas carol was originally written in German – as *Stille Nocht* – by Father Joseph Mohr. An Austrian headmaster, Franz Xaver Gruber, added the melody two years later, with the English translation by John Freeman Young dating to 1859.
Performed by Donna, as a medley with *Hark! The Herald Angels Sing* and *O Come All Ye Faithful*, when she appeared on *Bandstand* on 22nd December 1984.

Hit Versions:
Bing Crosby – no.8 in the UK in 1952, and no.54 on the Hot 100 in the States in 1960.
Mahalia Jackson – no.99 on the Hot 100 in 1962.
Dickies – no.47 in the UK in 1978.
Bros – no.2 in the UK in 1988.
Sinead O'Connor – no.60 in the UK in 1991.

SILVER GIRL

Written by Donna & David Foster in the 1980s – Donna performed the song during her 1986 concert tour, which she named after the song.

Donna did record a studio version of the song, produced by Davis Foster, but it remains unreleased.

SING ALONG (SAD SONG)

Written by Giorgio Moroder & Pete Bellotte, and recorded by Donna for her 1974 album, *LADY OF THE NIGHT* – released in the Netherlands only.

Produced by Pete Bellotte.

SLIDE OVER BACKWARDS

Written by Donna with Nathan DiGesare & Jakob Petren, and recorded by Donna for her 2008 album, *CRAYONS* – produced by DiGesare.

SMILE

Composed by Charlie Chaplin as the theme for his 1936 film, *MODERN TIMES* – lyrics were added by John Turner & Geoffrey Parsons in 1954, when the song was first recorded by Nat 'King' Cole.

Performed by Donna on her Greatest Hits Tour in 2005.

Hit Versions:
Nat 'King' Cole – no.2 in the UK in 1954.
Tony Bennett – no.73 on the Hot 100 in the States in 1959.
Betty Everett & Jerry Butler – no.42 on the Hot 100 and R&B chart in the States in 1965.
Robert Downey, Jr. – no.68 in the UK in 1993.
Michael Jackson – no.74 in the UK in 2009.

Donna was in Paris, France, to play a concert on 7th July 2009, so was unable to attend the 'A Celebration Of The Life Of Michael Jackson 1958-2009' memorial concert, staged at the Staples Center, Los Angeles. She did, however, pay tribute to Michael, and dedicated her performance of *Smile* – one of Michael's favourite songs – to his memory. She also added the song to her set list, for many of her concerts in the second half of 2009, and in 2010, always dedicating the song to Michael Jackson.

Performed by Donna when she appeared at the Nobel Peace Prize Concert, staged in Oslo, Norway, on 11th December 2009.

SO FINE

Written by Johnny Otis, and recorded by the Fiestas in 1959, as their debut single.

Donna & Brooklyn Dreams performed the song as part of a 1960s medley, when Donna hosted *The Midnight Special* TV show – aired in the States on 26th May 1978.

This was the opening song in the medley, it was followed by: *Maybe*, *My Girl*, *My Guy*, *The Way You Do The Things You Do*, *Good Lovin'*, *I Heard It Through The Grapevine* and *Heat Wave*.

Donna performed the same medley on her Bad Girls tour in 1979.

The Fiestas took the song to no.3 on the R&B chart and no.11 on the Hot 100 in the States.

SO SAID THE MAN

Written by Melouney & Parkinson, and recorded by Donna – as Donna Gaines – in 1971, as the B-side of her debut solo single, *Sally Go 'Round The Roses*.

Donna recorded both songs in London. 'I remember the whole thing,' she recalled, in a 2004 interview. 'We went over (from Germany) and recorded it (*Sally Go 'Round The Roses*) in the studio, but we didn't just do that song. We did another song called *So Said The Man*, which was this bizarre song about

meeting like a prophet – just some guy who could tell the future. And it was kind of an odd song. But, those were the two songs that I think I recorded in that period, but it didn't work out, so I moved back to Germany.'

SO THIS IS LONELY

Written by Donna in the late 1980s or early 1990s – she performed the song acoustically, accompanied by her husband Bruce Sudano on guitar, on BBC Radio in the UK in 1992. She also sang a medley of *Bad Girls* and *On The Radio*.

Remains unreleased.

SOME OF THESE DAYS

Written by Shelton Brooks, and recorded live by Donna at the Universal Amphitheatre, Los Angeles, as part of her *My Man Medley* – featured on her 1978 album, *LIVE AND MORE*.

The medley also featured *The Man I Love* and *I Got It Bad (And That Ain't Good)*.

SOMEDAY

Written by A. Menken & S. Schwartz, and featured in Walt Disney's 1996 animated film, *The Hunchback Of Notre Dame* – the North American edition of the soundtrack album featured All-4-One singing the song, while the European edition featured a version by Eternal.

Donna recorded the song for Disney's 1996 album, *MOUSE HOUSE:*

DISNEY'S MIXES – produced by Michael Becker & Marco Mamangeli.

Mouse House Remixes were released in the States as promo 12" and CD singles.

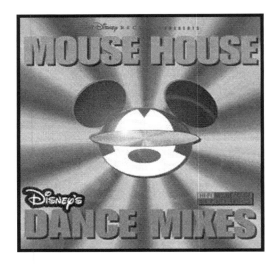

Official Versions:
Album Version.
Cox Euro Disney Mix.
Cox Euro Disney Club Mix.
Donna's 5AM Deep Mix.
Gypsy Classic Extended Mix.
Swingin' In The Summer Mix.
Swingin' In The Summer Club Mix.

SOMEONE TO WATCH OVER ME

Written by George & Ira Gershwin for the 1926 musical, *Oh, Kay!* – originally performed by Gertrude Lawrence.

Performed by Donna on her Mid Summer Nights Dream Tour in 1996-97, and on subsequent tours – a live version, recorded at the Hammerstein Ballroom, New York, on 4th January 1999, was included on the home video, *Live & More Encore!*

The video version was featured on the multi-artist compilation, *KEEPING THE DREAM ALIVE: RACE TO ERASE M.S.*, released in the States in 2001 (Epic EK 61402).

Other artists to have recorded the song include Ray Conniff, Ella Fitzgerald, Lena Horne, Melissa Manchester, Willie Nelson, Linda Ronstadt, Frank Sinatra, Rod Stewart, Sting, Barbra Streisand and Amy Winehouse.

SOMETHINGS IN THE WIND

Written by Giorgio Moroder & Pete Bellotte, and recorded by Donna in 1974 – produced by Bellotte.

B-side of *Denver Dream* – released in Belgium and the Netherlands.

The song, with the same melody but different lyrics, evolved into *Back In Love Again*.

SOMETHING'S MISSING

Song recorded by Paul Jabara, as a duet with Donna, for his 1978 album, *KEEPING TIME* – produced by Bob Esty.

However, at the request of Casablanca's Neil Bogart, Jabara re-recorded the song without Donna, and this version was included on *KEEPING TIME*.

The version featuring Donna remained unreleased until 1989, when it featured

on Paul Jabara's *GREATEST HITS ... AND MISSES* compilation.

SOMETIMES LIKE BUTTERFLIES

Written by Donna & Bruce Roberts, and recorded by Donna in 1982, during her sessions with producer Quincy Jones – failed to make her self-titled 1982 album.

B-side of *Love Is In Control (Finger On The Trigger)*.

The track was included on Mark Tara's 2004 album, *DIFFERENT LOVE*.

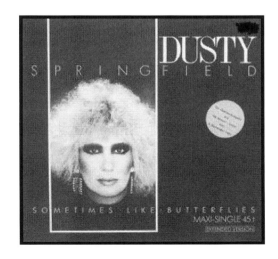

Dusty Springfield recorded a cover of the song in 1985 – it was released as a single, but wasn't a hit.

Donna's recording featured as a bonus track on the remastered released of the album *DONNA SUMMER*, as part of *THE CD COLLECTION* box-set, in 2014.

SOUNDS

Written by Gary William Friedman & Will Holt for the musical, *The Me Nobody Knows* – premiered at the Orpheum Theater, New York, on 18th May 1970.

Donna appeared – credited as Gayne Pierre – in the German production of the musical in 1970, titled *Ich Bin Ich*, and was part of the cast who performed this song on the English language version of the cast album.

The album also featured *Sounds (Reprise)*.

See also: *Schall*.

SPIRIT OF THE FOREST

Written by Kenny Young, and recorded by an all-star chorus – including Donna – in 1989, to raise funds for the Rainforest Appeal.

Numerous other artists were part of the all-star chorus, including Jon Anderson, Kate Bush, Belinda Carlisle, Rita Coolidge, Thomas Dolby, Fleetwood Mac, Debbie Harry, Joni Mitchell, Olivia Newton-John, Pink Floyd, Iggy Pop, Chris Rea, Ringo Starr, Kim Wilde and XTC.

A multi-artist, *We Are The World* type, music video was filmed.

The track featured on the 1994 album, *EARTHRISE: THE RAINFOREST ALBUM* – credited to Artists For Nature.

SPRING AFFAIR

Written by Donna with Pete Bellotte & Giorgio Moroder, and recorded by

Donna for her 1976 album, *FOUR SEASONS OF LOVE* – produced by Bellotte & Moroder.

This song, which opened Donna's album, represented spring – the beginning of a new relation.

Released as a single in North America and select European countries – with *Winter Melody*, it gave Donna her third no.1 on the Hot Dance Club Play chart in the States.

The single also achieved no.24 on the R&B chart and no.58 on the Hot 100 in the States, no.29 in Belgium and no.38 in Canada.

B-side of *I Remember Yesterday* in the UK.

Donna performed the song on *Soul Train* in 1976.

A live version, recorded at the Universal Amphitheatre, Los Angeles, featured on Donna's 1978 album, *LIVE AND MORE*.

Official Versions:
Album Version.
Spring Reprise (see below).
7" / Single Edit.
Live Version.

SPRING REPRISE

Reprise of *Spring Affair* – featured as the last track on Donna's 1976 album, *FOUR SEASONS OF LOVE*.

Released as a single in a limited number of countries, including Portugal.

STAMP YOUR FEET

Written by Donna with Danielle Brisebois & Greg Kurstin, and recorded by Donna for her 2008 album, *CRAYONS* – produced by Kurstin.

The song is also registered with the American Society of Composers, Authors & Publishers (ASCAP) under the title, '*Stamp*'.

Released as a single, the track gave Donna her 14th no.1 on the Hot Dance Club Play chart in the States.

The single also charted at no.88 in Germany.

Performed by Donna, backed by the top six female contestants, on the Season 7 finale of *American Idol* in 2008 – she also performed *Last Dance*, while the six contestants sang a medley of *She Works Hard For The Money*, *Hot Stuff* and *Bad Girls*.

'I did the show two or three years ago, when Fantasia won,' said Donna, 'and they've been asking me to come back. And so, this year, it worked out that my album was coming out and – they wanted to have a lot of surprises in the last show, and so (the producers called and asked),

"Do you wanna do the show?" And I'm like, "Hello! Of course!" … so I said I'd do it.'

Official Versions:
Album Version.
DiscoTech Mix.
DiscoTech Mixshow Edit.
Jason Nevins Radio Edit.
Jason Nevins Extended Mix.
Jason Nevins Mixshow.
Escape / Coluccio Radio Edit.
Escape / Coluccio Club Mix.
Escape / Coluccio Mixshow.
Granite & Sugarman Club Remix.
Granite & Sugarman Mixshow.
Ranny's Radio Edit.
Ranny's Radio Mix.
Ranny's Big Room Mix.
Ranny's Mixshow.

STAND BY YOUR MAN

Written by Tammy Wynette & Billy Sherrill, and recorded by Wynette for her 1968 album with the same title.

Donna performed the song, as part of a country medley, when she appeared as a guest on the *Eddie Rabbit Special* in 1982 – she also sang *I Can't Stop Loving You* and *Oh Lonesome Me* with Eddie Rabbit.

Tammy Wynette took the song to no.1 on the Country chart and no.19 on the Hot 100 in the States in 1968, and to no.1 in the UK in 1975.

STAR AGAINST THE NIGHT

Written by Donna & Nathan DiGesare, and recorded by Veronica Petrucci for the 1999 children's album, *SING ME TO SLEEP, MOMMY* – produced by DiGesare.

The album was sub-titled 'A Collection Of Original Ballads & Lullabies'.

STAR SPANGLED BANNER, THE

America's national anthem, with lyrics taken from the poem *Defence Of Fort McHenry*, written by Francis Scott Key in 1814. The melody came from a popular British drinking song, *The Anacreontic Song*, written by John

Stafford Smith. The song was renamed *The Star Spangled Banner*, and formally adopted as America's national anthem by congressional resolution, in March 1931.

Donna performed the anthem *a cappella* at the Major League Baseball All-Star Game, staged at Boston's Fenway Park on 13th July 1999.

Hit Versions:
José Feliciano – no.50 on the Hot 100 in 1969.
Whitney Houston – no.32 on the Hot 100 in the States in 1991.
Whitney Houston (reissue) – no.6 on the Hot 100, and no.30 on the R&B chart, in the States in 2001.

STARTING OVER AGAIN

Written by Donna with husband Bruce Sudano, and recorded by Dolly Parton for her 1980 album, *DOLLY DOLLY DOLLY*.

The song, which tells the tale of a couple splitting up after thirty-five years, was inspired by the divorce of Sudano's parents.

Although she has never recorded it herself, Donna did perform the song on several TV shows during the 1980s, including *The Tonight Show Starring Johnny Carson* and the *A Special Eddie Rabbit*, on which she also sang a medley of country songs.

'Dolly Parton recorded *Starting Over Again*,' said Bruce Sudano, 'because she saw Donna sing it on the Johnny Carson show. Donna was singing it on the Johnny Carson show because she thought that if she sang the song on TV and my parents saw it, maybe they wouldn't get divorced. That was her only reason for singing it.'

'We wrote it because of Bruce's parents' divorce,' Donna concurred, 'and because we were watching them struggle with their singleness. We knew they really needed to be together. They weren't seeing the forest for the trees. They were in their fifties when they were getting this divorce, and they'd been married since they were young adults. It was a very painful process for everybody involved.'

Dolly Parton took the song to no.1 on the Country chart, and to no.36 on the Hot 100, in the States.

Another country artist, Reba McEntire, recorded a cover of the song for her 1995 album, *STARTING OVER*. Her version achieved no.19 on the Country chart in the States.

Donna performed the song at the Legendary Songwriters Acoustic Concert, staged at Nashville's Ryman Auditorium on 3rd April 2001, when she was honoured by the Nashville Songwriters Association for her song-writing – she sang the song accompanied by her husband, Bruce Sudano, on piano.

STATE OF INDEPENDENCE

Written by Jon Anderson & Vangelis, and recorded by Jon & Vangelis for their 1981 album, *THE FRIENDS OF MR CAIRO*.

Recorded by Donna for her self-titled 1982 album, with an all-star chorus including Michael Jackson, Stevie Wonder, Lionel Richie, Brenda Russell, James Ingram, Kenny Loggins, Dionne Warwick & Christopher Cross.

Produced by Quincy Jones.

Donna wasn't actually present when the all-star chorus assembled in the studio. 'I was heavily pregnant and very ill in New York on the day they were due to record,' she explained. 'Quincy got everybody together, and he wanted me to fly into L.A., but I had a severe stomach virus and I was told by my doctor I couldn't leave … my sister went and stood in proxy for me, and there were wonderful pictures of my sister with all these celebrities. She was in her element.

I was so honoured. I mean, Michael was there, Dionne was there …'

'It's a song that really expresses what I've been feeling lately,' said Donna, when her self-titled album was released. 'It's got an optimism and sense of purpose that is based in reality.'

'He is such a professional,' said Donna, when she was asked about working with Michael Jackson. 'I had known Michael for many years. His family used to come and hang out backstage with me and go to my shows … Michael is probably one of the most sweet, humble people I have ever met in my life. He's hyper-insecure about people and who they liked. Did they like Michael, or did they like Michael the entertainer? I think that there was a real balancing act for him.'

As the second single lifted from Donna's eponymous album, the song charted at no.1 in the Netherlands, no.4 in Belgium, no.10 in Ireland, no.14 in the UK, no.30 in Australia, no.31 on the R&B chart and no.41 on the Hot 100 in the States and no.35 in Canada.

Official Versions:
Album Version.
7" / Single Edit.

The single was reissued in Europe in 1990, to promote Donna's *THE BEST OF...* compilation, and several new mixes were released. The single achieved no.45 in the UK.

1990 Remixes:
New Bass Mix.
New Bass Mix Edit.
No Drum Mix.
N-R-G Mix.
Quincy Mix.

The song was remixed and reissued again in 1996 – this version featured part of Martin Luther King's famous 'I have a dream' speech.

'It's my best remix ever,' said Eddie Gordon, 'coming together over two weeks in Olympic Studios in Barnes, South West London, with Steve 'Barney'

Chase. Thanks to Donna's husband, Bruce, we were given the original Quincy Jones master tapes from his Quest Studios, with the background vocals from Lionel Richie, Michael Jackson, James Ingram, Stevie Wonder, Dionne Warwick, Michael McDonald and more, so we have to take our time across the forty-eight tracks, to painstakingly rebuild those incredible vocals in the new mix.

'When we got Quincy's and Donna's approval for the inclusion of the Martin Luther King speech, we were thrilled, as that was how we wanted to deliver Donna back on radio in 1996. I heard it here on the radio in California last week, some twelve years later, and I was instantly surrounded by those great people and memories again. Wonderful, wonderful times.'

1996 Remixes:
Creation Mix.
Cuba-Libre Mix.
DJ Dero Vocal Mix.
Jules & Skins Vocal Mix.
Jules & Skins Dub Mix.
Murk Vocal Club Mix.

Murk-A-Dub Dub.
New Radio Millennium Mix.

A live version by Donna, with Ace Of Base's Jenny Berggren, was included on the 2005 album, *NIGHT OF THE PROMS* – this was a live compilation from the Belgian *Night Of The Proms* music festival.

A cover version by Moodswings, featuring Chrissie Hynde on vocals, was released in 1991. Titled *Spiritual High (State Of Independence)*, this version also sampled Martin Luther King, and first time out it charted at no.66 in the UK. A remixed version, issued in 1993, rose to no.47 in the UK.

STEP, STEP AWAY

Song recorded by Sunshine for their cancelled 1978 album, *WATCHIN' DADDY DANCE* – produced by Donna & Juergen Koppers.

Remains unreleased.

STOP! IN THE NAME OF LOVE

Written by Brian Holland, Lamont Dozier & Edward Holland, Jr., and recorded by the Supremes for their 1965 album, *MORE HITS BY THE SUPREMES*.

Donna sang the opening lines of the song before singing *Woman*, during her Hard For The Money tour in 1983. Donna's concert at the Pacific Amphitheatre, Los Angeles, was released on a home video, titled *A Hot Summer Night*.

Donna was scheduled to perform the song, as part of a Supremes medley, with Diana Ross & Mariah Carey, on *VH1 Divas 2000: A Tribute To Diana Ross, An Honors Concert For VH1's Save The Music*, staged at New York's Madison Square Garden on 9th April 2000. However, feeling there wasn't enough time to rehearse, Donna pulled out of the medley.

The Supremes took the song to no.1 on the Hot 100 and no.2 on the R&B chart in the States, and to no.7 in the UK.

STOP, LOOK AND LISTEN

Written by Donna with Michael Omartian & Greg Phillinganes, and recorded by Donna for her 1983 album, *SHE WORKS HARD FOR THE MONEY* – produced by Omartian.

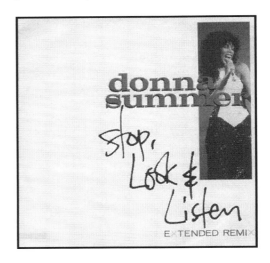

Released as the third single from the album in Europe, the song was only a minor it – it peaked at no.57 in the UK, but failed to chart in other countries.

Official Versions:
Album Version.
7" / Single Edit.
12" Version.

STOP ME

Written by Pete Bellotte & Keith Forsey, and recorded by Donna for her 1980 album, *THE WANDERER* – produced by Bellotte & Giorgio Moroder.

B-side of *The Wanderer*.

SUGAR DADDY

Written by Bruce Sudano, and recorded by former model Twiggy for her shelved 1979 album, *HEAVEN IN MY EYES* – produced by Donna & Juergen Koppers.

SUMMER FEVER

Written by Donna with Pete Bellotte & Giorgio Moroder, and recorded by Donna for her 1976 album, *FOUR SEASONS OF LOVE* – produced by Bellotte & Moroder.

SUNSET PEOPLE

Written by Pete Bellotte, Harold Faltermeyer & Keith Forsey, and recorded by Donna for her 1979 album, *BAD GIRLS* – produced by Bellotte & Giorgio Moroder.

Released as a single in several European countries, including the UK, but not in the States (where *Walk Away* was chosen instead) – it was released after Donna had quit her record company, Casablanca, and filed a lawsuit against them.

The single charted at no.46 in the UK, but failed to chart in other countries where it was issued.

The song featured in Donna's *The Donna Summer Special* TV movie, which aired in the States on 27th January 1980.

SUNSHINE

Written by V. Hicks, D. Ashton, L. Still, D. Bernard & V. Weber, and recorded by Sunshine for their cancelled 1978 album, *WATCHIN' DADDY DANCE* – produced by Donna & Juergen Koppers.

Remains unreleased.

SUPERNATURAL LOVE

Written by Donna with Bruce Sudano & Michael Omartian, and recorded by Donna for her 1984 album, *CATS WITHOUT CLAWS* – produced by Omartian.

The song was released as the second single from the album, but was only a minor hit – it achieved no.51 on the R&B chart and no.75 on the Hot 100 in the States.

Donna filmed a colourful music video with her husband, Bruce Sudano, in which they play a couple chasing each other through time – from the Stone Age to the then current New Wave.

SUPERSTAR

Written by Leon Russell & Bonnie Bramlett, and first recorded by Delaney & Bonnie in 1969 – best known for the version recorded by the Carpenters for their self-titled 1971 album.

Performed by Donna, accompanied on piano by Richard Carpenter, when she and the Carpenters were inducted into the Hollywood Bowl's Hall Of Fame on 18th June 2010.

'When they called, I was dumbfounded,' said Donna, when she was asked about her induction. 'When they asked me who I wanted to induct me, my first call was David Foster. He has been a big part of my musical career and he is a dear friend, and we have known each other since the beginning of my career … the other big, exciting thing for me, almost equal to the award, was being able to sing with Richard Carpenter. I mean, I am such a Carpenters fan, and I think that a lot of people in America are Carpenters fans because they grew up with them. I was just elated. It was a really beautiful evening. It will stay in my memory as sort of a high point.'

The following evening, at her concert in Indio, California, Donna reprised her performance of the song.

The Carpenters took the song to no. 2 on the Hot 100 in the States, and to no.18 in the UK.

SUZANNA

Written by Donna & Michael Omartian, and recorded by Donna for her 1984 album, *CATS WITHOUT CLAWS* – produced by Omartian.

B-side of *Supernatural Love* in the UK.

SWEET EMOTION

Written by Pete Bellotte & Sylvester Levay, and recorded by Donna for her shelved 1981 album, *I'M A RAINBOW* – produced by Bellotte & Giorgio Moroder.

The album was finally released in 1996.

SWEET ROMANCE

Written by Donna with Giorgio Moroder & Pete Bellotte, and recorded by Donna for her 1977 album, *ONCE UPON A TIME* – produced by Moroder & Bellotte.

SWING LOW, SWEET CHARIOT

Written by Wallis Willis, a Choctaw freedman, before 1862 – known as a

'Negro spiritual', that is, a religious song created by enslaved African people in the States.

Performed by Donna, with Lou Rawls, when she appeared on *The Midnight Special* TV show – the episode aired in the States on 20th May 1977.

The song has been a hit several times in recent years in the UK, largely thanks to the England rugby union team adopting it as their anthem.

Hit Versions:
Eric Clapton – no.19 in the UK in 1975.
Union feat. The England World Cup Squad – no.16 in the UK in 1991.
Ladysmith Black Mambazo feat. China Black – no.15 in the UK in 1995.
Russell Watson – no.38 in the UK in 1999.
UB40 & the United Colours Of Sound – no.15 in the UK in 2003.

Numerous other artists have recorded version of the song, including Louis Armstrong, Joan Baez, Harry Belafonte, Johnny Cash, Duke Ellington, Ella

Fitzgerald, Benny Goodman, Peggy Lee, Loretta Lynn, Johnny Mathis, Glenn Miller, Willie Nelson, Paul Robeson, Fats Waller and Stevie Wonder.

TAKE HEART

Written by Bruce Sudano & Nathan DiGesare, and recorded by Donna for the 2000 multi-artist album, *THE MERCY PROJECT*.

TAKE IT TO THE ZOO

Written by Donna with Bruce Sudano & Joe Esposito, and recorded by Sunshine for the 1978 soundtrack album, *THANK GOD IT'S FRIDAY* – produced by Arthur G. Wright.

Sunshine were a female trio – Donna's sisters Dara and Mary Ellen, with their cousin, Carlina Williams.

TAKE ME

Written by Donna with Pete Bellotte & Giorgio Moroder, and recorded by Donna for her 1977 album, *I*

REMEMBER YESTERDAY – produced by Bellotte & Moroder.

TALK TO ME

Written by Bruce Sudano & B. Incorvaia, and recorded by Sudano for his 1981 album, *FUGITIVE KIND* – backing vocals by Donna (credited as Donna Sudano).

TEARIN' DOWN THE WALLS

Written S. Garrett & T. Maiden, and recorded by Donna as a non-album track – produced by Michael Omartian.

The track was included on the 12" single of *Dinner With Gershwin* released in the UK.

Featured as a bonus track on the remastered release of the album *ALL*

SYSTEMS GO, as part of *THE CD COLLECTION* box-set, in 2014.

TEARING DOWN THE BERLIN WALL

One of three unreleased songs Donna mentioned she had written, for a new album, in a message to fans in July 2002 – the other two songs were *Rain On My Shoulders* and *Till You Get It*.

THANK YOU FOR BEING YOU

Written by Dennis Scott, and recorded by Donna as part of the ensemble for the 2005 tribute album to Fred 'Mister Rogers' Rogers, *SONGS FROM THE NEIGHBOUR-HOOD – THE MUSIC OF MISTER ROGERS* – produced by Scott.

Other artist to contribute to the album included Jon Secada, Amy Grant, B.J. Thomas, CeCe Winans, Crystal Gayle and Roberta Flack.

THAT'S THE WAY

Written by Giorgio Moroder & Keith Forsey, and recorded by Donna for the 2003 compilation, *THE JOURNEY – THE BEST OF* – produced by Moroder.

THEME FROM THE DEEP (DOWN, DEEP INSIDE)

See: *Down, Deep Inside (Theme From The Deep)*.

(THEME) ONCE UPON A TIME

See: *Once Upon A Time*.

THERE GOES MY BABY

Written by Benjamin Nelson (*aka* Ben E. King), Lover Patterson & George Treadwell, and originally recorded by the Drifters in 1959.

Recorded by Donna for her 1984 album, *CATS WITHOUT CLAWS* – produced by Omartian.

Chosen as the album's lead single, the song achieved no.20 on the R&B chart and no.21 on the Hot 100 in the States, no.22 in Canada, no.31 in the Netherlands, no.52 in Australia and no.99 in the UK.

In the music video, Donna was joined by her husband Bruce Sudano – they played a couple who are parted at the outbreak of World War II.

The Drifters took the song to no.1 on the R&B chart and no.2 on the Hot 100 in the States.

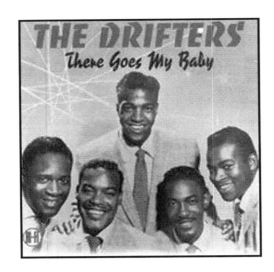

THERE WILL ALWAYS BE A YOU

Written and recorded by Donna for her 1979 album, *BAD GIRLS* – produced by Pete Bellotte & Giorgio Moroder.

B-side of *Dim All The Lights* & *On The Radio*.

'Of the not known songs,' replied Donna, when asked which songs she was most proud of writing, 'it would be *There Will Always Be A You*. That was written as a love song for my husband, and is very personal to me …

'For me, that was, poetically, one of the best songs that I ever wrote. I just love that song. I always say that people who really know me will regard that song. They're going to listen to that song and they're going to know that it's me.'

(THERE'S) ALWAYS SOMETHING THERE TO REMIND ME

Written by Burt Bacharach & Hal David – the original demo was recorded in 1963 by Dionne Warwick.

Donna performed the song, with host Eddy Mitchell, when she appeared on the French TV show *Numéro 1* – aired 29th January 1977. Mitchell sang his lines in French, while Donna sang hers in English.

Hit Versions:
Lou Johnson – no.49 on the Hot 100 in the States in 1964.
Sandie Shaw – no.1 in the UK, and no.52 on the Hot 100 in the States, in 1964.
Dionne Warwick – no.65 on the Hot 100 in the States in 1967.
R.B. Greaves – no.27 on the Hot 100 and no.50 on the R&B chart in the States in 1970.
Naked Eyes – no.8 on the Hot 100 in the States, and no.59 in the UK, in 1983.
Tin Tin Out featuring Espiritu – no.14 in the UK in 1995.

Other artists to have recorded the song include All Saints, Wayne Fontana, the Four Seasons, Patti LaBelle & the Bluebelles, Brenda Lee, Martha & the Vandellas, Johnny Mathis, Michael McDonald, Juice Newton, Dusty

Springfield, the Troggs and Don Williams.

THERE'S NO BUSINESS LIKE SHOW BUSINESS

Written by Irving Berlin for the 1946 musical, *Annie Get Your Gun*.

Donna performed the song, as part of a medley with *Love Is Here To Stay* and *The Man I Love*, on her Rainbow Tour in 1984. She also performed the song at select dates on her Silver Girl Tour two years later.

THEY CAN'T TAKE AWAY OUR MUSIC

Written by Lonnie Jordan, Papa Dee Allen, Harold Brown, B.B. Dickerson, Jerry Goldstein & Howard Scott, and recorded by Eric Burdon & War for their 1970 album, *THE BLACK-MAN'S BURDON*.

Recorded by the Veit Marvos Red Point Orchestra for a similarly titled album, released in Germany circa 1972-73 – Donna, at this time, was a member of the Veit Marvos Red Point Orchestra.

Eric Burdon & War took the song to no.50 on the Hot 100 in the States.

See also: *Back Off Boogaloo*.

THINKIN' 'BOUT MY BABY

Written by Donna with Jeffrey Lams & Keith Nelson, and recorded by Donna for her 1987 album, *ALL SYSTEMS GO* – produced by Donna, Lams & Nelson.

'I have a song on the new album called *Thinkin' 'Bout My Baby*,' said Donna, 'and to me, it's a song about a girl who's walking down the street. She's thinking about her boyfriend because she just had a fight with him, and she's looking for him. It's a nice song, a real mellow song. It's sort of like *Love To Love You...*, in a way, in that you can put it out in a room and it doesn't invade you. But, at the same time, it seduces you. It's simple, with nice vocals and a great saxophone solo – very musical.'

Donna revealed, '*Thinkin' 'Bout My Baby* was originally a ten minute cut. 'We cut it down to eight, and I had a right struggle with the (record) company for just eight. They said it was too long, but I said, you don't understand something – this is a song people are going to want to hear.'

THIS FORBIDDEN FRUIT

Written by Donna with Bruce Sudano, Al Kasha & Michael Omartian, for the as yet unpublished play Donna worked on with Sudano, Kasha & Omartian, *Ordinary Girl* – remains unreleased.

THIS GIRL'S BACK IN TOWN

Written by Paul Jabara & Bob Esty, and recorded by Jabara for his 1986 album, *DE LA NOCHE: THE TRUE STORY* – backing vocals by Donna.

THIS MASQUERADE

Written and recorded by Leon Russell, for his 1972 album, *CARNEY*.

Donna performed the song when she appeared on the Venezuelan TV special, *De Fiesta con Venevisión: Donna Summer en Concierto* (*A Celebration With Venevisión: Donna Summer In Concert*), in 1977.

Hit Version:
George Benson – no.3 on the R&B chart and no.10 on the Hot 100 in the States in 1976.

Other artists to have recorded the song include Shirley Bassey, Carpenters, Sergio Mendes, Helen Reddy and Kenny Rogers.

THIS TIME I KNOW IT'S FOR REAL

Written by Donna with Mike Stock, Matt Aitken & Pete Waterman, and recorded by Donna for her 1989 album,

ANOTHER PLACE AND TIME – produced by Stock, Aitken & Waterman.

Released as the lead single from the album, the song gave Donna her 14th – and to date final – Top 10 hit on the Hot 100 in the States, peaking at no.7.

The single was also successful outside the USA, achieving no.2 in Belgium, no.3 in Canada, Norway & the UK, no.4 in Ireland, no.5 in the Netherlands, no.6 in France, no.12 in Sweden, no.15 in Germany, no.20 in Japan and no.34 in Australia.

Donna performed the song, when she made only her second appearance of *Top Of The Pops* in the UK – the show aired on 9th March 1989. She also performed the song on *The Arsenio Hall Show* in the States in 1989.

RIAA Award: Gold (July 1989) = 500,000.

BPI Award: Silver (March 1989) = 200,000.

A heart-shaped 7" single was issued in the UK.

Official Versions:
Album Version.
Extended Remix.
Instrumental.

A cover version by Kelly Llorenna charted at no.14 in the UK in 2004.

A second cover version, by the Australian girl group Young Divas, was a no.2 hit in their homeland in 2006 – it was the no.6 best-selling single of the year in Australia.

THIS WORLD

Written by Gary William Friedman & Will Holt for the musical, *The Me Nobody Knows* – premiered at the Orpheum Theater, New York, on 18th May 1970.

Donna appeared – credited as Gayne Pierre – in the German production of the musical in 1970, titled *Ich Bin Ich*, and was part of the cast who performed this song on the English language version of the cast album.

TILL YOU GET IT

One of three unreleased songs Donna mentioned she had written, for a new album, in a message to fans in July 2002 – the other two songs were *Rain On My Shoulders* and *Tearing Down The Berlin Wall*.

TO PARIS WITH LOVE

Written by Donna & Bruce Roberts, and recorded by Donna – released as a digital single in 2010.

When originally announced, the song was titled, *Looking For Love* – and Donna has admitted the song was never intended to be released commercially.

'My daughter (Amanda) is a model with Louis Vuitton,' she explained, 'and I've been a patron of theirs since the beginning of my career, since I lived in Europe. I've had a long relationship with them and am friends with several designers for the company. They asked me to come and sing at the opening of their London store and I did, but because they had been so kind to my family, I wanted to do something for them, sort of as a payback, so I decided to write a song with a friend of mine and include their name.

'My co-writer in the process started playing it to some of his DJ friends, and they all started grovelling for it, so he said let's do some remixes.

'They liked the remixes, and started putting them out in the south of France. It started to snowball. It was never meant for release. All these DJs started playing it, and I didn't even know about it. And now it's on iTunes, and it's being picked up all over the world. I couldn't have made that happen if I was pushing that myself.'

A decision was taken to release the song as a digital single. 'I wanted to give my fans something special and exciting for the summer,' said Donna, 'and I couldn't think of a better theme than the glamour and allure of Paris. I want people to feel transported, whether they're listening on the dance floors of Ibiza or on their head-phones at work. The idea is to let them escape into that magic world.'

Released digitally, remarkably, the single went all the way to no.1 on Billboard's Hot Dance Club Songs chart in the States, giving Donna her 16th chart topper. This meant Donna had hit no.1 on the chart in five different decades – a unique achievement.

Official Versions:
Original Version.
Original Version Radio Edit.
Craig C's Master Blaster.
Craig C's Radio Blaster Remix.
Mendy Radio Edit.
Mendy Club Mix.
WaWa Radio Edit.
WaWa Extended.
Eddie Amador Remix.
Eddie Amador Break It Down Remix.
Eddie Amador Dub.
DJ DLG Lazo Disco Mix.
DJ DLG Lazo Disco Instrumental.
Automatic Panic Remix.
Automatic Panic Dub.
Uner Extended Remix.

Uner Remix.
David Herrero Vocal Remix.

'It was a dream come true for me,' said Automatic Panic, 'and I am grateful and blessed to be a part of a project with the legendary and talented Donna Summer. I had a lot of fun remixing the already hot track, *To Paris With Love*, and now everyone gets to hear my version, which is super raw, hot and sexy.'

TO TURN THE STONE

Written by Giorgio Moroder & Pete Bellotte, and recorded by Donna for her shelved 1981 album, *I'M A RAINBOW* – produced by Moroder & Bellotte.

The album was finally released in 1996.

Frida, formerly of ABBA, recorded a version of the song for her 1982 solo album, *SOMETHING'S GOING ON* – as a single, it charted at no.8 in Belgium & the Netherlands, and no.52 in Germany.

TOKYO

Written by Donna with Michael Omartian & Bruce Sudano, and recorded by Donna for her 1983 album, *SHE WORKS HARD FOR THE MONEY* – produced by Omartian.

B-side of *Stop, Look And Listen.*

TOO MUCH FOR THE LADY

Written by Donna with Bruce Sudano, Joe Esposito & Eddie Hokenson, and recorded by Brooklyn Dreams for their 1979 album, *JOY RIDE* – produced by Juergen Koppers.

TRUE LOVE

Written by Donna with Bruce Sudano, Joe Esposito & B. Incorvaia, and recorded by Sudano for his 1981 album, *FUGITIVE KIND* – backing vocals by Donna (credited as Donna Sudano).

TRUE LOVE SURVIVES

Written by Donna & Pete Bellotte, and recorded by Donna for her shelved 1981 album, *I'M A RAINBOW* – produced by Bellotte & Giorgio Moroder.

The album was finally released in 1996.

TRY A LITTLE TENDERNESS

Written by Harry Woods & Irving King (*aka* James Campbell & Reginald Connelly) in 1932, and originally recorded by the Ray Noble Orchestra.

This is one of the songs Donna performed regularly in 1965-66, as a member of the rock band, the Crow.

Performed by Donna, with Joss Stone, at *Save The Music: A Concert To Benefit The VH1 Dave The Music Foundation*, staged at New York's Beacon Theater on 12th April 2005 – the concert aired on VH1 five days later. Donna also sang *Last Dance*.

Hit Versions:
Ted Lewis – no.6 on the Pop chart in the States in 1933.
Otis Redding – no.4 on the R&B chart and no.46 on the Hot 100 in the States, and no.25 in the UK, in 1967.
Ohio Players – no.40 on the R&B chart in the States in 1981.

Other artists to have recorded the song include Michael Bublé, Bing Crosby, Etta James, Al Jarreau, Frankie Laine, Nina Simone, Frank Sinatra, Rod Stewart, Mel Tormé, Three Dog Night and Tina Turner.

TRY ME, I KNOW WE CAN MAKE IT

Written by Donna with Pete Bellotte & Giorgio Moroder, and recorded by Donna for her 1976 album, *A LOVE TRILOGY* – produced by Bellotte & Moroder.

Length of album version: 17:59 minutes.

The single, with the B-side *Wasted*, gave Donna her second no.1 on the Hot Dance Club Play in the States, where it also achieved no.35 on the R&B chart and no.80 on the Hot 100.

The single peaked at no.42 in Germany, but it failed to chart in most countries.

Donna performed the song on *American Bandstand* and *Dick Clark's New Year's Rockin' Eve* in 1976.

A live version, recorded at the Universal Amphitheatre, Los Angeles, featured on Donna's 1978 album, *LIVE AND MORE*.

Featured in the 1977 film, *Looking For Mr Goodbar*.

Donna included the song in her *The Donna Summer Special* TV movie, which aired in the States on 27th January 1980.

Official Versions:
Album Version.
7" / Radio Edit.
Live Version.

TUNNEL OF LOVE

Written and recorded by Kiss's Gene Simmons, for his 1978 album: *KISS:*

GENE SIMMONS – produced by Simmons & Sean Delaney, with backing vocals by Donna.

TURN THE BEAT AROUND

Written by Gerald & Peter Jackson, and recorded by Vicki Sue Robinson for her 1976 album, *NEVER GONNA LET YOU GO*.

Performed by Donna, with Chaka Khan & Gloria Estefan, at their 'Three Divas On Broadway' benefit concert, staged at Manhattan's Lunt-Fontanne Theater on 11th December 1996. Donna, on the evening, was under doctor's orders with 'flu symptoms, so her vocal participation in the concert was minimal.

Mid-way through the song, the three divas were joined on stage by the artist formerly known as Prince, with his guitar – and, as the song ended, he bowed respectfully in front of Donna, Chaka & Gloria. Donna, with the other two divas, also sang *I'm Every Woman*.

Hit Versions:

Vicki Lee Robinson – no.10 on the Hot 100 in the States in 1976.

Gloria Estefan – no.13 on the Hot 100 in the States in 1994.

UN-BREAK MY HEART

Written by Diane Warren, and recorded by Toni Braxton for her 1996 album, *SECRETS* – produced by David Foster.

Donna performed the song as a duet with Seal, as part of a medley, when she appeared at the *David Foster & Friends* concert, staged at the Mandalay Bay Events Center, Las Vegas, on 15th October 2010 – the medley also featured *Crazy* and *On The Radio*.

The medley featured on the 2011 album, *HIT MAN RETURNS*, credited to David Foster & Friends. The release also included a DVD or Blu-ray home video of the concert.

Toni Braxton took the song to no.1 on the Hot 100 in the States, for an impressive 11 weeks; the single also achieved no.2 on the R&B chart in the States, and no.2 in the UK.

UNCONDITIONAL LOVE

Written by Donna & Michael Omartian, and recorded by Donna for her 1983 album, *SHE WORKS HARD FOR THE MONEY* – produced by Omartian.

Backings vocals by Musical Youth – the young, British reggae group also joined Donna in the music video, in which she played a school teacher.

Released as the second single from the album, the song achieved no.3 in Zimbabwe, no.9 on the R&B chart and no.43 on the Hot 100 in the States, no.14 in the UK, no.24 in New Zealand, no.28 in Canada & Ireland and no.57 in Australia.

Official Versions:
Album Version.
7" / Single Edit.
12" Extended Remix.

VALLEY OF THE MOON

An audio clip of this song was posted on Donna's official web-site – however, it remains unreleased.

VIRGIN MARY

Written by Giorgio Moroder & Pete Bellotte, and recorded by Donna in 1975 – produced by Bellotte.

Released as a single in the Netherlands only (Groovy GR 1215).

VOICES CRYIN' OUT

Written by Donna & Harold Faltermeyer, and recorded by Donna for her 1987 album, *ALL SYSTEMS GO* – produced by Faltermeyer.

'I started writing it about people who are hungry,' said Donna, 'and then it ended up being about kids my daughter's age. I think the lyrics to the song are the best on the album.'

WALK AWAY

Written by Pete Bellotte & Harold Faltermeyer, and recorded by Donna for her 1979 album, *BAD GIRLS* – produced by Bellotte & Giorgio Moroder.

Released as a single in the States after Donna has resigned from, and filed a lawsuit against, her record company, Casablanca – initially, it was promoted as a double A-side with *Could It Be Magic*.

The single – with only *Walk Away* listed – charted at no.35 on the R&B chart and no.36 on the Hot 100.

Official Versions:
Album Version.
12" Extended Version.

WALK HAND IN HAND

Written by B. Brodersen, and heard on bootleg recordings of Donna's shelved 1981 album, *I'M A RAINBOW* – the track wasn't featured on the album, when it was finally released in 1996.

The track, which may have been recorded during Donna's sessions with Quincy Jones in 1982, remains unreleased on any of Donna's albums. However, it has been released on: *DISCO ROUND 2*, a various artists compilation released in Germany in 1982.

WALK ON (KEEP ON MOVIN')

Written by Pete Bellotte & Giorgio Moroder, and recorded by Donna for her shelved 1981 album, *I'M A RAINBOW* – produced by Bellotte & Moroder.

The album was finally released in 1996.

WANDERER, THE

Written by Donna & Giorgio Moroder, and recorded by Donna for her 1980 album with the same title – produced by Moroder & Pete Bellotte.

Lead single from the album – in the States, it charted at no.3 on the Hot 100, no.8 on the Hot Dance Club Play chart and no.13 on the R&B chart.
Outside the USA, the single achieved no.3 in Canada, no.5 in New Zealand & South Africa, no.6 in Australia, no.9 in Sweden, no.10 in Zimbabwe, no.17 in Belgium, no.26 in the Netherlands, no.48 in the UK and no.63 in Japan.

Donna performed the song when she appeared on the TV show, *The Tomorrow Show*, in 1980.

RIAA Award: Gold (December 1980) = 1 million.

WASSERMANN (AQUARIUS)

Written James Rado & Gerome Ragni (book and lyrics) & Galt MacDermot (music) for the controversial 'tribal love-rock' musical, *Hair*.

Donna appeared in the German production of the musical in 1968, titled *Haare*, and was part of the cast who performed this song on stage and on the cast album.

Released as a single in Germany (Polydor International 53107) – failed to chart.

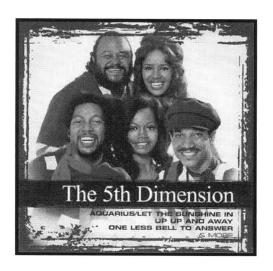

The Fifth Dimension took a medley of *Aquarius / Let The Sunshine In* to no.1 on the Hot 100 in the States in 1969 – the single also achieved no.6 on the R&B chart and no.11 in the UK.

WASTED

Written by Pete Bellotte & Giorgio Moroder, and recorded by Donna for her 1976 album, *A LOVE TRILOGY* – produced by Bellotte & Moroder.

B-side of *Winter Melody* in the UK.

WATCHIN' DADDY DANCE

Written by Donna & Bruce Sudano, and recorded by Sunshine for their cancelled 1978 album with the same title – produced by Donna & Sudano.

Donna revealed, in her autobiography *Ordinary Girl: The Journey*, she originally penned the song with her sisters, having been inspired by watching her father dance with her mother.

Remains unreleased.

WAY WE WERE, THE

Written by Alan Bergman, Marilyn Bergman & Marvin Hamlisch, and recorded by Barbra Streisand for the 1973 film of the same title, which starred Streisand and Robert Redford.

A live version was recorded by Donna at the Universal Amphitheatre, Los Angeles, for her 1978 album, *LIVE AND MORE*.

Hit Versions:
Barbra Streisand – no.1 on the Hot 100 in the States, and no.31 in the UK, in 1974.
Gladys Knight & The Pips (medley) – no.4 in the UK, and no.6 on the R&B chart and no.11 on the Hot 100 in the States, in 1975.
Manhattans (medley) – no.33 on the R&B chart in the States in 1979.

Other artists to have recorded the song include Shirley Bassey, Whitney Houston and Barry Manilow.

WAY YOU DO THE THINGS YOU DO, THE

Written by Smokey Robinson & Bobby Rogers, and recorded by the Temptations for their 1964 album, *MEET THE TEMPTATIONS*.

Donna & Brooklyn Dreams performed the song as part of a 1960s medley, when Donna hosted *The Midnight Special* TV show – aired in the States on 26th May 1978.

Other songs in the medley: *So Fine, Maybe, My Girl, My Guy, Good Lovin', I Heard It Through The Grapevine* and *Heat Wave.*

Donna performed the same medley on her Bad Girls tour in 1979.

Hit Versions:
Temptations – no.11 on the Hot 100 in the States in 1964.
Daryl Hall, John Oates with David Ruffin & Eddie Kendrick (medley) – no.20 on the Hot 100 and no.40 on the R&B chart in the States in 1985.
UB40 – no.49 in the UK in 1991.

WE WISH YOU A MERRY CHRISTMAS

This is a popular 16th century English carol Donna sang with several other artists on *Solid Gold Christmas* on 22nd

December 1984 – the Student Choir of the Hillcrest Drive Magnet School opened the carol, and as well as Donna other participating artists included Peabo Bryson, John Davidson, Suzanne Somers, Crystal Gayle, John Schneider, and Peter, Paul & Mary.

WE'RE GONNA WIN

Written by Paul Jabara & Jay Asher, and recorded by Jabara – with vocals by Donna – for his 1986 album, *DE LA NOCHE.* However, the song failed to make the final track listing, and remains unreleased.

WE'VE COME THIS FAR BY FAITH

Popular gospel hymn Donna and her sisters often used to sing as young children.
Donna revealed, in a message to fans following the passing of her father in December 2004, this was a favourite family song.

'I have been blessed to be the daughter of a great man who God allowed to live to the ripe age of 80,' wrote Donna. 'He has been a force in my life and a mentor. His name was Andrew Gaines and I had the privilege of being his child. On December 14th at 3 o'clock central time, at his home in Nashville, my father made the ultimate transition and went home to his heavenly reward after a long battle with lung disease.

'There were two services for him, one in Nashville and one on the 17th at my childhood church, Grant A.M.E. in Boston. It was a very warm and heartfelt service. My brother, sisters and I sang our favourite family song, *We've Come This Far By Faith*.'

WHAT A DIFFERENCE A DAY MADE

Originally written in Spanish, as *Cuando Vuelva A Tu Lado*, by Mexican composer María Méndez Grever in 1934.

The English lyrics were penned by Stanley Adams, and the best known version of the song was recorded by Dinah Washington in 1959.

Donna revealed, in her autobiography *Ordinary Girl: The Journey*, this was a song she mastered as a young girl, to please her father, as he loved the song so much.

Hit Versions:
Dorsey Brothers Orchestra – no.5 on the Pop chart in the States in 1934.
Dinah Washington – no.4 on the R&B chart and no.8 on the Hot 100 in the States in 1959.
Esther Phillips – no.6 in the UK, and no.10 on the R&B chart and no.20 on the Hot 100 in the States, in 1975.

The track is also known by the title: *What A Difference A Day Makes*.

Other artists to have recorded the song include Jamie Cullum, Aretha Franklin, Eydie Gorme, Luis Miguel and Sarah Vaughan.

WHAT A FOOL BELIEVES

Written by Michael McDonald & Kenny Loggins, and recorded by the Doobie Brothers for their 1978 album, *MINUTE BY MINUTE*.

Donna performed the song, with Kenny Rogers, as part of a Grammy nominations medley, when she appeared at the Grammy Awards, staged at the Shrine Auditorium, Los Angeles, on 27th February 1980.

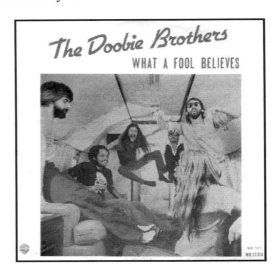

The Doobie Brothers took the song to no.1 on the Hot 100 and no.72 on the R&B chart in the States, and to no.31 in the UK.

See also: *Grammy Nominations Medley*.

WHAT CHILD IS THIS

Written by William Chatterton Dix, and recorded by Donna, as part of *Christmas Medley*, for her 1994 album, *CHRISTMAS SPIRIT* – produced by Michael Omartian.

The medley also featured *Do You Hear What I Hear* & *Joy To The World*.

WHAT IS IT YOU WANT

Written by Donna with Keith Diamond, Anthony Smith, Donna Wyant, Vince Lawrence & Dave Resnik, and recorded by Donna for her 1991 album, *MISTAKEN IDENTITY* – produced by Diamond.

WHATEVER YOUR HEART DESIRES

Written by Donna with Mike Stock, Matt Aitken & Pete Waterman, and recorded by Donna for her 1989 album, *ANOTHER PLACE AND TIME* – produced by Stock, Aitken & Waterman.

WHAT'S LOVE GOT TO DO WITH IT

Written by Terry Britten & Graham Lyle, and recorded by Tina Turner for her 1984 album, *PRIVATE DANCER*.

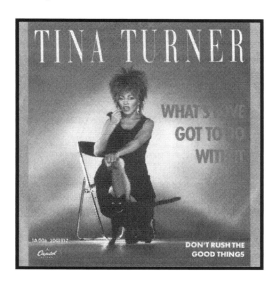

'I had *What's Love Got To Do With It* for two years,' revealed Donna, in a 1999 interview, 'and I didn't do it. I realised after hearing what Tina did with it that had I sung the song it would have never sounded that way. Her raspiness, and the sensitivity of the song, is what made the match.'

The song was originally recorded – but not released until 2000 – by Bucks Fizz.

Tina Turner took the song to no.1 on the Hot 100 and no.2 on the R&B chart in the States, and to no.3 in the UK.

WHEN I LOOK UP

Written by Cedric Caldwell, Victor Caldwell & H. Hill, and recorded by Donna with Darwin Hobbs for Hobb's 2000 gospel album, *VERTICAL* – produced by Cedric & Victor Caldwell.

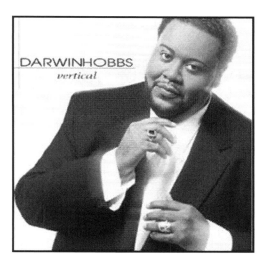

WHEN LOVE CRIES

Written by Donna with Keith Diamond, Paul Chiten, Larry Henley & Anthony Smith, and recorded by Donna for her 1991 album, *MISTAKEN IDENTITY* – produced by Diamond.

Lead single from the album in most countries, excluding the UK, where it wasn't issued.

The single charted at no.18 on the R&B chart and no.77 on the Hot 100 in the States.

Official Versions:
Album Version.
Single Version Remix.
12" Mix.
Instrumental.
Club Mix.
Radio Mix.

Radio Edit.
Summertime Mix / Vocal Club Dub.
ISA Extended Remix.
Vocal Club Mix.

WHEN LOVE TAKES OVER YOU

Written by Mike Stock, Matt Aitken & Pete Waterman, and recorded by Donna for her 1989 album, *ANOTHER PLACE AND TIME* – produced by Stock, Aitken & Waterman.

The track was released as a single in select countries, not including the States – it was a minor hit in the UK, achieving no.72.

Official Versions:
Album Version.
Dave Ford 7".
Dave Ford Extended Remix.
Dave Ford Instrumental.
Pete Hammond Original 12" Mix.

WHEN THE DREAM NEVER DIES

Written by Michael & Stormie Omartian, and recorded by Donna, as Elizabeth, for the 2000 original cast album, *CHILD OF THE PROMISE* – produced by Michael Omartian.

WHENEVER THERE IS LOVE

Written by Bruce Roberts & Sam Roman (*aka* MCA's chair, Edgar Bronfman, Jr.), and recorded by Donna as a duet with Roberts for the 1996 film soundtrack, *DAYLIGHT* – produced by Roberts & David Foster.

'Someone called me with this song,' said Donna. 'Bruce Roberts, who I've written songs with before and who wrote *Enough Is Enough*. I said OK, well, send me the song. And then David Foster called me, who I've known for years, and he said, "Donna, you gotta do this song!" Then a third person called me, so I thought I better listen to this song.

'I listened to the song – thought it was fantastic. So we got together, put the

tracks down with David (Foster), and they took the tracks back to LA, and then they did a dance mix with Junior Vasquez in New York.'

Released as a single in a limited number of countries, including Germany and the States.

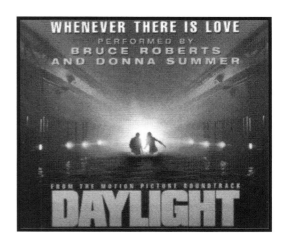

The single failed to enter the Hot 100 in the States, but it did achieve no.9 on the 'bubbling under' section of the chart.

A French version of the duet titled *Tant Quil Y Aura L'Amour*, was released as a single in France, and a Spanish version, *El Verdadero Amor*, was included on the Spanish release of *Daylight* on DVD.

Official Versions:
Soundtrack Version.
Club Mix.
Club Dub.
Riff Dub.
Tribal Beats.
Instrumental.
7" Edit.
French Version.
Spanish Version.

WHERE I SHOULD BE

Song recorded by Sunshine for their cancelled 1978 album, *WATCHIN' DADDY DANCE* – produced by Donna & Juergen Koppers.

Remains unreleased.

WHERE WOULD I BE WITHOUT YOU

This was one of two unreleased songs mentioned in *Contemporary Christian Music* in June 1981, as a song Donna had recorded for her shelved album, *I'M A RAINBOW* – the other was *You'll Never Walk Alone*.

WHISPERING WAVES

Written by Pete Bellotte & Giorgio Moroder, and recorded by Donna for her 1975 album, *LOVE TO LOVE YOU BABY* – produced by Bellotte.

B-side of *Could It Be Magic*.

WHITE BOYS

Written James Rado & Gerome Ragni (book and lyrics) & Galt MacDermot (music) for the controversial 'tribal love-rock' musical, *Hair*.

Donna appeared in the German production of the musical in 1968, titled *Haare*, and was part of the cast who performed this song on stage and on the cast album.

WHITE CHRISTMAS

Written by Irving Berlin for the film, *Holiday Inn*, and recorded by Bing Crosby in Los Angeles on 29th May 1942 – it hit no.1 in the States and went on to become to the no.1 best-selling non-charity single of all time.

Donna performed the song *a cappella*, in a German hotel ballroom, on New Year's Eve 1975.

Recorded by Donna for her 1994 album, *CHRISTMAS SPIRIT* – produced by Michael Omartian.

Other hit versions:
Ravens – no.9 on the R&B chart in the States in 1948.
Mantovani – no.6 in the UK in 1952.
Drifters – no.2 on the R&B chart in 1954 (with several re-entries in later years).
Pat Boone – no.29 in the UK in 1957.
Andy Williams – no.1 on the Christmas Singles chart in the States in 1963.
Otis Redding – no.12 on the Christmas Singles chart in 1968.
Freddie Starr – no.41 in the UK in 1975.
Darts – no.48 in the UK in 1980.
Jim Davidson – no.52 in the UK in 1980.
Keith Harris & Orville – no.40 in the UK in 1985.
Max Bygraves – no.71 in the UK in 1989.

WHO DO YOU THINK YOU'RE FOOLIN'

Written Pete Bellotte, Sylvester Levay & Jerry Rix, and recorded by Donna for her 1980 album, *THE WANDERER* – produced by Bellotte & Giorgio Moroder.

This was the third and last single released from the album – it charted at no.8 on the Hot Dance Club chart and no.40 on the Hot 100 in the States, and no.100 in Australia.

WINTER MELODY

Written by Donna with Pete Bellotte & Giorgio Moroder, and recorded by Donna for her 1976 album, *FOUR*

SEASONS OF LOVE – produced by Bellotte & Moroder.

This song represented winter on Donna's concept album – that is, coming to terms with a relationship that has ended.

With *Spring Affair*, the single gave Donna her third no.1 on the Hot Dance Club Play chart in the States, where it charted at no.21 on the R&B chart and no.43 on the Hot 100.

The single also achieved no.20 in Ireland, no.27 in the UK and no.41 in Canada.

Donna performed the song on *Soul Train* in 1976.

Official Versions:
Album Version.
7" / Single Edit.

WITH A LITTLE HELP FROM MY FRIENDS

Written by John Lennon & Paul McCartney, and recorded by the Beatles for their 1967 album, *SGT. PEPPER'S LONELY HEARTS CLUB BAND*.

Performed by Donna on her Greatest Hits Tour in 2005.

Hit Versions:
Joe Cocker – no.1 in the UK, and no.68 on the Hot 100 in the States, in 1968.
Beatles (with *Sgt. Pepper's Lonely Hearts Club Band*) – no.63 in the UK, and no.71 on the Hot 100 in the States, in 1978.
Wet Wet Wet – no.1 in the UK in 1988.
Sam & Mark – no.1 in the UK in 2004.

When, in one interview, Donna was asked to name her all-time favourite album, she replied: 'Probably *ABBEY ROAD*. The Beatles caused pop to turn a corner, and people started paying much more attention to lyrics. A lot of music before them was lyrically very corny, but they went a lot deeper, they started writing about things people didn't really write about. Their use of terminology and phraseology within the structure of a song was very different for the times – even now they hold up.'

WITH YOUR LOVE

Written by Donna with Giorgio Moroder & Pete Bellotte, and recorded by Donna for the 1978 soundtrack album, *THANK GOD IT'S FRIDAY* – produced by Moroder & Bellotte.

B-side of *Last Dance*.

Donna performed the song when she appeared on *American Bandstand* in 1978 – she was the first person to act as guest host on the long running show.

WOMAN

Written by Donna with Bruce Sudano, Michael Omartian & Greg Phillinganes, and recorded by Donna for her 1983 album, *SHE WORKS HARD FOR THE MONEY* – produced by Omartian.

B-side of *Unconditional Love*.

WOMAN IN ME, THE

Written by John Bettis & Michael Clark, and recorded by Donna for her self-titled 1982 album – produced by Quincy Jones.

The track featured backing vocals by James Ingram.

This was the third and last single lifted from the album. It achieved no.7 in the Netherlands, no.18 in Belgium & Canada, no.30 on the R&B chart and no.33 on the Hot 100 in the States and no.62 in the UK.

A limited edition translucent blue vinyl 12" single was issued in the UK.

WORDS

An audio clip of this song was posted on Donna's official web-site – however, it remains unreleased.

WORK IT

One of three unreleased songs Donna mentioned she had written, for a new album scheduled for July 2002, in her 2001 holiday message to fans – the other two songs were *Rain On My Shoulders* and *Only Words*.

WORK THAT MAGIC

Written by Donna with Keith Diamond, Paul Chiten, Larry Henley & Anthony Smith, and recorded by Donna for her 1991 album, *MISTAKEN IDENTITY* – produced by Diamond.

'When we started writing *Work That Magic*,' said Donna, 'Keith Diamond had just fallen in love, so we were writing from a frame of reference of real intensity and passion.'

Released as the lead single from the album in the UK, in place of *When Love Cries*, which was preferred in most other countries – the single achieved no.74.

Donna performed the song when she appeared as a guest on the British TV show, *The Terry Wogan Show*, in 1991.

Official Versions:
Album Version.
ISA Remix.
Extended ISA Remix (*aka* ISA Full
  Length Remix).
Capricorn ISA Remix.

WORKING THE MIDNIGHT SHIFT

Written by Donna with Giorgio Moroder & Pete Bellotte, and recorded by Donna for her 1977 album, *ONCE UPON A TIME* – produced by Moroder & Bellotte.

WORTH THE WAIT

Written by Donna & Bruce Sudano.

Donna performed this song live occasionally, but it is not known if a studio recording exists.

Remains unreleased.

WOUNDED

Written by Giorgio Moroder & Pete Bellotte, and recorded by Donna for her 1974 album, *LADY OF THE NIGHT* – released in the Netherlands only.

Produced by Pete Bellotte.

B-side of *Lady Of The Night*.

YOU ARE SO BEAUTIFUL

Written by Billy Preston & Bruce Fisher, and recorded by Preston for his 1974 album, *THE KIDS & ME*.

Performed by Donna when she appeared at the European *Night Of The Proms* in 2007 – staged in Rotterdam, in the Netherlands.

Joe Cocker's cover version achieved no.5 on the Hot 100 in the States in 1975.

YOU ARE THE SUNSHINE OF MY LIFE

Written and recorded by Stevie Wonder, for his 1973 album, *TALKING BOOK*.

As part of a tribute to Stevie, Donna joined Lionel Richie, Tina Arena, Ray Parker, Jr., Quincy Jones, Sheena Easton & Glen Campbell, to sing the song at the American Music Awards on 25th January 1982. Joined by Ella Fitzgerald, Donna and the other artists also performed Stevie's *Isn't She Lovely* as *Isn't He Lovely*.

Stevie Wonder took the song to no.1 on the Hot 100 and no.3 on the R&B chart in the States, and to no.7 in the UK.

YOU GOT ME BELIEVING

Written by Donna & Bruce Sudano – registered with the American Society of Composers, Authors & Publishers (ASCAP), but never released.

YOU GOTTA BE RICH

Written by Donna with Al Kasha & Michael Omartian, for the as yet unpublished play Donna worked on with Bruce Sudano, Kasha & Omartian, *Ordinary Girl* – remains unreleased.

Performed by Donna on her Live & More Encore Tour in 1999 – however, the song wasn't included on Donna's *Live & More Encore!* album or on the accompanying home video.

(YOU MAKE ME FEEL LIKE A) NATURAL WOMAN

Written by Carole King, Gerry Goffin & Jerry Wexler, and recorded by Aretha Franklin for her 1968 album, *ARETHA: LADY SOUL*.

Donna performed the song on her Greatest Hits Tour in 2005.

Hit Versions:
Aretha Franklin – no.2 on the R&B chart, and no.8 on the Hot 100, in the States

in 1967.

James Ingram – no.30 on the R&B chart in the States in 1990 (as *(You Make Me Feel Like A) Natural Man)*.

Mary J. Blige – no.23 in the UK, and no.39 on the R&B chart and no.95 on the Hot 100 in the States, in 1995.

YOU TO ME

Written by Pete Bellotte & Sylvester Levay, and recorded by Donna for her shelved 1981 album, *I'M A RAINBOW* – produced by Bellotte & Giorgio Moroder.

The album was finally released in 1996.

YOU'LL NEVER WALK ALONE

Written by Richard Rodgers & Oscar Hammerstein, for their 1945 musical, *Carousel*.

This was one of two unreleased songs mentioned in *Contemporary Christian Music* in June 1981, as a song Donna had recorded for her shelved album, *I'M A RAINBOW* – it was replaced by *Don't Cry For Me Argentina*, and remains unreleased.

Hit Versions:

Gerry & The Pacemakers – no.1 in the UK in 1963.

Patti LaBelle – no.34 on the Hot 100 in the States in 1964.

Elvis Presley – no.44 in the UK, and no.90 on the Hot 100 in the States, in 1968.

Crowd – no.1 in the UK in 1985.

Isley Brothers – no.25 on the R&B chart in the States in 1989.

Robson & Jerome – no.1 in the UK in 1996.

José Carreras, Placido Domingo & Luciano Pavarotti – no.35 in the UK in 1998.

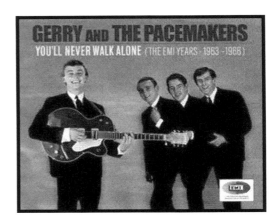

Other artists to have recorded the song include Louis Armstrong, Shirley Bassey, Chris de Burgh, Johnny Cash, Ray Charles, Perry Como, the Crusaders, Doris Day, Aretha Franklin, Tom Jones, Alicia Keys, Mario Lanza, Olivia Newton-John, Nina Simone, Frank Sinatra, Barbra Streisand, Gene Vincent, Dionne Warwick and Tammy Wynette.

YOUR LOVE IS SO GOOD TO ME

Written by Donna & Bruce Sudano – registered with the American Society of Composers, Authors & Publishers (ASCAP), but never released.

YOU'RE SO BEAUTIFUL

Written by Donna with Nathan DiGesare & Tony Moran, and recorded by Donna for the 2003 compilation, *THE JOURNEY – THE BEST OF...* – produced by DiGesare & Moran.

Donna first mentioned the song in her 2001 holiday message to fans, and she wasn't pleased when an early version of the song leaked on the internet. 'It was out there, and we couldn't stop it,' she said. 'Of course, it has since been completed.'

Released as a promo 12" single in the States, where the song climbed to no.5 on the Hot Dance Club Play chart.

Official Versions:
Glenn Friscia Club Mix.
Glenn Friscia Dub mix.
Glenn Friscia Radio Edit.
Friscia & Lamboy Beautiful Vocal Mix.
Tony Moran Vocal Mix.
Tony Moran Dub.
Tony Moran Radio Edit.
Tony & Mac's Dancefloor Journey Mix.
Ultimate Club Mix.

YOU'VE BEEN LYIN'

Song former model Twiggy recorded for her shelved 1979 album, *HEAVEN IN MY EYES* – produced by Donna & Juergen Koppers.

The album was finally released in 2007, and included an up-dated remix by OUTpsiDER, titled *U Bin Lyin'*.

YOU'VE GOT A FRIEND

Written and originally recorded by Carole King, for her 1971 album, *TAPESTRY*.

Donna performed the song, as a duet with Rita Coolidge, at *The Music For UNICEF Concert: A Gift For Song*, staged at the United Nations General Assembly, New York, on 9th January 1979 – the concert aired the following day in the States, however, the concert was edited and only a few seconds of Donna's duet with Rita Coolidge was aired.

Hit Versions:
James Taylor – no.1 on the Hot 100 in the States, and no.4 in the UK, in 1971.
Roberta Flack & Donny Hathaway – no.8 on the R&B chart, and no.29 on the Hot 100, in the States in 1971.
Big Fun & Sonia – no.14 in the UK in 1990.
Brand New Heavies – no.9 in the UK in 1997.

Other artists to have recorded the song include Petula Clark, Ella Fitzgerald, Aretha Franklin, Al Green, Michael Jackson, Tom Jones, Johnny Mathis, Alanis Morissette, Dusty Springfield, Barbra Streisand and Andy Williams.

PART 2: THE ALBUMS

Here, Donna's albums are listed chronologically within each category.

Catalogue numbers, release dates, track listings and producer(s) are given for each album, together with other information, including:

- Chart positions achieved in the USA (Pop & R&B), UK and other countries.

- USA sales awards by the RIAA (Recording Industry Association of America).

- UK sales awards by the BPI (British Phonographic Industry).

- American Music Awards, Grammy Awards & selected other awards and nominations.

- Hit singles lifted from the album (in the USA and/or UK).

Studio Albums

Donna's debut album is little known as, originally, it was only released in one country.

LADY OF THE NIGHT

USA: Not Released.
UK: Not Released.

Lady Of The Night/Born To Die/Friends/Full Of Emptiness/Domino/The Hostage/

Wounded/Little Miss Fit/Let's Work Together Now/Sing Along (Sad Song)

Produced by Pete Bellotte.

Donna's debut album was recorded in Germany, and released in the Netherlands only in 1974, on the Groovy record label (LGR 8301).

The album, boosted by two Top 5 singles, achieved no.27 in the Netherlands.

The album was reissued on CD in several countries in 1995, and again in 1999 – the latter, with the original sleeve artwork (as above). One track, *Full Of Emptiness*, was omitted from the CD releases, as it also featured on Donna's second album, *LOVE TO LOVE YOU BABY*.

Hit Singles:
The Hostage.
Lady Of The Night.

LOVE TO LOVE YOU BABY

USA: Oasis OCLP 5003 (1975).
UK: GTO GTLP 008 (1975).

Love To Love You Baby/Full Of Emptiness/Need-A-Man Blues/Whispering Waves/Pandora's Box/Full Of Emptiness (Reprise)

Produced by Pete Bellotte.

This album – Donna's first international release – was originally issued in 1975 in Germany (Atlantic ATL 50198) and the Netherlands (PolyGram 9128 039), with a different track listing:

Love To Love You Baby/Lady Of The Night/Pandora's Box/Need-A-Man Blues/The Hostage

On both versions of the album, *Love To Love You Baby* was 16:50 minutes, and filled the entire first side of the vinyl album.

Boosted by the inclusion of the title track, the album charted at no.6 on the R&B chart and no.11 on the Billboard 200 in the States, no.6 in Italy, no.7 in Australia & Sweden, no.9 in Norway, no.16 in the UK, no.23 in Germany and no.64 in Japan.

RIAA Award: Gold (January 1976) = 500,000.

BPI Award: Gold (January 1977) = £250,000 (pre-1979, album certifications were based on monetary value in the UK, rather than the number of units).

Hit Singles:
Love To Love You Baby.

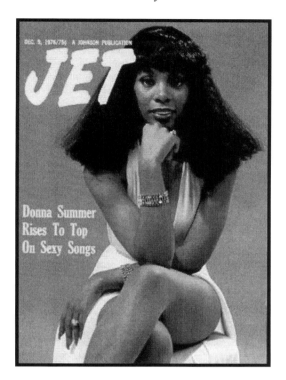

'Donna originally didn't want to do dance music at all,' admitted Giorgio Moroder. 'I mean, I knew her as a great singer with an incredible voice, so when we did the demo for *Love To Love You Baby* it was very different for her to be singing in that soft, breathy way. She hadn't sung that way for me before, and she wasn't too interested in disco. Ballads and musical numbers were more her style, but then that record took off and we had a bit of a problem.

'For the second album, which was moderately successful, we wanted to record disco tunes and we wanted to use her proper voice, but we didn't want to change the formula too much. She therefore stayed sexy, but a little less so, while using a little more voice, and then for the third album she really sang like we knew she could.'

A LOVE TRILOGY

USA: Oasis OCLP 5004 (1976).
UK: Casablanca CAL 2055 (1976).

Try Me, I Know We Can Make It/Intro: Prelude To Love/Could It Be Magic/ Wasted/Come With Me

Produced by Giorgio Moroder & Pete Bellotte.

The 'love trilogy' in the title referred to the three parts of the opening song: *Try Me... I Know... We Can Make It*.

Donna's second international album followed the style and format of the first, with the opening, 17:59 minute track taking up the whole of the first side of vinyl.

With no major hit single to boost sales, the album failed to match the success of Donna's previous album in most countries. It achieved no.1 in Italy & Spain, no.8 in Austria, no.9 in Norway, no.16 on the R&B chart and no.21 on the Billboard 200 in the States, no.18 in Sweden, no.24 in Germany, no.32 in Australia and no.41 in the UK.

RIAA Award: Gold (June 1976) = 500,000.

BPI Award: Gold (November 1977) = £250,000.

Hit Singles:
Could It Be Magic.
Try Me, I Know We Can Make It.

FOUR SEASONS OF LOVE

USA: Casablanca NBLP 7038 (1976).
UK: GTO GTLP 018 (1976).

Spring Affair/Summer Fever/Autumn Changes/Winter Melody/Spring Reprise

Produced by Giorgio Moroder & Pete Bellotte.

This concept album told the story of a love affair through the four seasons.

The longest track on the album was *Spring Affair*, at 8:30 minutes – short, compared with the opening track on Donna's previous two albums, but still long compared to most songs released around the same time.

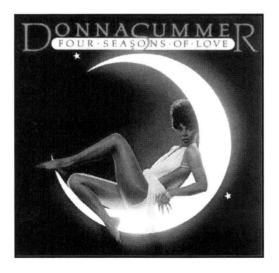

The album peaked at no.1 in Italy, no.13 on the R&B chart and no.29 on the

Billboard 200 in the States, no.31 in Germany and no.40 in Sweden.

RIAA Award: Gold (November 1976) = 500,000.

BPI Award: Silver (January 1977) = £150,000.

Hit Singles:
Spring Affair.
Winter Melody.

I REMEMBER YESTERDAY

USA: Casablanca NBLP 7056 (1977).
UK: GTO GTLP 025 (1977).

I Remember Yesterday/Love's Unkind/ Back In Love Again/I Remember Yesterday (Reprise)/Black Lady/Take Me/Can't We Just Sit Down (And Talk It Over)/I Feel Love

Produced by Giorgio Moroder & Pete Bellotte.

As the title suggests, the concept of this album was Donna 'remembering yesterday', with songs on the first side of the album in particular representing styles of music from different decades:

- 1940s – *I Remember Yesterday.*
- 1950s – *Love's Unkind.*
- 1960s – *Back In Love Again.*

I Feel Love, which gave Donna one of her biggest international hits, and her first and only UK no.1, represented 'the future' of music, as Donna, Giorgio Moroder and Pete Bellotte saw it.

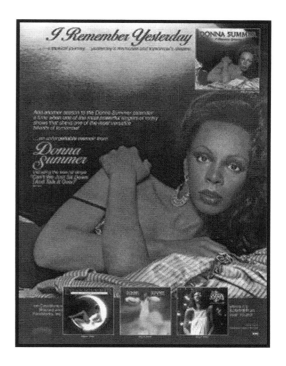

The album saw Donna beginning to move away from her 'lady of love' image, on her way to becoming the 'Queen of Disco'.

The album was Donna's most successful of all-time in the UK, in terms of chart position: it rose to no.3.

The album achieved no.1 in Italy (Donna's third chart topper in a row), no.2 in Zimbabwe, no.3 in Austria, no.5 in Norway, no.7 in Germany, no.11 on the R&B chart and no.18 on the Billboard 200 in the States, no.12 in New Zealand, no.13 in Sweden and no.77 in Japan.

RIAA Award: Gold (July 1977) = 500,000.

BPI Award: Gold (August 1977) = £250,000.

Hit Singles:
Can't We Just Sit Down (And Talk It Over).
I Feel Love.
I Remember Yesterday.
Love's Unkind.
Back In Love Again.

The album has been reissued in some countries, re-titled *I FEEL LOVE.*

ONCE UPON A TIME

USA: Casablanca NBLP 7078 (1977).
UK: Casablanca CALD 5003 (1977).

LP1: *Once Upon A Time/Faster And Faster To Nowhere/Fairy Tale High/Say Something Nice/Now I Need You/ Working The Midnight Shift/Queen For A Day*

LP2: *If You Got It Flaunt It/A Man Like You/Sweet Romance/(Theme) Once Upon A Time/Dance Into My Life/Rumour Has It/I Love You/Happily Ever After/ (Theme) Once Upon A Time*

Produced by Giorgio Moroder & Pete Bellotte.

This was Donna's first double album, and the four sides of vinyl were titled 'Act One', 'Act Two', 'Act Three' and 'Act Four'. It was the last album she recorded at Musicland Studios, Germany, where Bob Esty was brought in to arrange the album.

'Giorgio gave me a tape of him singing la-la-la, accompanied by a little keyboard,' said Esty. 'That was it. Then I went into a studio, did a synthesizer demo of the whole album, and flew to his Musicland Studio in Munich.' Donna was on tour at the time. '(On her return) she listened to the tape of music I had arranged, and wrote the entire album with Pete Bellotte in just a few days.'

Donna went on to record the album in just four night sessions – originally, it was going to be titled *CINDERELLA*.

The album was issued in a gatefold sleeve, and the track listing in the inner sleeve was printed in the form of a *libretto* – that is, like text used for a ballet, musical or opera.

'You have to get people's attention some kind of way, but I'm not just sex, sex, sex,' stated Donna, around this time. 'I would never want to be a one dimensional person like that. It's like if you have a coat that's red, yellow and white. You don't call it a red coat or a yellow one or a white one, you call it a multi-coloured coat. It has three colours in it. Same with me. I can sing songs like *Love To Love You Baby*, but I can also sing ballads, light opera, things from musical comedies, church hymns – all kinds of songs.

'Plus, I can write, act and think. Like the multi-coloured coat, I'm multi-dimensional, and I don't want to be known for just one thing.'

The album itself told a 'rag-to-riches', Cinderella-like story, through modern day music. Donna, it was reported at the time, hoped to turn her album into a musical and take it to Broadway, but this never materialised.

Donna has described the album as 'the first record I can really say is a part of me.'

The album achieved no.2 in Italy, no.9 in Norway, no.11 in Zimbabwe, no.13 on the R&B chart and no.26 on the Billboard 200 in the States, no.24 in the UK, no.31 in Japan and no.44 in Australia.

RIAA Award: Gold (December 1977) = 250,000.

BPI Award: Gold (November 1977) = £250,000.

Hit Singles:
I Love You.
Rumour Has It.

Donna, in the late 1970s, was finding her success – and the demands of her record company – increasingly difficult to cope with. Things came to a head in early 1979.

'It got bad enough for me to say, "I got to either get out of this business, or do something about my life",' Donna later recalled. 'It was a turning point for me. I really felt like I wasn't going to make it.

'You can't travel day and night, party day and night, go to this place and that place, and have no real sleep pattern over a period of two or three years, and survive it without being on serious drugs – and that's only going to last so long, too. You'll either have a heart attack if you keep it up, or your liver is going to give out.

'My husband (Bruce Sudano) hates for me to say this, because he doesn't want me to sound like I was a drug addict or anything, but I was taking some really heavy anti-depressant type medicines. I wasn't sleeping. I didn't know at the time I was allergic to caffeine, and caffeine would make me stay awake for days at a time. Every time I would drink Coca Cola, it was like taking speed. So I'd be up, and I couldn't sleep when I was travelling. I'd be awake all night, then I'd go and do a gig, and I'd sleep maybe four hours in two or three days.

'My husband, who was then my boyfriend, was really uptight about it. He felt like it was going to kill me. So they gave me medicines to help me go to sleep, and one to keep me awake, and I was just all over the place. I got desperate. I said, "God, I can't go on like this. This is not it. I want to have children. I want to have a normal life again".'

BAD GIRLS

USA: Casablanca NBLP 7150 (1979).
UK: Casablanca CALD 5007 (1979).

LP1: *Hot Stuff/Bad Girls/Love Will Always Find You/Walk Away/Dim All The Lights/Journey To The Centre Of Your Heart/One Night In A Lifetime/Can't Get To Sleep At Night*

LP2: *On My Honor/There Will Always Be A You/All Through The Night/My Baby Understands/Our Love/Lucky/Sunset People*

Produced by Pete Bellotte & Giorgio Moroder.

Donna feels her third double album in a row, finally, helped her to break away from the 'lady of love' image. 'I think *BAD GIRLS* turned it around,' she said. 'I was becoming more sassy. The original image was a victim of femininity. When the *BAD GIRLS* album came out, I was able to make other statements and be other women.'

This was Donna's most successful album in the States: it rose to no.1 on the Billboard 200 on 16th June 1979, and held for top spot for six non-consecutive weeks. The album also achieved three weeks at no.1 on the R&B chart – it was her only R&B chart topping album.

Outside the States, the album charted at no.2 in Italy, no.3 in New Zealand, Norway & Sweden, no.6 in Australia, no.7 in Germany, no.8 in the Netherlands, no.9 in Japan, no.15 in Zimbabwe and no.23 in the UK.

RIAA Award: 2 x Platinum (December 1993) = 1 million.

BPI Award: Silver (July 1979) = 60,000.

No.2 best-selling album of 1979 in the USA (behind Supertramp's *BREAKFAST IN AMERICA*).

Grammy Award:
Best Rock Vocal Performance, Female –
Hot Stuff.

Grammy Award nominations:
Album Of The Year.
Best Pop Vocal Performance, Female –
Bad Girls.
Best R&B Vocal Performance, Female –
Dim All The Lights.
Best Disco Recording – *Bad Girls*.

Hit Singles:
Hot Stuff.
Bad Girls.
Dim All The Lights.
Walk Away.
Sunset People.

Despite its success, by the time *BAD GIRLS* was released, Donna felt increasingly unhappy with the direction she was being forced to take, with both her career and her life. She had never been comfortable with the 'lady of love' image and, increasingly, she felt she was being exploited by her record company, Casablanca.

The final straw, so far as she was concerned, came when Neil Bogart reneged on his promise to hold back *No More Tears (Enough Is Enough)* for a couple of weeks, so that it wouldn't compete with *Dim All The Lights* – a song Donna had composed all by herself, and was headed for no.1 on the Hot 100, before her duet with Barbra Streisand grabbed the top spot ahead of it.

'Everyone was telling me that Casablanca was ripping me off,' said Donna, speaking in 1987, 'but I didn't find out until much later. My records were black-marketed severely. At one point, I think I was one of the top three black-marketed artists. And we're talking mega-bucks here. The black market pressings were often better than the tapes my company was pressing, so they had to have real material from somewhere. I don't think they could have gotten it anywhere else but Casablanca.'

In leaving the label, Donna issued a $10 million lawsuit against Casablanca – $5 million in punitive damages and $5 million in actual damages. Donna became the first act to sign to David Geffen's new Geffen Records label – initially, however, having reaffirmed her faith in God in October 1979, Donna was keen to sign with a Christian record company.

'I was trying to separate and start myself in that direction,' she stated, 'but I met so many obstacles. I actually had trouble getting on a gospel label. A lot of people were defensive and it was very strange.

'Instead of being more forgiving, or whatever it takes, and saying, "Hey, look, this is a person who could potentially sell a lot of records", we didn't get that reaction … and when that didn't come through, we realised that it had to be God's desire for it (*THE*

WANDERER) to be the record that it was.'

The first vinyl disc was released as a CD album in its own right in Germany in 1995, titled *BAD GIRLS* (Karussell 512 115-2).

THE WANDERER

USA: Geffen GHS 2000 (1980).
UK: Warner Bros K99124 (1980).

The Wanderer/Looking Up/Breakdown/ Grand Illusion/Running For Cover/Cold Love/Who Do You Think You're Foolin'/ Nightlife/Stop Me/I Believe In Jesus

Produced by Giorgio Moroder & Pete Bellotte.

Donna's first album for her new record label saw her moving away from the disco sound that had brought her success. 'David (Geffen) wanted me to do a dance record at that point,' she said. 'I was in a transition emotionally. Everything was shifting in my life. It was very difficult,

extremely … I found myself in a serious mental and physical condition after being worked to death – nearly dying …

'I was either going to OD on some kind of medication, or I kept having these flashes of doing something crazy – like taking too many of the pills I had to take because I was always so depressed.'

Donna turned her life around by re-affirming her faith in God, and becoming a born-again Christian. 'I believed in God my whole career,' she said, 'my whole life, since I was a little girl. God in that sense wasn't new … being a Christian doesn't make me perfect. I have chosen to live my life in a way that will be an asset to others, as well as to my children and myself. If someone wants to misconstrue that with all the baloney about Christianity and people who profess to be Christian but are not, that's their problem. Christianity does not make you perfect: it's about asking

God to hold you to the commitment to be perfect in a way.'

Originally, Donna planned the album as a double, but David Geffen decided to test the market first with a single disc.

'The problem with Donna's album,' observed Geffen, after the album's release, 'is that it's a rock record, but rock stations aren't playing it because of a prejudice against black artists and female artists. When you look at a rock station playlist and can't find a single black act, I think there's something radically wrong – and it has nothing to do with Donna Summer. And Donna has the misfortune, in terms of rock radio, to be both black and a woman.'

The change in direction brought Donna's run of American no.1 albums to an end, but the album still performed respectably in the States, rising to no.12 on the R&B chart and no.13 on the Billboard 200.

The album was generally less well received outside the States, where it achieved no.5 in Zimbabwe, no.7 in Italy, no.15 in Sweden, no.16 in New Zealand, no.18 in Australia & Norway, no.22 in Japan, no.54 in Germany and no.55 in the UK.

RIAA Award: Gold (December 1980) = 500,000.

Grammy Award nominations:
Best Rock Vocal Performance, Female –
  Cold Love.
Best Inspirational Performance –
  I Believe In Jesus.

The album ranked no.2 on Rolling Stone magazine's prestigious listing of the best albums of 1980, behind Bruce Springsteen's *THE RIVER*.

'If you're an artist, you have to do your artistry,' said Donna, regarding the album's reception. 'Sometimes, there's a conflict and people don't want your artistry to be what it is, and so you make the adjustment to try to please them.

'At that point, I wasn't trying to please anyone but myself. That's not my best-selling record, but at the same time, I think it certainly was one I felt that I was being true to myself. I was not allowing myself to be pigeon-holed, where people were trying to put me, but I was taking them with me on this journey. We were going to 'wander' around, and we were going to go to places that they hadn't been with me. That's what *THE WANDERER* meant to me.'

Hit Singles:
The Wanderer.
Cold Love.
Who Do You Think You're Foolin'.

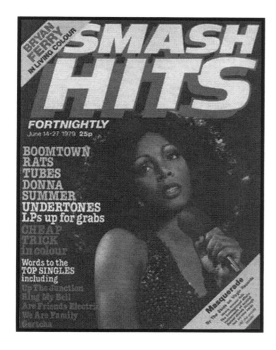

I'M A RAINBOW

USA: Casablanca/Mercury 314 532 869-2 (1996).

UK: Casablanca/Mercury 314 532 869-2 (1996), Driven By The Music DBTMCD207 (2CD remastered, 2014).

I Believe (In You)/True Love Survives/You To Me/Sweet Emotion/Leave Me Alone/Melanie/Back Where You Belong/People Talk/To Turn The Stone/Brooklyn/I'm A Rainbow/Walk On (Keep On Movin')/Don't Cry For Me Argentina/Runner With The Pack/Highway Runner/Romeo/End Of The Week/I Need Time

Produced by Giorgio Moroder & Pete Bellotte.

Although released in 1996, this album – what was planned as a double album – was originally recorded in 1981.

'Everybody is subject to the rules of the game that they play,' said Donna, when she was interviewed just before the album was due for release in 1981. 'I have two producers who write a lot of my songs, and they are not Christians. I have been with them since the beginning, and I am still subject to them in some ways, so until the whole situation is altered there aren't going to be any drastic, drastic, drastic, drastic changes. There are going to be subtle changes.'

'The record company wanted me to make different kinds of songs and records,' Donna said, explaining why her album was shelved. 'They didn't think the old way was working. They thought my time with Giorgio had run out. *THE WANDERER* album did very well, but when Giorgio and I went to record the next album, they stopped us mid-way, because they didn't like it.

'They used one of the songs, *Romeo*, on the *FLASHDANCE* album, but they said the rest of the songs wouldn't make it. That's when they made me switch producers.'

Donna, understandably, was angry and upset by Geffen's rejection of her work. 'David Geffen didn't think there was enough dance music on the album,' she said. 'It wasn't what he was looking for. It was like having a miscarriage. I don't go into the studio to have an album canned.'

Donna wasn't happy about being forced to switch producers, either. 'Giorgio was my mentor, my guide,' she said. 'He was like – well, I wouldn't dare call him my father, because he would kill me, but he was like my father in the business. All of a sudden, they were taking away everything that was true and dear to me, and putting me with people I didn't know.

'As for the record company, it just didn't work out. It was one of those situations where they didn't have the confidence they needed to have in me. David (Geffen) desperately wanted to sign me as his first act, and he did. I love David. I used to go to his house to write songs. I don't know at what point things started to go awry, but they did … it might have happened when he got into making *Cats* and then movies, and just got interested in other things. When I joined his company, he made all kinds of promises: "I'm going to put you in movies, blah,

blah, blah." He never did, and it became apparent to me that I had made a major mistake. But that's okay, I had six or seven years to sit home with my kids, and hang out on my ranch.'

Looking back, Giorgio Moroder admitted, 'I personally don't think it (the album) was very good. If I could go back now, first of all, I would not have done a double album. Of the eighteen songs, I would have picked the ten best ones. I never did think that we had a hit single on that album.'

Moroder described *Don't Cry For Me Argentina* as 'the only good song on the album.'

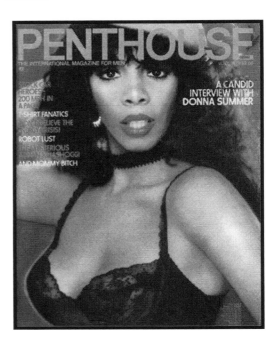

PolyGram, after acquiring the rights to all Donna's albums recorded for Geffen and Atlantic, took the decision to finally release *I'M A RAINBOW*. However, it's unlikely the album that was issued was exactly the same version that would have been released in 1981

Not surprisingly, given it was actually 15 years old, the album wasn't heavily promoted and didn't chart.

I'M A RAINBOW was remastered and reissued, as a double CD, in 2014.

DONNA SUMMER

USA: Geffen GHS 2005 (1982).
UK: Warner Bros K99163 (1982).

Love Is In Control (Finger On The Trigger)/Mystery Of Love/The Woman In Me/State Of Independence/Livin' In America/Protection/(If It) Hurts Just A Little/Love Is Just A Breath Away/Lush Life

Produced by Quincy Jones.

David Geffen, having rejected Donna's *I'M A RAINBOW* album, was keen for Donna to record a soul/R&B album – so, having split Donna and her usual co-writers/producers Giorgio Moroder & Pete Bellotte, he teamed her up with Quincy Jones.

'Of course, I had to like everything on the album,' said Donna, 'but it was Quincy that really searched out the tunes, and he really worked hard to find just the right ones.'

'It was hard for me,' Donna admitted, 'because I was used to just sitting down and writing. This time I had to trust Quincy's judgement. He picked most of the songs. He solicited the material from various people. I was never more dormant as a creative contributor.'

Jones, whose next project was Michael Jackson's *THRILLER*, has revealed Donna's album took seven months to record.

'Before we started on *THRILLER*,' he said, 'I was working on Donna Summer's second Geffen album. I thought it would take four months, but it went seven ... by the time I finished Summer's record, we only had eight weeks to do *THRILLER*. Sometimes that's better. You don't have time to sit there and get paralysis from analysis – you just go with your best instincts.'

In the States, the album charted at no.6 on the R&B chart and no.20 on the Billboard 200.

Elsewhere, it achieved no.3 in the Netherlands, no.8 in Sweden, no.10 in South Africa, no.12 in Norway, no.13 in the UK, no.19 in Austria, no.27 in Japan, no.37 in Germany, no.40 in Italy, no.45 in Australia and no.47 in New Zealand.

RIAA Award: Gold (September 1982) = 500,000.

Grammy Award nominations:
Best Rock Vocal Performance, Female – *Protection*.
Best R&B Vocal Performance, Female – *Love Is In Control (Finger On The Trigger)*.

A picture disc album was issued in the UK.

Hit Singles:
Love Is In Control (Finger On The Trigger).
State Of Independence.
The Woman In Me.

Although the album was successful, ultimately, Donna didn't enjoy working with Quincy Jones.

'Quincy Jones is a great producer,' she stated. 'It is difficult to produce someone like myself, who has a pre-established image. At the time, there were a lot of different opinions. There was my opinion, the record company's opinion, and so many different ways to go that, yes, there were many conflicts.'

'I was pregnant when Quincy produced my last album,' she said, 'and I wanted to be at home, knitting socks rather than recording.'

SHE WORKS HARD FOR THE MONEY

USA: Mercury 821 265 (1983).
UK: Mercury MERL21 (1983).

She Works Hard For The Money/Stop, Look And Listen/He's A Rebel/Woman/ Unconditional Love/Love Has A Mind Of Its Own/Tokyo/People, People/I Do Believe (I Fell In Love)

Produced by Michael Omartian.

Donna, at this time, was still in dispute with her former label, Casablanca Records, who had been taken over by PolyGram. As part of the settlement, Donna agreed to give the label one more album, so this album was given to PolyGram, who released it on their Mercury label.

Multi-Grammy winning Michael Omartian was Donna's choice of producer – like her, he was a born-again Christian, and unlike Quincy Jones he encouraged her to involve herself in the whole creative process.

The album was recorded at Hollywood's United Western Studios and two L.A.

studios, Lion Share Studios and Rhema Studio. Donna wrote or co-wrote every track on the album.

The album returned Donna to the Top 10 in the States, achieving no.5 on the R&B chart and no.9 on the Billboard 200.

In other countries, the album peaked at no.3 in Zimbabwe, no.6 in South Africa, no.8 in Sweden, no.11 in the Netherlands, no.12 in Norway, no.14 in Germany, no.21 in Australia, no.27 in Japan, no.28 in the UK, no.46 in Italy and no.47 in New Zealand.

RIAA Award: Gold (August 1983) = 500,000.

Grammy Award:
Best Inspirational Performance –
He's A Rebel.

Grammy Award nomination:
Best Pop Vocal Performance, Female –
She Works Hard For The Money.

Hit Singles:
She Works Hard For The Money.
Unconditional Love.
Stop, Look And Listen.
Love Has A Mind Of Its Own.

The success of the album didn't please PolyGram or Geffen – PolyGram, as the follow-up wouldn't be theirs, and Geffen because it was felt Donna should have saved some of her stronger material for them. David Geffen did, however, recruit the album's producer, Michael Omartian, to produce Donna's follow-up as well.

CATS WITHOUT CLAWS

USA: Geffen GHS 24040 (1984).
UK: Warner Bros 250 806 (1984).

Supernatural Love/It's Not The Way/ There Goes My Baby/Suzanna/Cats Without Claws/Oh Billy Please/Eyes/ Maybe It's Over/I'm Free/Forgive Me

Produced by Michael Omartian.

To David Geffen's annoyance, Donna's second album with Michael Omartian was less well received than her first, and

Donna's liner notes spoke volumes on their deteriorating relationship:

'To David Geffen – thanks for staying out of the kitchen this time. Now I hope you like the meal.'

In the States, the album charted at no.24 on the R&B chart and no.40 on the Billboard 200.

Elsewhere, the album peaked at no.10 in Sweden, no.15 in the Netherlands & Norway, no.29 in Italy, no.33 in Japan, no.39 in Germany, no.69 in the UK and no.91 in Australia.

Grammy Award:
Best Inspirational Performance –
 Forgive Me.

Hit Singles:
There Goes My Baby.

Supernatural Love.
Eyes.

The album, together with *DONNA SUMMER* and *THE WANDERER*, was reissued as part of a vinyl box-set, titled *THE BOX*, in 1984.

ALL SYSTEMS GO

USA: Geffen GHS 24102 (1987).
UK: Warner Bros 252 953 (1987).

All Systems Go/Bad Reputation/Love Shock/Jeremy/Only The Fool Survives/ Dinner With Gershwin/Fascination/ Voices Cryin' Out/Thinkin' 'Bout My Baby

Produced by Harold Faltermeyer, except:

- *Bad Reputation* produced by Peter Bunetta & Rick Chudacoff.
- *Dinner With Gershwin* produced by Richard Perry.
- *Thinkin' 'Bout My Baby* produced by Donna, Keith Nelson & Jeffrey Lams.

The tracks on what proved to be Donna's final album released on the Geffen label were recorded between 1983 and 1987, mostly in Germany.

'Going back to Munich was great,' said Donna. 'I had the same kind of feeling that I had the first time I worked there.'

In the States, the album charted at no.53 on the R&B chart, but became her first album to peak outside the Top 100 on the Billboard 200, when it stalled at no.122.

The album failed to chart in many countries, including the UK, but it did register at no.27 in Italy & Sweden, no.49 in the Netherlands and no.69 in Japan.

Hit Singles:
Dinner With Gershwin.
All Systems Go.

Looking back, Donna admitted the album 'doesn't sound like me at all. It's kind of synthetic. No, that sounds terrible. It's kind of homogenised – no, that sounds worse! I don't know how to say it … high tech?'

David Geffen wasn't satisfied with the album, either – and he chose to drop Donna from Geffen's roster.

ANOTHER PLACE AND TIME

USA: Atlantic 81917 (1989).
UK: Warner Bros 255 976 (1989).

I Don't Wanna Get Hurt/When Love Takes Over You/This Time I Know It's For Real/The Only One/In Another Place And Time/Sentimental/Whatever Your Heart Desires/Breakaway/If It Makes You Feel Good/Love's About To Change My Heart

Produced by Stock, Aitken & Waterman.

Having been released from her contract with Geffen Records, Donna was free to work with whoever she chose on her new album. Her husband Bruce Sudano suggested the hugely successful British song-writing team of Mike Stock, Matt Aitken & Pete Waterman.

'When Donna first started working with us,' said Waterman, 'I think there was culture shock on both sides. At first, there was some friction as we tried to bridge the gap, but Donna soon understood that our squabbles were a way of achieving a final result.

'She has a quick ear for music and can learn a song in no time at all. Donna possessed the ability to take what we had written, go behind the microphone and take it three times further than anything we had achieved. Just to hear that voice coming back at you through the monitors was absolutely fantastic.'

Once it was completed, Donna was free to take her new album to any record company she chose – this resulted in a bidding war, which was won by Ahmet Ertugen, for Atlantic Records.

The striking cover image was Donna's idea. 'I'm an artist and I wanted to represent myself in a new way,' she explained. 'I was just sick of looking at myself, and I wanted to do something extreme, so I decided to paint my face like I would paint a picture. I wanted to paint my face white, completely white. Actually, there were several different shots for that, that didn't get used. Originally, I wrapped my head in red toile with bright red lipstick on – it was incredibly striking. I haven't used those pictures yet, but I am going to use them someday in a photobook I'm planning. I love those shots. I think it was a kind of courageous move, and definitely a step aside for me, but I'm glad I did it.'

'It's a very 80s sounding record,' said Donna, 'but it's the closest thing to my big hits with Giorgio (Moroder). Stock-Aitken-Waterman probably sound closer to Giorgio, in general, than anyone else has since I was with him … they are much better than people give them credit for. Their desire is to create a Motown for the 90s – discovering new talent and developing that. I'm the exception at this point.'

Unusually, Donna only co-wrote two tracks on the album. 'I didn't really have less creative control on this record,' she stated. 'Anywhere they wrote without me was only because I told them to write the song. I'd say, "Look, I want to go to a polo match – you write" and they did. They didn't say, "You can write only this much and we're going to do the rest." It wasn't anything like that … people's reaction to the record is really good. I'm surprised, almost. I like it, but you never know what's going to happen until you get it out there. Being with Atlantic is like running into an oasis. There's plenty of water, food and excitement. It's great, and it's been an emotional thrust.'

The album enjoyed better sales than its predecessor, and achieved no.16 in Sweden, no. 17 in the UK, no.19 in the

Netherlands, no.49 in Germany, no.53 on the Billboard 200 and no.71 on the R&B chart in the States, no.92 in Japan and no.95 in Australia.

BPI Award: Gold (June 1989) = 100,000.

Hit Singles:
This Time I Know It's For Real.
I Don't Wanna Get Hurt.
Love's About To Change My Heart.
When Love Takes Over You.
Breakaway.

A disagreement between Donna and Stock, Aitken & Waterman meant a second album together didn't happen, as had been planned – songs the British song-writing team had penned for Donna were subsequently recorded by Lonnie Gordon.

One of the songs written for Donna, *Happenin' All Over Again*, gave Lonnie Gordon a no.4 hit in the UK in 1990; a re-recording peaked at no.98 on the Hot 100 in the States in 1993.

MISTAKEN IDENTITY

USA: Atlantic 82285 (1991).
UK: Warner Bros 75159 (1991).

Get Ethnic/Body Talk/Work That Magic/ When Love Cries/Heaven's Just A Whisper Away/Cry Of A Waking Heart/ Friends Unknown/Fred Astaire/Say A Little Prayer/Mistaken Identity/What Is It You Want/Let There Be Peace

Produced by Keith Diamond.

The UK edition of the album featured *Work That Magic (ISA Full Length Remix)* in place of the original version of the song.

The album's title and urban feel was reflected in the sleeve design, which saw Donna sporting a blonde wig and a black leather jacket.

The album was recorded at a number of different studios, in both Los Angeles and New York.

'Originally, I wasn't going to work with Keith (Diamond) as a producer,' said Donna. 'We met in Nashville and were just going to write some songs together, but we got going on such a roll that we decided to work it out so he could produce the whole album.'

Generally, the change to a more urban style wasn't well received, and as a result the album became Donna's first to fail to enter the Billboard 200 in the States. The album did register on the R&B chart, but only just – it peaked at no.97.

The album wasn't a hit in the UK or in any other major market, either.

Hit Singles:
When Love Cries.
Work That Magic.

CHRISTMAS SPIRIT

USA: Mercury 314 522 694-2 (1994).
UK: Spectrum 522 6942 (1999).

White Christmas/The Christmas Song/O Come All Ye Faithful/Christmas Is Here/ Christmas Medley (What Child Is This/ Do You Hear What I Hear/Joy To The World/I'll Be Home For Christmas/ Christmas Spirit/Breath Of Heaven/O Holy Night/Lamb Of God

Produced by Michael Omartian.

'I have longed to make a Christmas album,' said Donna. 'Every year I start off planning to do one, but then February and March roll around, and it doesn't happen – my life takes off and I never get a chance to do it.

'We did a lot of the final cuts right around Easter, so that was peculiar … Michael Omartian did a wonderful job producing, and I absolutely adored playing with the Nashville Symphony Orchestra. When they first started playing *White Christmas*, tears just welled in my eyes and I had to leave the room, because it sounded so beautiful, and it had taken so long to finally start this project. It was just a wonderful feeling, and I think that comes across on the record.'

The album was released in the UK in 1999, with a different sleeve design.

The album was reissued in North America in 2005, as part of the 20th Century Masters series, as *THE BEST OF – THE CHRISTMAS COLLECTION* (Mercury B0005126-02).

Following the release of her Christmas album, Donna parted company with her record company.

'There comes a point when you get tired of doing what everyone else wants you to do,' she said. 'They want you to make a record the way they think it should be made. I want to make the kinds of records now the way I want to make them. I'd rather be doing my own thing than be stuck with a company that doesn't support me. Until I find the relationship that I'm looking for, I don't want to be signed to a label. I have to at least try once to do the record I want to do.'

One project Donna was keen to see released was the cast recording for her musical, *Ordinary Girl* – however, it didn't happen, and Donna eventually signed with Sony's Epic Records label, and her first project for her new label was a live album, *LIVE & MORE ENCORE!*

'Donna Summer brings a lot to the table,' said Frank Ceraolo, senior director of marketing and A&R at Epic, 'especially an overwhelming amount of artistry. Without question, she brings a level of excitement back to dance music. She epitomises what a true dance artist is. While she may have done new wave, rock and R&B in the past, the root of what she is, is dance.'

Donna's association with Sony's Epic label was short-lived, and didn't result in a new studio album being released. Donna signed with another Sony imprint, Burgundy Records, in 2006.

'It feels good,' she said. 'They will help us to define who I am now. We must find this out, as I am a lot of things. These days, I am much more socially and politically aware. The world has changed over the past several years. There are levels of the human psyche I'd like to address.'

Donna spoke about the possibility of including some covers on her new album, possibly including a Marvin Gaye song. Donna further revealed, prior to his death in April 1984, she had been planning to record some duets with Gaye. 'I have always loved his work,' she said. 'I was listening to his music the other day. His songs are relevant, touching and gripping. A couple of them would make for very timely covers.'

CRAYONS

USA: Burgundy 8869722992 2 (2008).
UK: Burgundy 8869730725 2 (2008).

Stamp Your Feet/Mr Music/Crayons/The Queen Is Back/Fame (The Game)/Sand On My Feet/Drivin' Down Brazil/I'm A Fire/Slide Over Backwards/Science Of Love/Be Myself Again/Bring Down The Reign/It's Only Love

Producers:

- *Stamp Your Feet*, *Crayons* & *Drivin' Down Brazil* produced by Greg Kurstin.
- *Mr Music* & *The Queen Is Back* produced by J. R. Rotem.
- *Fame (The Game)*, *Sand On My Feet* & *Science Of Love* produced by Toby Gad.
- *I'm A Fire* & *It's Only Love* produced by Sebastian Arocha Morton.
- *Slide Over Backwards* produced by Nathan DiGesare.
- *Be Myself Again* produced by Lester Mendez.
- *Bring Down The Reign* produced by Jamie Houston.

It's Only Love wasn't included on the USA edition of the album.

Japanese Bonus Track: *I'm A Fire (Rod Carrillo Leave It On The Floor Mix)*.

This was Donna's first studio album of new songs since 1991, and was recorded between 2006 and 2008.

'I had no idea it had been that long,' said Donna, in a 2010 interview. 'The funny thing is, I'm always writing. I'm writing songs all the time. I go in and out of the studio constantly. But for some reason I didn't even realise that it had been that long. When someone said seventeen years, I'm like, "What are you – out of your mind?!" They said no, it's been seventeen years since you had a studio album out.

'I'm thinking that's impossible when, in fact, they were right. I mean, I put out some compilations, a Christmas album, that sort of thing, but a real full-out studio album I hadn't done. But by the end of this year, I will have released a standards album and a full-out dance album. I'll get off the road shortly after Labor Day (6th September 2010) and then, hopefully by the middle to the end of September, I'll start selecting the songs and getting the production situation ready.

'It took me over a year and three months to finish. It's like having a baby without giving birth – it would have been easier to get pregnant!'

'*CRAYONS* reflects me in transition,' said Donna, 'and I think when you are in transition, you will sample or look into a lot of different things. I'm not one thing anymore. Things don't need a category. If you like it, play it. Period. The category should be music, not age, not colour, period. If it comes from India, or China, or whatever, why does it need to have a category …

'CRAYONS is named CRAYONS primarily because when you were a little kid and you got your first box of crayons – you open them up and there you go, you start scribbling on everything in sight. You're like a force to reckon with after you get you first crayon, so the concept is, we're free when we're little kids, we're out of the box, we don't have any restrictions. And this album, for me, is an out of the box album. I set no restrictions, except that no two songs could be the same.'

Donna revealed, 'I have over a hundred songs or more. I was actually getting ready to record seven years ago – I had about forty songs, but then 9/11 happened, and nothing seemed right after that. It changed everything, so we didn't use any of those songs on CRAYONS.'

The album was released through the Sony imprint, Burgundy. 'I had been offered several deals over the years,' said Donna, 'but my career started on a small label, Casablanca, and I'm very comfortable with that. You actually know the people who are working on your record and they know you. It's more like a family.'

However, Donna did have to make a stand against stereotyping. 'I think they (the record company) would have preferred it to be one kind of an album,'

she admitted, 'but I don't care. Sometimes, it's really more important to make the statement, because I think maybe fewer people hear that statement, but it's still being heard. I've had musicians come up to me and say, "Man, the concept of that album has made me free. It has helped me to be free." I think that's the point.'

In the States, the album debuted on the R&B chart at no.5 and the Billboard 200 at no.17 – on both charts, this represented the highest ever debut by Donna.

Outside the States, the album achieved no.46 in Italy and no.73 in Germany.

Reissues with Bonus Tracks

BAD GIRLS: DELUXE EDITION

USA: Chronicles/Mercury B00000683 (2003).
UK: Universal 9860357 (2003).

Bonus Track:
Bad Girls (Demo Version)

Bonus CD: 12" Singles & More
I Feel Love (12" Version)/Last Dance/ MacArthur Park Suite (12" Single Mix)/ Hot Stuff (12" Version)/Bad Girls (12" Version)/Walk Away (12" Version)/Dim All The Lights (12" Version)/No More Tears (Enough Is Enough)/On The Radio (Long Version)

All the tracks on the bonus CD, except *MacArthur Park Suite (12" Single Mix) & On The Radio (Long Version)* featured on the 1987 compilation, *THE DANCE COLLECTION*.

THE WANDERER

USA: Not Released.
UK: Driven By The Music
   DBTMCD001 (2014).

Bonus tracks: *Who Do You Think You're Foolin' (Stereo Edit)/Cold Love (Edit)*

This was one of seven of Donna's albums remastered and reissued in 2014,

and six of the released featured bonus tracks (the exception was *I'M A RAINBOW* which, as originally intended, was issued as a double album).

The seven albums were also released together in a box-set titled *THE CD COLLECTION*. A vinyl version of the box-set, titled *THE VINYL COLLECTION*, was also released – however, no bonus tracks were included on this release.

DONNA SUMMER

USA: Not Released.
UK: Driven By The Music
   DBTMCD002 (2014).

Bonus tracks: *Sometimes Like Butterflies/ Love Is In Control (Finger On The Trigger) (7" Version)/(Dance Remix)/ (Instrumental Feat. Ernie Watts On Saxophone Solo)/State Of Independence (7" Version)/(N.R.G. Mix)/(New Radio Millennium Mix)*

CATS WITHOUT CLAWS

USA: Not Released.
UK: Driven By The Music
    DBTMCD003 (2014).

Bonus tracks: *Face The Music/Eyes (7"
Remix Edit)/Supernatural Love
(Extended Dance Remix)/Eyes (Extended
Mix)/I'm Free (Extended Mix)*

ALL SYSTEMS GO

USA: Not Released.
UK: Driven By The Music
    DBTMCD004 (2014).

Bonus tracks: *Tearin' Down The Walls/
All Systems Go (Edit)/(Extended Remix)/
Dinner With Gershwin (Edit)/(Extended
Version)/(Instrumental)/Only The Fool
Survives (Edit)*

ANOTHER PLACE AND TIME

USA: Not Released.
UK: Driven By The Music
    DBTMCD305 (2014).

Bonus CD1: *Breakaway (Power Radio
Mix)/(Extended Power Mix)/(Remix –
Full Version)/(Remix Edit)/(Instrumental
Remix Edit)/I Don't Wanna Get Hurt
(Phil Harding 12" Version)/(Instru-
mental)/(7" Remix)/(Pete Hammond
Original 12" Version)/If It Makes You
Feel Good (Pete Hammond Remix
Instrumental)/Sentimental (Instru-
mental)/This Time I Know It's For Real
(Extended Remix)/(Instrumental)*

Bonus CD2: *When Love Takes Over You
(Dave Ford 7")/(Dave Ford Extended
Remix)/(Dave Ford Instrumental)/(Pete
Hammond Original 12" Mix)/The Only
One (Instrumental)/Whatever Your Heart
Desires (Instrumental)/Love's About To
Change My Heart (Clivilles & Cole 12"
Mix)/(Clivilles & Cole 7" Mix)/
(Extended Remix)/(Instrumental)/(Love*

Dub)/(Dub)/(Loveland's Full-On 7"
Radio Edit)/(PWL 7" Mix)

MISTAKEN IDENTITY

USA: Not Released.
UK: Driven By The Music
   DBTMCD006 (2014).

Bonus tracks: *When Love Cries (Single Version Remix)/(Vocal Club Dub Aka*

Summertime Remix)/Work That Magic (ISA Extended Remix)

Cast & Soundtrack Albums

HAARE (HAIR)

USA: Not Released.
UK: Not Released.

Donna, as Donna Gaines, featured on five tracks:

Wassermann(Aquarius)/Luft (Air)/White Boys/Schweben Im Raum (Walking In Space)/Finale (We Starve Look/Flesh Failures)

Donna's recording debut was released in Germany only, in German, in 1968 (Polydor International 249266).

The album achieved no.4 on the German albums chart, where it spent 64 weeks on the Top 40.

ICH BIN ICH
(THE ME NOBODY KNOWS)

USA: Not Released.
UK: Not Released.

Donna, under the pseudonym Gayn Pierre, featured on six tracks of this German cast album, released in 1970:

Licht Singt (Light Sings)/(Hätt Ich Eine Million Dollars (If I Had A Million Dollars)/Fuge (Fugue)/Schall (Sounds)/ Schwarz (Black)/Schall (Reprise)

An English language version was also released in 1970, with Donna once again credited as Gayn Pierre. Donna featured on eight tracks:

Light Sings/This World/How I Feel/If I Had A Million Dollars/Sounds/Fugue/ Sounds (Reprise)/Black

GODSPELL

USA: Not Released.
UK: Not Released.

Donna, reverting back to as Donna Gaines, featured on two tracks of this German cast album (Reprise 44176), released in 1971:

Oh, Segne Gott Mein Seel (O Bless The Lord)/Du Bist Das Licht Der Welt (Light Of The World)

Although Donna was only credited with backing vocals on two tracks, she actually also sang backing vocals on several other tracks.

Helmuth Sommer, Donna's first husband, was also credited as one of the performers on this album.

The album was reissued on CD Germany in the 1990s (Reprise 158 919) – on this release, Donna was credited as Donna Summer.

THE DEEP

USA: Casablanca NBLP 7060 (1977).
UK: Casablanca CAL 2018 (1977).

Donna: *Theme From The Deep (Down, Deep Inside)/Theme From The Deep (Down, Deep Inside) (A Love Song)*

Other Artists: *Return To The Sea – 2033 A.D.* (John Barry)/*Theme From The Deep (Instrumental)* (John Barry)/*Disco Calypso* (Beckett)

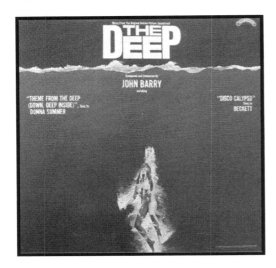

This film soundtrack was released on translucent blue vinyl in some countries, including Germany and the USA.

The soundtrack achieved no.39 in New Zealand, no.63 in Australia and no.70 on the Billboard 200 in the States.

Hit Singles:
Down, Deep Inside
  (Theme From The Deep).

The album was reissued, as part of a 2CD set, in 2010 by Intrada (Special Collection Volume 143).

The second CD featured the original soundtrack album, while the first CD was the complete original motion picture score:

First Discovery (Main Title)/More Discovery/The Coin; The Vial; The Chase/Your Ship Is Dead; Here You'll Need This; Second Dive; Eel Attack/

VooDoo/Tower; Helpless/Three Key Lock; All Yours/Soft Kisses; Dive Preparations/Third Dive/Trouble/Shark Bait (Original Version); Coffin Discovers; Death Grip/Kevin Dead; Goodbye Coffin/After Explosion/Final Dive; Final Eel Attack; End Credits

The Intrada Special Collection release was a limited edition of 3,000 copies.

THANK GOD IT'S FRIDAY

USA: Casablanca NBLP 7099 (1978).
UK: Casablanca TGIF 100 (1978).

LP1 (Donna): *With Your Love/Last Dance*

LP1 (Other Artists): *Thank God It's Friday* (Love & Kisses)/*After Dark* (Pattie Brooks)/*Disco Queen* (Paul Jabara)/*Find My Way* (Cameo)/*Too Hot Ta Trot* (Commodores)/*Leatherman's Theme* (Wright Bros. Flying Machine)/*I Wanna Dance* (Marathon)

LP2 (Donna): *Last Dance (Reprise)*

LP2 (Other Artists): *Take It To The Zoo* (Sunshine)/*Sevilla Nights* (Santa Esmeralda)/*You're The Most Precious Thing In My Life* (Love & Kisses)/*Do You Want The Real Thing* (D.C. LaRue)/*Trapped In A Stairway* (Paul Jabara)/*Floyd's Theme* (Natural Juices)/*Lovin', Livin' And Givin'* (Diana Ross)/*Love Masterpiece* (Thelma Houston)

One-Sided 12" (Donna): *Je T'Aime ... Moi Non Plus*

The album was more successful, both critically and commercially, than the film it accompanied, rising to no.6 on the R&B chart and no.10 on the Billboard 200 in the States.

The album also achieved no.3 in New Zealand, no.4 in Zimbabwe, no.10 in Sweden, no.17 in the Netherlands, no.21 in Australia, no.34 in Germany and no.40 in the UK.

RIAA Award (June 1978): Platinum = 500,000.

BPI Award (August 1978): Silver = £150,000.

Academy Award:
  Song Of The Year – *Last Dance*.

Golden Globe:
  Best Original Song – *Last Dance*.

Grammy Award:
Best R&B Vocal Performance, Female – *Last Dance*.

Hit Singles (Donna):
Last Dance.

Hit Singles (Other Artists):
Too Hot Ta Trot.
Thank God It's Friday.
Lovin', Livin' And Givin'.

CHILD OF THE PROMISE

USA: Sparrow 724385170225 (2000).
UK: Not Released.

Donna: *Elizabeth Recitative/When The Dream Never Dies/Mary And Elizabeth Recitative/I Cannot Be Silent*

Donna was joined by Crystal Lewis on *Mary And Elizabeth Recitative* and *I Cannot Be Silent*.

Other Artists: *The Way It Will Be* (Howard Hewett, Richard Marx & David Pack)/*You Will Call His Name* (Russ Taff)/*After All These Years* (Michael Crawford)/*Zacharias And Gabriel Recitative* (Michael Crawford & Russ Taff)/*Gabriel And Mary Recitative* (Russ Taff & Crystal Lewis)/*Let It Be To Me* (Crystal Lewis)/*The Mary I Know* (Steven Curtis Chapman)/*Townspeople At The Temple* (Christopher Beatty *et al*)/*He Will Prepare The Way* (Michael Crawford)/*Townspeople At Joseph's House* (Christopher Beatty et al)/*Children In The Stable* (Joel Evrist & Elizabeth Stewart)/*Joseph And Mary Recitative* (Steven Curtis Chapman & Crystal Lewis)/*I Wanted All That For You* (Steven Curtis Chapman & Crystal Lewis)/*Nothing Ever Happens To A Shepherd* (Wayne Watson, Bob Carlisle, Michael Smith & Gary Chapman)/*Glory To God* (Russ Taff & Celebration Choir)/*Shepherd's Recitative* (Wayne Watson, Bob Carlisle, Michael Smith & Gary Chapman)/*We Have Come To Worship Him* (Wayne Watson, Bob Carlisle, Michael Smith & Gary Chapman)/*Wise Men And Herod* (Steve Crawford, Jody McBrayer, Michael Passons & Danny Gans)/*I Have To Do What I Have To Do* (Danny Gans)/*Joseph And Simeon Recitative* (Steve Curtis Chapman & Vince Gill)/*What My Eyes Have Seen* (Vince Gill & Amy Grant)/*Wise Men Recitative I* (Steve Crawford, Jody McBrayer & Michael Passons)/*We Have Seen The Light* (Steve Crawford, Jody McBrayer & Michael Passons)/*Wise Men Recitative II* (Steve Crawford, Jody McBrayer & Michael Passons)/*Joseph, Mary And Prophets Recitative* (Steve Curtis Chapman, Crystal Lewis, Howard Hewett, Richard Marx & David Pack)/*Child Of The Promise* (Steven Curtis Chapman, Crystal Lewis & Celebration Choir).

Produced by Michael Omartian.

Sub-titled 'A Musical Story Celebrating The Birth Of Christ'

This musical was the brainchild of producer Norman Miller who, after preparing for the final performance of *The Young Messiah* at the Citadel of David, Jerusalem, was invited to create a new event for Bethlehem 2000.

'Upon returning to the United States,' said Miller, 'I met with Sparrow Records' Peter York, and together we decided to ask multi-Grammy winning producer songwriter, Michael Omartian, and his equally talented wife and million selling author, Stormie Omartian, to write this musical.'

'Stormie and I knew this was a wonderful opportunity to work together,' said Michael Omartian, 'and be able to honour the Lord in more than just a song. We envisioned this as a large historical body of work that could hopefully be performed anywhere, from the smallest churches to the largest arenas.'

Donna was cast in the role of Elizabeth, wife of Zacharias and mother of John the Baptist. The cast also included:

- Howard Hewett as Isaiah The Prophet.
- Richard Marx as Micah The Prophet.
- David Pack as Jeremiah The Prophet.
- Michael Crawford as Zacharias.
- Russ Taff as Gabriel.
- Steven Curtis Chapman as Joseph.
- Crystal Lewis as Mary.
- Amy Grant as Anna.
- Danny Gans as Herod.
- Vince Gill as Simeon.

Following the album's release, the musical toured 20 major cities across the United States, in November and December 2000. However, most of the artists who recorded the cast album, including Donna, were not a part of the tour – the two exceptions were Steven Curtis Chapman and Crystal Lewis.

A year later, the musical had its European premiere in the UK, and in August 2005 the production was released for amateur licensing.

A similarly titled book, written by Stormie Omartian and illustrated by Jack Terry, was published it 2000 – it told the story of the nativity, and paid tribute to the birth of Jesus.

'This is the Christmas story set to music for all people of all ages,' said Stormie Omartian. 'I hope that all who do see and hear it will walk away with a fresh sense that God loved us enough to keep his promise and come to Earth to show us that no matter how dark our world becomes, his light can never be put out.'

Live Albums

LIVE AND MORE

USA: Casablanca NBLP 7119-2 (1978).
UK: Casablanca CALD 5006 (1978).

LP1: *Once Upon A Time/Fairy Tale High/Faster And Faster To Nowhere/ Spring Affair/Rumour Has It/I Love You/ Only One Man/I Remember Yesterday/ Love's Unkind/My Man Medley (The Man I Love/I Got It Bad And That Ain't Good/Some Of These Days)/The Way We Were/Mimi's Song*

LP2: *Try Me, I Know We Can Make It/ Love To Love You Baby/I Feel Love/Last Dance/MacArthur Park Suite (MacArthur Park/One Of A Kind/Heaven Knows/MacArthur Park (Reprise))*

Produced by Giorgio Moroder & Pete Bellotte.

All the tracks – except *MacArthur Park Suite* – were recorded live at Donna's concert at the Universal Amphitheatre, Los Angeles, in June 1978, during her Once Upon A Time Tour.

Although she performed it regularly in concert around this time, Donna's stunning rendition of Leon Russell's *A Song For You* wasn't included on the album.

Donna has admitted one of her reasons for wanting to do a live album was to prove she really could sing. 'It was always rumoured that disco singers can't sing,' she said. 'It was all hype from studios, the engineers and the producers. It was all producers' magic. I just felt that having come from a real history of theatre and music, it was time for me to get up there and sing. I had been touring for a while, and my record company really felt it was important for me to do a live album, to show all the colours that they felt were there.'

As well as singing songs she had recorded, Donna chose to showcase other musical styles as well – jazzy numbers like *I Got It Bad (And That Ain't Good)* and *The Man I Love*, and ballads such as *The Way We Were* and her own *Mimi's Song*, which she dedicated to her young daughter. Before Donna sang the song, Mimi joined her mother on stage, to say 'goodnight'.

This was Donna's second double album in a row, and on 11th November 1978 it rose to no.1 on the Billboard 200 – her first chart topping album.

The album also charted at no.4 on the R&B chart in the States, and achieved no.4 in New Zealand, no.14 in Italy, no.16 in the UK, no.17 in the Netherlands, no.27 in Australia and no.52 in Japan.

RIAA Award: Platinum (October 1978) = 500,000.

BPI Award: Gold (November 1978) = 100,000.

Grammy Award nomination:
Best Pop Vocal Performance, Female –
    MacArthur Park.

A promotional vinyl picture disc titled *THE BEST OF LIVE AND MORE* was released in the States (Casablanca NBPIX 7119), with the following track listing:

MacArthur Park Suite (MacArthur Park/ One Of A Kind/Heaven Knows/ MacArthur Park (Reprise))/Try Me, I Know We Can Make It/Love To Love You Baby/I Feel Love/Last Dance

Hit Singles:
MacArthur Park.
Heaven Knows.

When the album was reissued on CD in 1987, the running time was too long to fit on a single CD, therefore the lengthy *MacArthur Park Suite* was replaced with the shorter (but extended) *Down, Deep Inside (Theme From The Deep)*.

A BLUE LIVE LADY

Italy: Buccaneer BUC 048 (1993).

MacArthur Park/Love Is In Control (Finger On The Trigger)/No More Tears (Enough Is Enough)/Unconditional Love/ Romeo/Don't Cry For Me Argentina/On The Radio/Forgive Me/Woman/Dim All The Lights/Sunset People/Bad Girls/Hot

Stuff/Last Dance/She Works Hard For The Money/State Of Independence

This little known live album was recorded at Donna's concert at the Pacific Amphitheater, Los Angeles, California, on 22nd July 1983 – the same concert was released on home video as *A Hot Summer Night* in 1983.

LIVE & MORE ENCORE!

USA: Epic 66910 (1999).
UK: Epic 494532 2 (1999).

MacArthur Park/This Time I Know It's For Real/I Feel Love/On The Radio/No More Tears (Enough Is Enough)Dim All The Lights/She Works Hard For The Money/Bad Girls/Hot Stuff/My Life/Last Dance/Love Is The Healer/I Will Go With You

Donna's second international live album featured edited highlights of her VH1 televised concert staged at the Hammerstein Ballroom, New York, on 4th February 1999 – reportedly, VH1 officials were astounded by Donna's 'single take' approach to the concert.

Initially, VH1 had approached Donna, with a view to her participating in the second 'Divas Live' concert, which also featured Whitney Houston, Tina Turner, Cher, Brandy and LeAnne Rimes. However, during further negotiations, it was agreed Donna should do her own concert special.

The album included one live performance of a song Donna hadn't released before, *My Life*, and she performed *No More Tear (Enough Is Enough)* as a duet with her new record label mate, Tina Arena.

The album also included two new studio recordings, *Love Is The Healer* and *I Will Go With You (Con Te Partiró)*.

The album achieved no.30 in Italy, no.33 on the R&B chart and no.43 on the Billboard 200 in the States and no.75 in Germany.

Grammy Award nomination:
Best Dance Recording –
    I Will Go With You (Con Te Partiró).

Nashville Music Award:
    Best R&B Album.

Hit Singles:
I Will Go With You (Con Te Partiró).

The concert was also released on DVD, and it featured five songs Donna performed on the night that were omitted from the CD: *Someone To Watch Over Me, If There Is Music There, Riding*

Through The Storm, I Don't Wanna Work & Nobody.

The concert, as released on DVD – though not in the correct running order – was released on CD in the Netherlands in 2008, as *LIVE FROM NEW YORK* (Phantom 1419402):

This Time I Know It's For Real/No More Tears (Enough Is Enough)/I Feel Love/ Dim All The Lights/Someone To Watch Over Me/She Works Hard For The Money/If There Is Music There/ MacArthur Park/Riding Through The Storm/Bad Girls/Hot Stuff/Don't Wanna Work/My Life/Nobody/Last Dance

The concert was released as a double album in Germany in 2013, titled LIVE FROM NEW YORK CITY (Delta N 70 005).

LP1: *On The Radio/This Time I Know It's For Real/No More Tears (Enough Is Enough)/I Feel Love/Dim All The Lights/ Someone To Watch Over Me/She Works Hard For The Money/If There Is Music*

There/MacArthur Park/(Riding) Through The Storm

LP2: *Bad Girls/Hot Stuff/Don't Wanna Work/My Life/Nobody/Last Dance*

Posthumous Remix Album

LOVE TO LOVE YOU DONNA

USA: Verve B0019066-02 (2013).
UK: Verve 0602537506552 (2013).

Love To Love You Baby (Giorgio Moroder Feat. Chris Cox Remix)/Dim All The Lights (Duke Dumont Remix)/Hot Stuff (Frankie Knuckles & Eric Kupper As Director's Cut Signature Mix)/I Feel Love (Afrojack Remix)/Love Is In Control (Finger On The Trigger) (Chromeo & Oliver Remix)/Sunset People (Hot Chip Dub Edit)/Working The Midnight Shift (Holy Ghost! Remix)/Bad Girls (Gigamesh Remix)/Macarthur Park (Laidback Luke Remix)/I Feel Love (Benga Remix)/On The Radio (Jacques Greene Remix)/Last Dance (Masters At Work Remix Short Version)/La Dolce Vita

This was the first international posthumous release credited to Donna, and featured remixed versions of some of her hits, plus one previously unreleased recording, *La Dolce Vita*, which was credited to Donna & Giorgio Moroder.

Controversially, the album's liner notes confirmed *Working The Midnight Shift* featured 'additional vocals by Tiffany Roth' – but the remix appeared not to feature any vocals by Donna.

The album made its debut on the Billboard 200 at no.97, but slipped out of the chart after just one week. Disappointingly, the album failed to enter the chart in the UK and most other countries.

Box-Sets

THE BOX

USA: Geffen 9080/3 (1984).
UK: Not Released.

Vinyl box-set of three albums originally released on the Geffen label, namely:

- *CATS WITHOUT CLAWS*
- *DONNA SUMMER*
- *THE WANDERER*

A RETROSPECTIVE

USA: PolyGram BX45120 (1994).
UK: Not Released.

This box-set came in two formats: 9 x 7" singles and 12 x 12" singles, each with back-to-back hits. The 7" singles were:

- *Last Dance/I Love You*
- *On The Radio/Dim All The Lights*
- *Bad Girls/I Feel Love*
- *MacArthur Park/Love To Love You Baby*
- *Hot Stuff/Heaven Knows*
- *She Works Hard For The Money/Unconditional Love*
- *Could It Be Magic/Try Me, I Know We Can Make It*
- *Walk Away/Rumour Has It*
- *The Wanderer/Stop Me*

The 12" singles were:

- *Bad Girls/I Feel Love*
- *Come With Me/Try Me, I Know We Can Make It*
- *Could It Be Magic/Spring Affair*
- *Hot Stuff/Heaven Knows*
- *Last Dance/I Love You*
- *MacArthur Park/Love To Love You Baby*

- *Melody Of Love (Wanna Be Loved)/The Christmas Song*
- *On The Radio/Dim All The Lights*
- *She Works Hard For The Money/Unconditional Love*
- *The Wanderer/Who Do You Think You're Foolin'*
- *Walk Away/Rumour Has It*

CHRONICLES

USA: Mercury B0004821-02 (2005).
UK: Not Released.

Box-set with three of Donna's early albums on CD, namely:

- *LOVE TO LOVE YOU BABY*
- *A LOVE TRILOGY*
- *FOUR SEASONS OF LOVE*

THE VINYL COLLECTION

USA: Not Released.
UK: Driven By The Music
  DBTMLPBOX01 (2014).

Box-set of seven of Donna's albums, remastered and reissued on vinyl:

- *THE WANDERER*
- *DONNA SUMMER*
- *CATS WITHOUT CLAWS*
- *ALL SYSTEMS GO*
- *ANOTHER PLACE AND TIME*
- *MISTAKEN IDENTITY*
- *I'M A RAINBOW*

I'M A RAINBOW, as was originally intended, was released as a double album.

All the albums featured the original track listings, with no bonus tracks.

The box-set included an LP booklet with extensive liner notes, a poster and a sheet music facsimile.

THE CD COLLECTION

USA: Not Released.
UK: Driven By The Music
  DBTMCDBOX01 (2014).

Box-set of seven of Donna's albums, remastered and reissued on 10 CDs, including two CDs of remixes from *ANOTHER PLACE AND TIME*:

- *THE WANDERER*
- *DONNA SUMMER*
- *CATS WITHOUT CLAWS*
- *ALL SYSTEMS GO*
- *ANOTHER PLACE AND TIME*
- *MISTAKEN IDENTITY*
- *I'M A RAINBOW*

As with the accompanying vinyl release, *I'M A RAINBOW* was released on two CDs. Unlike the vinyl release, however, with the exception of *I'M A RAINBOW* each album featured bonus tracks.

THE WANDERER
Bonus tracks: *Who Do You Think You're Foolin' (Stereo Edit)/Cold Love (Edit)*

DONNA SUMMER
Bonus tracks: *Sometimes Like Butterflies/ Love Is In Control (Finger On The Trigger) (7" Version)/(Dance Remix)/ (Instrumental Feat. Ernie Watts On Saxophone Solo)/State Of Independence*

(7" Version)/(N.R.G. Mix)/(New Radio Millennium Mix)

CATS WITHOUT CLAWS
Bonus tracks: *Face The Music/Eyes (7" Remix Edit)/Supernatural Love (Extended Dance Remix)/Eyes (Extended Mix)/I'm Free (Extended Mix)*

ALL SYSTEMS GO
Bonus tracks: *Tearin' Down The Walls/ All Systems Go (Edit)/(Extended Remix)/ Dinner With Gershwin (Edit)/(Extended Version)/(Instrumental)/Only The Fool Survives (Edit)*

ANOTHER PLACE AND TIME
Bonus CD1: *Breakaway (Power Radio Mix)/(Extended Power Mix)/(Remix – Full Version)/(Remix Edit)/(Instrumental Remix Edit)/I Don't Wanna Get Hurt (Phil Harding 12" Version)/(Instrumental)/(7" Remix)/(Pete Hammond Original 12" Version)/If It Makes You Feel Good (Pete Hammond Remix Instrumental)/Sentimental (Instrumental)/This Time I Know It's For Real (Extended Remix)/(Instrumental)*

ANOTHER PLACE AND TIME
Bonus CD2: *When Love Takes Over You (Dave Ford 7")/(Dave Ford Extended Remix)/(Dave Ford Instrumental)/(Pete Hammond Original 12" Mix)/The Only One (Instrumental)/Whatever Your Heart Desires (Instrumental)/Love's About To Change My Heart (Clivilles & Cole 12" Mix)/(Clivilles & Cole 7" Mix)/ (Extended Remix)/(Instrumental)/(Love Dub)/(Dub)/(Loveland's Full-On 7" Radio Edit)/(PWL 7" Mix)*

MISTAKEN IDENTITY
Bonus tracks: *When Love Cries (Single Version Remix)/(Vocal Club Dub Aka Summertime Remix)/Work That Magic (ISA Extended Remix)*

Sometimes Like Butterflies, *Face The Music* and *Tearin' Down The Walls* all featured on an album by Donna for the first time.

The ten CDs were packaged in hardback case bound books, and the box-set included six exclusive postcards.

The seven remastered albums in the box-set were also made available individually.

Compilations

BEST OF DISCO

France: Atlantic 50 336 (1976).

This compilation was credited to Donna Summer, Roberta Kelly & Giorgio (Moroder).

Trouble Maker (Roberta Kelly)/*Try Me, I Know We Can Make It/I Wanna Funk With You Tonight* (Giorgio)/*Knights* (sic) *In White Satin* (Giorgio)/*Could It Be Magic/Oh L'Amour* (Giorgio)/*Love To Love You Baby*

STAR COLLECTION

Germany: Midi MID 20 109 (1977).

Love To Love You Baby/Try Me, I Known We Can Make It/Winter Melody/Spring Affair/Could It Be Magic/Wasted

THE GREATEST HITS OF

USA: Not Released.
UK: GTO GTLP 028 (1977).

I Feel Love/Could It Be Magic/Winter Melody/Wasted/Try Me, I Know We Can Make It/I Remember Yesterday/Spring Affair/Love's Unkind/Love To Love You Baby

Donna's first major UK compilation achieved no.4 in the album chart.

BPI Award: Gold (December 1977) = £250,000.

GREATEST HITS

Germany: Atlantic ATL 50433 (1977).
Netherlands: Groovy GRL 25029 (1977).

I Feel Love/Could It Be Magic/Love To Love You Baby/Try Me, I Know We Can Make It/Lady Of The Night/I Remember Yesterday/The Hostage/Spring Affair/Virgin Mary/Winter Melody

Donna's first compilation issued in Germany and the Netherlands, with different sleeve designs, charted at no.30 in the latter, but didn't chart in Germany.

DISCO QUEEN

Germany: Global 30 566 4 (1977).

Love To Love You Baby/Love's Unkind/ Lady Of The Night/Rumour Has It/The Hostage/I Feel Love/Once Upon A Time/ A Man Like You/Could It Be Magic/I Remember Yesterday

LO MEJOR DE (THE BEST OF)

Argentina: Casablanca 981 2382 (1978).

I Feel Love/Once Upon A Time/Love To Love You Baby/Spring Affair/Could It Be Magic/I Remember Yesterday/Down, Deep Inside (Theme From The Deep)/ Come With Me

LO MEJOR DE (THE BEST OF) VOLUME 2

Argentina: Casablanca 80016 (1978).

Rumour Has It/Need-A-Man Blues/Fairy Tale High/Try Me, I Know We Can Make It/Take Me/Winter Melody/Faster And Faster To Nowhere/I Love You

THE BEST OF

Germany: Sonocord 27 074-4 (1978).

I Feel Love/Try Me, I Know We Can Make It/Back In Love Again/Wasted/ Love To Love You Baby/Come With Me/ Need-A-Man Blues/Take Me

ON THE RADIO: GREATEST HITS VOLUMES I & II

USA: Casablanca NBLP 7191 (1979).
UK: Casablanca NB 7070 (1979).

LP1: *One The Radio/Love To Love You Baby/Try Me, I Know We Can Make It/I Feel Love/Our Love/I Remember Yesterday/I Love You/Heaven Knows/ Last Dance*

LP2: *MacArthur Park/Hot Stuff/Bad Girls/Dim All The Lights/Sunset People/ No More Tears (Enough Is Enough)/On The Radio (Long Version)*

Donna's first international compilation album was a double – her fourth in a row. Two brand new tracks were featured: *On The Radio* and a duet with Barbra Streisand, *No More Tears (Enough Is Enough)*.

Significantly, the compilation was the last album Donna released on Casablanca Records, before she quit the label and signed with Geffen Records.

When it rose to no.1 on the Billboard on 5th January 1980, the compilation gave Donna a hat-trick of chart toppers – remarkably, all three were double albums, and included one studio album, one live album and one compilation.

Donna thus became the first female artist to score three consecutive no.1's on the Billboard 200, and to this day she remains the only solo artist to take three double albums in a row to the top of the chart – Donna apart, only the Beatles have achieved this feat.

The compilation achieved no.2 in New Zealand, no.4 on the R&B chart in the States, no.12 in Zimbabwe, no.15 in Italy, no.16 in Australia, no.20 in Japan, no.21 in the Netherlands, no.24 in the UK, no.29 in Sweden, no.39 in Norway and no.42 in Germany.

RIAA Award: 2 x Platinum (December 1993) = 1 million.

BPI Award: Gold (November 1979) = 100,000.

Grammy Award nomination:
Best Pop Vocal Performance, Female – *On The Radio*.

For a short time, the compilation was also released as two individual LPs in some countries, including Canada, France and the Netherlands, titled *GREATEST HITS VOLUME ONE* and *GREATEST HITS VOLUME TWO*.

The first vinyl disc was released as a CD album in its own right in Germany in 1995, titled *I FEEL LOVE* (Karussell 512 114-2).

Following Donna's passing in May 2012, *ON THE RADIO – GREATEST HITS VOLUMES I & II* re-entered the Billboard 200 in the States at no.73, but it climbed no higher.

WALK AWAY

USA: Casablanca NBLP 7244 (1980).
UK: Not Released.

Bad Girls/Hot Stuff/On The Radio/I Feel Love/Walk Away/Last Dance/Sunset People/MacArthur Park/Our Love

Sub-titled: *COLLECTOR'S EDITION – THE BEST OF 1977-1980.*

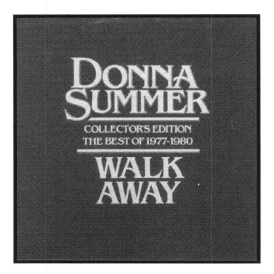

The album charted at no.50 on the Billboard 200 and no.54 on the R&B chart in the States, and no.78 in Japan.

THE SUMMER COLLECTION

USA: Mercury 826144-1 (promo, 1985).
UK: Mercury MERH 84 (1985).

She Works Hard For The Money/Bad Girls/On The Radio/Stop, Look And Listen/Last Dance/MacArthur Park/Heaven Knows/Unconditional Love/I Love You/No More Tears (Enough Is Enough)

This compilation was reissued in Japan in 1991 with a different sleeve.

THE DANCE COLLECTION

USA: PolyGram 830 534-1/2 (1987).
UK: Not Released.

LP1: *I Feel Love (Promo 12" Mix)/With Your Love (Promo 12" Mix)/Last Dance (12" Mix)/MacArthur Park Suite*

LP2: *Hot Stuff (12" Mix)/Bad Girls/Walk Away (12" Mix)/Dim All The Lights (12" Mix)/ No More Tears (Enough Is Enough) (Album Version)*

Sub-titled 'A Compilation of Twelve inch Singles' – as this suggests, it brought together the extended remixes that originally featured on Donna's 12" singles.

A single CD version was also released, which omitted *Bad Girls*, the one track that wasn't an extended 12" mix.

12"ERS

Japan: WEA WMC5-28 (1990).

This Time I Know It's For Real (12" Version)/I Don't Wanna Get Hurt (12" Version)/Love's About To Change My Heart (12" Version)/When Loves Takes Over You (12" Version)

THE BEST OF

USA: Not Released.
UK: Warner Bros WX 397 (1990).

*I Feel Love/MacArthur Park/Hot Stuff/
The Wanderer/Love's Unkind/On The
Radio/State Of Independence/
Breakaway/Love Is In Control (Finger
On The Trigger)/Dinner With Gershwin/I
Don't Wanna Get Hurt/This Time I Know
It's For Real/Love's About To Change
My Heart*

The album achieved no.24 in the UK.

BPI Award: Gold (December 1990) =
100,000.

THE COMPLETE HITS

Japan: Mercury PHCR-3177-80 (1991).

CD1: *Love To Love You Baby/Need-A-
Man Blues/Try Me, I Know We Can
Make It/Prelude To Love/Could It Be
Magic/Down, Deep Inside (Theme From
The Deep)*

CD2: *Once Upon A Time/Faster And
Faster To Nowhere/Fairy Tale High/Say
Something Nice/Rumour Has It/I Love
You/Happily Ever After/Last Dance/
MacArthur Park Suite/The Way We Were*

CD3: *Spring Affair/Summer Fever/
Autumn Changes/Winter Melody/I
Remember Yesterday/Love's Unkind/
Back In Love Again/I Remember
Yesterday (Reprise)/Can't We Just Sit
Down (And Talk It Over)/I Feel Love*

CD4: *Hot Stuff/Bad Girls/Dim All The
Lights/Walk Away/Sunset People/No
More Tears (Enough Is Enough)/On The*

Radio/She Works Hard For The Money/
Unconditional Love/Love Has A Mind Of
Its Own

This 4CD box-set, released only in
Japan, came with a 72 page booklet.

DANCE COLLECTION

France: Phonogram (1991).

*On The Radio/Try Me, I Know We Can
Make It/I Feel Love/Our Love/I
Remember Yesterday/I Love You/Heaven
Knows/Last Dance/MacArthur Park/Hot
Stuff/Bad Girls/Dim All The Lights/
Sunset People*

BEST

Japan: TF T-2010 (1991).

*Once Upon A Time/Faster And Faster To
Nowhere/Fairy Tale High/Say Something
Nice/MacArthur Park/Love To Love You
Baby/Now I Need You/I Feel Love/Queen
For A Day/A Man Like You/Sweet
Romance/Rumour Has It/I Love You/*

*Happily Ever After/I Remember
Yesterday/Last Dance*

THE ANTHOLOGY

USA: Casablanca 518 144-2 (1993).
UK: Casablanca 518 144-2 (1993).

*CD1: Love To Love You Baby/Could It
Be Magic/Try Me, I Know We Can Make
It/Spring Affair/Love's Unkind/I Feel
Love/Once Upon A Time/Rumour Has It/
I Love You/Last Dance/MacArthur Park/
Heaven Knows/Hot Stuff/Bad Girls/Dim
All The Lights/Sunset People*

*CD2: No More Tears (Enough Is
Enough)/On The Radio/The Wanderer/
Cold Love/I'm A Rainbow/Don't Cry For
Me Argentina/Love Is In Control (Finger
On The Trigger)/State Of Independence/
She Works Hard For The Money/
Unconditional Love/There Goes My
Baby/Supernatural Love/All Systems Go/
This Time I Know It's For Real/I Don't
Wanna Get Hurt/When Love Cries/
Friends Unknown/Carry On*

'It was a good feeling,' replied Donna, when asked how she felt about going through her old material, for this compilation. 'It made me feel like wherever my life is at this moment, or whatever I've gone through in recent years, that I did something that was worthwhile. It made me feel like I shouldn't always be so down on myself. I can be proud of my career, which frees me up to do things besides music.'

This compilation was most notable for the inclusion of two tracks from Donna's *I'M A RAINBOW* album, which, at the time, was unreleased: the title track and *Don't Cry For Me Argentina*.

This was also the first of Donna's albums to include *Carry On*, her collaboration with Giorgio Moroder, plus the promotional single version of *MacArthur Park*.

ENDLESS SUMMER

USA: Mercury 314 526 178-2 (1994).
UK: Mercury 526 217-2 (1994).

USA Edition:
Melody Of Love (Wanna Be Loved)/Love To Love You Baby/Could It Be Magic/I Feel Love/Last Dance/MacArthur Park/ Heaven Knows/Hot Stuff/Bad Girls/Dim All The Lights/No More Tears (Enough Is Enough)/On The Radio/The Wanderer/ Love Is In Control (Finger On The Trigger)/State Of Independence/She Works Hard For The Money/This Time I Know It's For Real/Any Way At All

UK Edition:
Melody Of Love (Wanna Be Loved)/Love To Love You Baby/Could It Be Magic/I Feel Love/Love's Unkind/I Love You/Last Dance/MacArthur Park/Hot Stuff/Bad Girls/No More Tears (Enough Is Enough)/On The Radio/Love Is In Control (Finger On The Trigger)/State Of Independence/She Works For The Money/ Unconditional Love/This Time I Know It's For Real/I Don't Wanna Get Hurt/Any Way At All

Sub-titled 'Donna Summer's Greatest Hits'.

This compilation featured two previously unreleased songs, *Melody Of Love (Wanna Be Loved)* and *Any Way At All*.

The album charted at no.10 in New Zealand and no.37 in the UK.

The album was released in France, as *GREATEST HITS*, in 1995 – the two new songs were omitted, and replaced with the 1995 remix of *I Feel Love*.

Following Donna's passing in May 2012, *ENDLESS SUMMER* charted at no.90 in the States and no.154 in the UK.

THIS TIME I KNOW IT'S FOR REAL

USA: Not Released.
UK: WEA 9548-31823-2 (1993).

This Time I Know It's For Real/Cats Without Claws/Say A Little Prayer/ Maybe It's Over/Love Is Just A Breath Away/The Woman In Me/All Systems Go/ Running For Cover/Who Do You Think You're Foolin'/There Goes My Baby/

Supernatural Love/Suzanna/When Love Takes Over You/Cold Love

This was a budget compilation of '14 classic tracks' – however, the CD sleeve on some pressings incorrectly stated '16 classic tracks'.

GREATEST HITS

France: Mercury 528 943-2 (1995).

I Feel Love (1995 Remix)/Love To Love You Baby/Could It Be Magic/Love's Unkind/I Love You/Last Dance/ MacArthur Park/Hot Stuff/Bad Girls/No More Tears (Enough Is Enough)/On The Radio/Love Is In Control (Finger On The Trigger)/State Of Independence/ Unconditional Love/This Time I Know It's For Real/I Don't Wanna Get Hurt/I Feel Love (Original Version)

MASTER SERIE (MASTER SERIES)

France: Podis 534 285-2 (1997).

I Feel Love/(She Works Hard For The Money/Love To Love You Baby/Walk Away/Don't Cry For Me Argentina/On The Radio/Winter Melody/Need-A-Man Blues/Bad Girls/No More Tears (Enough Is Enough)/I Do Believe (I Fell In Love)/ Rumour Has It/Full Of Emptiness/With Your Love/My Baby Understands/People, People/Can't We Just Sit Down (And Talk It Over)/Could It Be Magic

She Works Hard For The Money/ Unconditional Love/There Goes My Baby/Supernatural Love/All Systems Go/This Time I Know It's For Real/I Don't Wanna Get Hurt/When Love Cries/ Friends Unknown/Carry On

GREATEST HITS

USA: Mercury 314 558 795-2 (1998).
UK: Not Released.

THE VERY BEST OF

France: PolyGram 518 144-2 (1997).

CD1: *Love To Love You Baby/Could It Be Magic/Try Me, I Know We Can Make It/Spring Affair/Love's Unkind/I Feel Love/Once Upon A Time/Rumour Has It/I Love You/Last Dance/MacArthur Park/ Heaven Knows/Hot Stuff/Bad Girls/Dim All The Lights/Sunset People*

CD2: *No More Tears (Enough Is Enough)/On The Radio/The Wanderer/ Cold Love/I'm A Rainbow/Don't Cry For Me Argentina/Love Is In Control (Finger On The Trigger)/State Of Independence/*

Love To Love You Baby/Could It Be Magic/I Feel Love/Last Dance/Hot Stuff/ Bad Girls/On The Radio/The Wanderer/ Love Is In Control (Finger On The Trigger)/State Of Independence/She Works Hard For The Money/This Time I Know It's For Real

GREATEST HITS didn't chart when it was released but, following Donna's passing in May 2012, it spent a solitary week at no.194 on the Billboard 200.

THE COLLECTION

Germany: Spectrum 554 386-2 (1998).

She Works Hard For The Money/When Love Takes Over You/I Don't Wanna Get Hurt/The Woman In Me/Mystery Of Love/ My Baby Understands/Hot Stuff/This Time I Know It's For Real/Livin' In America/If It Makes You Feel Good/All Through The Night/Full Of Emptiness/ Our Love

MASTER SERIES

USA: Not Released.
UK: PolyGram 534 285-2 (1998).

I Feel Love/She Works Hard For The Money/Love To Love You Baby/Walk Away/Don't Cry For Me Argentina/On The Radio/Winter Melody/Need-A-Man Blues/Bad Girls/No More Tears (Enough Is Enough)/I Believe (I Fell In Love)/ Rumour Has It/Full Of Emptiness/With Your Love/My Baby Understands/People, People/Can't We Just Sit Down (And Talk It Over)/Could It Be Magic

GOLDEN SONGS –
MTV HISTORY 2000

Germany: Sony (1999).

Could It be Magic/I Feel Love/Love To Love You Baby/Melody Of Love (I Wanna Be Loved)/When Love Cries/ Friends Unknown/No More Tears (Enough Is Enough)/This Time I Know It's For Real/Spring Affair/Hot Stuff/I'm A Rainbow/Don't Cry For Me

Argentina/Heaven Knows/Carry On/Bad Girls/I Don't Wanna Get Hurt/Any Way At All/Once Upon A Time/MacArthur Park/Last Dance

GOLDEN COLLECTION 2000

Netherlands: Lighthouse MLN 07/102 (2000).

Love To Love You Baby/Could It Be Magic/Spring Affair/I Feel Love/I Love You/Hot Stuff/Bad Girls/No More Tears

(Enough Is Enough)/On The Radio/I'm A Rainbow/Don't Cry For Me Argentina/ Love Is In Control (Finger Of The Trigger)/State Of Independence/She Works Hard For The Money/This Time I Know It's For Real

GOLDEN STARS

Germany: Casablanca 65 906 0 (2000).

Hot Stuff/On The Radio/Love To Love You Baby/She Works Hard For The Money/Unconditional Love/On My Honor/Dim All The Lights/I Feel Love/ Bad Girls/I Remember Yesterday/There Will Always Be A You/MacArthur Park/ Rumour Has It/I Love You/Love Has A Mind Of Its Own/No More Tears (Enough Is Enough)

MILLENNIUM EDITION

Germany: Mercury 542302 (2000).

Love To Love You Baby/She Works Hard For The Money/I Feel Love/Walk Away/ On The Radio/Don't Cry For Me

Argentina/Winter Melody/Need-A-Man Blues/Bad Girls/I Do Believe (I Fell In Love)/No More Tears (Enough Is Enough)/Rumour Has It/Full Of Emptiness/With Your Love/My Baby Understands/People, People/Can't We Just Sit Down (And Talk It Over)/Could It Be Magic

ORO – GRANDES EXITOS
(GOLD – GREATEST HITS)

Argentina: Universal 542228-2 (2002).

Love To Love You Baby/She Works Hard For The Money/I Feel Love/Walk Away/On The Radio/Don't Cry For Me Argentina/Winter Melody/Need-A-Man Blues/Bad Girls/I Do Believe (I Fell In Love)/No More Tears (Enough Is Enough)/Rumour Has It/Full Of Emptiness/With Your Love/My Baby Understands/People, People/Can't We Just Sit Down (And Talk It Over)/Could It Be Magic

LES LEGENDES DU DISCO
(THE LEGENDS OF DISCO)

France: Universal 068 862-2 (2003).

Donna:
Love To Love You Baby/Hot Stuff/Bad Girls/Last Dance/I Feel Love/Could It Be Magic/I Love You/Love Is In Control (Finger On The Trigger)/Love's Unkind/Unconditional Love/MacArthur Park/State Of Independence/On The Radio/She Works Hard For The Money

This two CD compilation featured one CD by Donna and one CD by Diana Ross.

THE BEST OF – THE MILLENNIUM COLLECTION

USA: Mercury 440 063 609 2 (2003).
UK: Not Released.

Love To Love You Baby/I Feel Love/Last Dance/MacArthur Park/Hot Stuff/Bad Girls/Dim All The Lights/No More Tears (Enough Is Enough)/On The Radio/Love Is In Control (Finger On The Trigger)/ She Works Hard For The Money

THE JOURNEY – THE VERY BEST OF

USA: UTV Records B0001009-02 (2003).
UK: Mercury 0602498628584 (2003).

USA Edition:
Love To Love You Baby/Could It Be Magic/I Feel Love/I Love You/Last Dance/MacArthur Park/Heaven Knows/ Hot Stuff/Bad Girls/Dim All The Lights/ No More Tears (Enough Is Enough)/On The Radio/The Wanderer/Love Is In Control (Finger On The Trigger)/State Of Independence/She Works Hard For The Money/This Time I Know It's For Real/I Will Go With You (Con Te Partiró)/ That's The Way/Dream-A-Lot's Theme (I Will Live For Love)

USA Bonus CD:
I Feel Love (12" Version)/Hot Stuff (12" Version)/This Time I Know It's For Real (12" Extended Remix)/You're So Beautiful (Ultimate Club Mix)

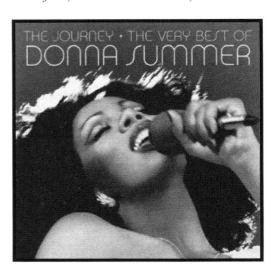

UK Edition:
Love To Love You Baby/Could It Be Magic/I Feel Love/Down, Deep Inside (Theme From 'The Deep')/Love's Unkind/I Love You/Last Dance/ MacArthur Park/Heaven Knows/Rumour Has It/Hot Stuff/Bad Girls/No More Tears (Enough Is Enough)/On The Radio/ Love Is In Control (Finger On The Trigger)/State Of Independence/She Works Hard For The Money/Dinner With Gershwin/This Time I Know It's For Real

UK Bonus CD:
Love To Love You Baby (Original 12"/ Album Version)/I Feel Love (Patrick Cowley Mix)/Hot Stuff (Original 12")/

No More Tears (Enough Is Enough) (Original 12"/Album Version)/On The Radio (Original 12"/Foxes Soundtrack Version)/Melody Of Love (Wanna Be Loved) (Morales Classic Club Mix)/ That's The Way/Dream-A-Lot's Theme (I Will Live For Love)

A one CD edition, minus the bonus CD, was also released in the UK.

The compilation featured three new songs: *Dream-A-Lot's Theme (I Will Live For Love)*, *That's The Way* and *You're So Beautiful*.

The release of the compilation was timed to coincide with the publication of Donna's autobiography, *Ordinary Girl: The Journey*.

'I am in such a good place right now,' said Donna. 'My life story, which I've been wanting to tell for a long, long time, is finally out there – and it's accompanied by a soundtrack of my musical journey …

'The disc works as a great backdrop to the book. Some of the new songs were finished within the last month or so – *Beautiful* was done a while ago. In fact, I probably have about forty or fifty new songs that I've worked on. I was with Sony for a couple of years, but I felt I was floundering over there, but I kept writing anyway. Right now, I'm talking to a few companies, including UMG, and I'm hoping we can work something out. I don't want to close the door with possible record deals.'

The album achieved no.6 in the UK, no.27 in Norway, and no.65 on the R&B

chart and no.111 on the Billboard 200 in the States.

BPI Award: Gold (June 2004) = 100,000.

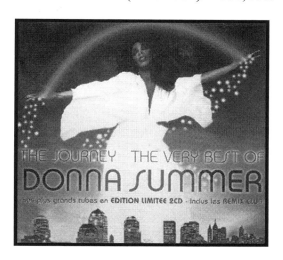

Following Donna's passing in May 2012, *THE JOURNEY – THE VERY BEST OF* charted at no.88 (a new peak) in the States and no.67 in the UK.

THE ULTIMATE COLLECTION

Netherlands: Universal CCM 980 927-7 (2003).

CD1: *The Hostage/Lady Of The Night/ Love To Love You Baby/Full Of Emptiness/Could It Be Magic/Try Me, I Know We Can Make It/Spring Affair/ Winter Melody/I Feel Love/Down, Deep Inside (Theme From The Deep)/I Remember Yesterday/Love's Unkind/ Back In Love Again/I Love You/Rumour Has It*

CD2: *Last Dance/MacArthur Park/Hot Stuff/Bad Girls/Dim All The Lights/ Sunset People/On The Radio/The Wanderer/State Of Independence/Love Is*

In Control (Finger On The Trigger)/The Woman In Me/She Works Hard For The Money/Dinner With Gershwin/This Time I Know It's For Real/Melody Of Love (Wanna Be Loved)

CD3: *Love To Love You Baby (Live)/Last Dance (Live)/Je T'Aime ... Moi Non Plus/ Heaven Knows/No More Tears (Enough Is Enough)/Unconditional Love/State Of Independence (New Radio Millennium Mix)/I Feel Love (Masters At Work 86th St. Mix)/I Will Go With You (Con Te Partiró)*

This re-mastered Dutch 3CD box-set included the full length versions of *Love To Love You Baby*, *No More Tears (Enough Is Enough)* and *Je T'Aime ... Moi Non Plus*, the 12" versions of *Down, Deep Inside (Theme From The Deep)*, *Last Dance* and *Hot Stuff*, plus a promo 12" mix of *MacArthur Park*.

The live versions of *Love To Love You Baby* and *Last Dance* on CD3 were taken from Donna's 1978 album, *LIVE AND MORE*.

Disappointingly, given how comprehensive the track selection was as a whole, a very short, 3:11 minute edit of *I Feel Love* was included on CD1.

The first two discs were reissued in the Netherlands in 2006 (Universal 9842977), as *THE VERY BEST OF*.

GOLD

USA: Hip-O Records 000271902 (2005).
UK: Almighty CDALMY 120 (2005).

CD1: *Love To Love You Baby/Could It Be Magic/Try Me, I Know We Can Make It/Spring Affair/Love's Unkind/I Feel Love/I Love You/Last Dance/MacArthur Park/Heaven Knows/Hot Stuff/Bad Girls/ Dim All The Lights/Sunset People/No More Tears (Enough Is Enough)/On The Radio*

CD2: *The Wanderer/Love Is In Control (Finger On The Trigger)/State Of Independence/She Works Hard For The Money/Unconditional Love/There Goes My Baby/Supernatural Love/Dinner With*

*Gershwin/All Systems Go/This Time I
Know It's For Real/I Don't Wanna Get
Hurt/Love's About To Change My Heart/
When Love Cries/Carry On/Melody Of
Love (Wanna Be Loved)/I Will Go With
You (Con Te Partiró)/Dream-A-Lot's
Theme (I Will Live For Love)/You're So
Beautiful*

THE BEST OF – THE MILLENNIUM COLLECTION VOLUME 2

USA: Hip-O Records 000820402
(2007).
UK: Not Released.

*Could It Be Magic/Spring Affair/I Love
You/Heaven Knows/The Wanderer/State
Of Independence/There Goes My Baby/
This Time I Know It's For Real/Melody
Of Love (Wanna Be Loved)/I Will Go
With You (Con Te Partiró)/I Got Your
Love*

CLASSIC

USA: Not Released.
UK: Spectrum UMC 5424 (2008).

*Love To Love You Baby/She Works Hard
For The Money/I Feel Love/Walk Away/
On The Radio/Don't Cry For Me
Argentina/Winter Melody/Need-A-Man
Blues/Bad Girls/I Do Believe (I Fell In
Love)/No More Tears (Enough Is
Enough)/Rumour Has It/Full Of
Emptiness/With Your Love/My Baby*

Understands/People, People/Can't We Just Sit Down (And Talk It Over)/Could It Be Magic

The same compilation was released in other countries, with a different sleeve design and titled *CLASSIC – THE UNIVERSAL MASTERS COLLECTION*.

THE COLLECTION

USA: Not Released.
UK: Spectrum WITUN029 (2008).

Could It Be Magic/Love To Love You Baby/Full Of Emptiness/Back In Love Again/Last Dance/Heaven Knows/Dim All The Lights/One Night In A Lifetime/ On The Radio/Sunset People/Spring Affair/Try Me, I Know We Can Make It/ Unconditional Love/She Works Hard For The Money/Stop, Look And Listen

This budget compilation sold exclusively in Woolworths stores, as part of their 'WorthIt!' series of albums.

BEST SELECTION

Japan: Universal UICY 8185 (2009).

Hot Stuff/Bad Girls/No More Tears (Enough Is Enough)/Love To Love You Baby/Last Dance/On The Radio/ MacArthur Park/The Wanderer/She Works Hard For The Money/I Feel Love/ Heaven Knows/Dim All The Lights/ Could It Be Magic/Love Is In Control (Finger On The Trigger)/Unconditional Love/There Goes My Baby/State Of Independence/This Time I Know It's For Real/Any Way At All

GREATEST HITS OF THE DISCO QUEEN

USA: Burgundy 4607147910740 (2012).
UK: Not Released.

CD1: *Hot Stuff/I Feel Love/Bad Girls/ Love To Love You Baby/Spring Affair/ Last Dance/Could It Be Magic/Try Me, I Know We Can Make It/Love's Unkind/I Love You/MacArthur Park/I Remember Yesterday/Heaven Knows/Dim All The Lights/No More Tears (Enough Is Enough)/On The Radio/The Wanderer*

CD2: *Sunset People/Love Is In Control (Finger On The Trigger)/She Works Hard For The Money/There Goes My Baby/Supernatural Love/Dinner With Gershwin/This Time I Know It's For Real/I Don't Wanna Get Hurt/Love's About To Change My Heart/Carry On/Melody Of Love (Wanna Be Loved)/I Will Go With You (Con Te Partiro)/Love Is The Healer/The Power Of One/Stamp Your Feet/Fame (The Game)/I'm A Fire/To Paris With Love*

PLAYLIST – THE VERY BEST OF

USA: Epic/Legacy 88883710842 (2013).
UK: Not Released.

MacArthur Park/This Time I Know It's For Real/I Feel Love/On The Radio/No More Tears (Enough Is Enough)/If There Is Music There/Riding Through The Storm/Don't Wanna Work/Nobody/Dim All The Lights/She Works Hard For The Money/Bad Girls/Hot Stuff/Last Dance

ICON

USA: Mercury B0015598-02 (2013).
UK: Not Released.

Hot Stuff/Bad Girls/She Works Hard For The Money/On The Radio/Love To Love You Baby/I Feel Love/MacArthur Park/ Heaven Knows/Dim All The Lights/Could It Be Magic/Last Dance

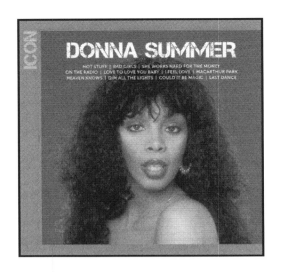

I FEEL LOVE – THE COLLECTION

USA: Not Released.
UK: Spectrum SPECXX2105 (2013).

CD1 (The Classics): *I Feel Love/Love To Love You Baby/Bad Girls/Hot Stuff/Love Is In Control (Finger On The Trigger)/ MacArthur Park/Love's Unkind/Down, Deep Inside (Theme From 'The Deep')/ On The Radio/I Remember Yesterday/ Could It Be Magic/Back In Love Again/ Rumour Has It/I Love You/Last Dance/ Heaven Knows/Dim All The Lights/She*

Works Hard For The Money/ Unconditional Love

CD2 (12" & Extended Mixes): *I Feel Love (Patrick Cowley Mega Mix)/Je T'Aime (Moi Non Plus) (12" Version)/ Down, Deep Inside (Theme From 'The Deep') (12" Version)/MacArthur Park Suite: MacArthur Park/One Of A Kind/Heaven Knows (12" Version)/No More Tears (Enough Is Enough) (12" Version)/Sunset People/Our Love*

PART 3:
THE HOME VIDEOS

Donna's first official home video showcased her live in concert, and was released in 1983.

A HOT SUMMER NIGHT

USA: RCA/Columbia (1983).
UK: Channel 5 CFV 00242 (1983).

MacArthur Park/Love Is On Control (Finger On The Trigger)/Unconditional Love/Romeo/Don't Cry For Me

Argentina/On The Radio/Forgive Me/ Woman/Medley (Dim All The Lights/ Sunset People/Bad Girls/Hot Stuff)/Last Dance/She Works Hard For The Money/ State Of Independence/Reprise

Woman featured lines from *One Night Only* and the Supremes classic, *Stop! In The Name Of Love.*

Donna was joined by Musical Youth, to sing *Unconditional Love*, and her daughter Mimi sang the opening lines, then joined her mother, on *State Of Independence*. Donna was backed by her sisters, Dara Bernard and Mary Ellen Bernard.

This concert was recorded live at the Pacific Amphitheatre, Los Angeles, on 22nd July 1983, during the 2nd leg of Donna's Hard For The Money Tour in 1983.

One song Donna performed at the concert, *No More Tears (Enough Is Enough)*, was omitted from the home video.

The concert was also released on Laser Disc (Pioneer Artists PA-84-083) in the States.

ENDLESS SUMMER

USA: PolyGram 800 632 353-2 (1994).
UK: PolyGram 632 352-3 (1994).

Donna Summer Medley (Dim All The Light/Hot Stuff/Bad Girls/Last Dance)/ She Works Hard For The Money/ Unconditional Love/State Of Independence/The Wanderer/Dinner With Gershwin/Supernatural Love/There Goes My Baby/Love's About To Change My Heart/This Time I Know It's For Real/ MacArthur Park/On The Radio/Last Dance/Melody Of Love

This home video, like the compilation album with the same title, carried the sub-title 'donna summer's greatest hits'.

The compilation brought together many – but not all – of Donna's music videos, plus live in concert footage of *MacArthur Park*, *On The Radio* and *Last Dance*, taken from her concert was recorded live at the Pacific Amphitheatre, Los Angeles, on 22nd July 1983 – this was originally released on home video as *A Hot Summer Night*.

The home video achieved no.37 on Billboard's Music Videos chart.

LIVE & MORE ENCORE!

USA: Sony 50202 (1999).
UK: Sony 201982 9 (1999).

MacArthur Park/This Time I Know It's For Real/I Feel Love/On The Radio/ Someone To Watch Over/If There Is Music There/No More Tears (Enough Is Enough)/Riding Through The Storm/

Don't Wanna Work/Nobody/Dim All The Lights/She Works Hard For The Money/ Bad Girls/Hot Stuff/My Life/Last Dance

In addition to the above concert footage, filmed at Donna's concert at the Hammerstein Ballroom, New York, on 4th January 1999, the DVD also included:

- Lyrics
- Biography
- Discography
- Chart Positions
- *I Will Go With You (Con Te Partiró)* – video
- *I Will Go With You (Con Te Partiró)* – remix video

The home video spent five weeks on Billboard's Music Video chart, peaking at no.15.

LIVE & MORE ENCORE! re-entered Billboard's Music Videos chart in June 2012, following Donna's passing, and peaked at no.8 – a seven place improvement on its original chart peak.

The DVD has been reissued under a number of different, usually with a 10 song track list, with most of the newer songs omitted:

I Feel Love/On The Radio/No More Tears (Enough Is Enough)/Dim All The Lights/ She Works Hard For The Money/ MacArthur Park/Bad Girls/Hot Stuff/My Life/Last Dance

The reissues include:

- *LIVE* (2004)
- *LIVE AT MANHATTAN CENTRE, 1999* (2004)
- *DONNA SUMMER* (2006)

- *IN CONCERT* (2007)
- *LIVE FROM NEW YORK* (2008)

THE BEST OF – THE DVD COLLECTION

USA: Universal B000197109 (2004).
UK: Not Released.

*She Works Hard For The Money/
Unconditional Love/There Goes My
Baby/This Time I Know It's For Real/
Love's About To Change My Heart*

This budget release brought together five
of Donna's music videos from the 1980s
– it spent a solitary week on Billboard's
Music Videos chart at no.22.

PART 4:
THE MUSICALS, FILMS & TV SHOWS

Donna was only 19 years old when she auditioned for a role in the Broadway production of the rock musical, *Hair*.

She was successful – but, initially, she was offered the role of Sheila, as the understudy to Melba Moore. However, keen to be onstage rather than watching from the wings each night, Donna was more interested in being part of the European production of *Hair*. She was offered the lesser role of Dionne, a student protester, and given the choice between England, France and Germany, she chose the latter.

Musicals

HAIR

Written by James Rado & Gerome Ragni, with music by Galt MacDermot, *Hair* is a rock musical that made its debut at Joseph Papp's Public Theater in October 1967, followed by its Broadway debut in April 1968.

The musical focused on the 'tribe' – young, politically active hippies living in New York City, who are fighting against conscription at the time of the Vietnam War.

With a racially-integrated cast, the musical was hugely controversial, thanks to its anti-American sentiment, portrayal of illegal drug taking and sexuality, and a nude scene.

Donna flew to Munich, Germany, on 28th August 1968. Initially, she signed a six month contract, for the German production – titled *Haare* – which opened on 24th October 1968, and played six nights per week.

Among the cast, with Donna, was a young singer called Liz Mitchell – who went on to become the lead singer of Boney M.

'Her (Donna's) talent was obviously enormous,' said Dagmar, *Haare*'s assistant director. 'She had a lot of confidence in her singing. Donna was creative and fun and easy to work with. She got along with everyone. What I remember most is she often played the clown.'

Asked about the infamous nude scene in the musical, Donna stated, 'It was not meant to be sexual in any way. We stood naked to comment on the fact that society makes more of nudity than killing. We worry more about someone walking around half-dressed than somebody who's walking around shooting people.'

However, Donna's age meant her participation in the controversial scene was short-lived. 'I did it once or twice,' she said, 'but then I guess the official people discovered they were doing a nude scene there, and they made us stay within the restrictions. There were a few of us that were under twenty-one, and we weren't allowed to do it. But we could look – and we did!'

A cast album, in German, was recorded. Donna, who was still known as Donna Gaines at the time, featured on five tracks:

- *Wassermann (Aquarius)*
- *Luft (Air)*
- *White Boys*
- *Schweben Im Raum (Walking In Space)*
- *Finale (We Starve Look/Flesh Failures)*

The cast album was released in Germany in 1968.

At the end of her first six months, Donna re-signed for another year.

'*Hair* was the break that brought me to Europe,' she said, 'which I did for a year and a half, then I went to the Vienna Folk Opera and did two musicals there.'

The two musicals Donna did with the Vienna Folk Opera were *Porgy And Bess* and *Show Boat*.

PORGY AND BESS

Based on the novel *Porgy*, written by DuBose Heyward, and the similarly titled play he wrote with his wife, Dorothy, *Porgy And Bess* is an opera first performed in 1935 – it was composed by George Gershwin (music) and Ira Gershwin & DuBose Heyward (lyrics).

Set in the 1920s in the fictitious Catfish Row in Charlestown, South Carolina, the opera focuses on a disabled African-American beggar, Porgy, as he tries to rescue Bess from Crown and Sportin' Life, her violent lover and a drug dealer, respectively.

The two best known songs in the opera are *Summertime* and *It Ain't Necessarily So*.

SHOW BOAT

Like *Porgy And Bess*, *Show Boat* was based on a novel: *Show Boat* by Edna Ferber, published in 1926.

Ferber's novel was turned into a musical by Jerome Kern (music) and Oscar Hammerstein II (lyrics).

The musical is set on a Mississippi show boat, the *Cotton Blossom*, between 1880 and 1927, and explores such themes as tragic love and racial prejudice. After a pre-Broadway tour that started on 15th November 1927, the musical opened on Broadway on 27th December, and was hugely popular.

The most well-known song in the musical, *Ol' Man River*, was written especially for Paul Robeson (who played the character Joe).

After *Show Boat*, Donna was offered – and accepted – a lead role in the Hamburg production of *The Me Nobody Knows*.

THE ME NOBODY KNOWS

Written by Gary William Friedman (music) & Will Holt (lyrics), this was a musical about under-privileged children living in New York City.

The musical premiered at New York's Orpheum Theater on 18th May 1970, and moved to Broadway's Helen Hayes Theater on 18th December 1970.

A cast album of the German production – titled *Ich Bin Ich* – was released in 1970. Donna, under the pseudonym 'Gayn Pierre', featured on six tracks:

- *Licht Singt (Light Sings)*
- *(Hätt Ich Eine Million Dollars (If I Had A Million Dollars)*
- *Fuge (Fugue)*
- *Schall (Sounds)*
- *Schwarz (Black)*
- *Schall (Reprise)*

An English language version of the album was also released in 1970, with Donna featured on eight tracks:

- *Light Sings*
- *This World*
- *How I Feel*
- *If I Had A Million Dollars*

- *Sounds*
- *Fugue*
- *Sounds (Reprise)*
- *Black*

The cast of *Ich Bin Ich* also included Donna's husband-to-be, Austrian Helmuth Sommer – the couple also joined the cast of *Godspell* together, for a tour through German speaking countries.

GODSPELL

Written by Stephan Schwartz & John-Michael Tebelak in 1970, this musical opened off-Broadway on 17th May 1971, and it didn't move to Broadway until June 1976.

A German cast album, on which both Donna Gaines and Helmuth Sommer were credited, was released in Germany in 1971. Donna was credited on two tracks:

- *Oh, Segne Gott Mein Seel (O Bless The Lord)*
- *Du Bist Das Licht Der Welt (Light Of The World)*

Although not credited, Donna also featured on backing vocals on several other tracks.

THE BLACK EXPERIENCE

After *Godspell*, Donna and Helmuth Sommer took up an offer to go to Italy, to do a little known show called *The Black Experience*.

As Donna recalled in her autobiography, *Ordinary Girl: The Journey*, it wasn't the happiest of experiences.

'I didn't like anything about it,' she wrote. 'The production was poorly done, and the accommodations for the actors were terrible.'

As soon as the show closed, Donna and Helmuth returned to Vienna – where he asked her to marry him.

ORDINARY GIRL

This is an unpublished, autobiographical musical Donna worked on for well over a decade, prior to her passing.

In July 1998, it was announced the musical would begin its pre-Broadway

North American tour in Chicago, in the last week of April 1999. This was to be followed by dates in Cleveland, Miami, Baltimore, Toronto and Boston, before the musical arrived on Broadway in the fall of 1999.

The musical was scheduled to be co-produced by Steve Leber Productions & Back Row Productions – a TV special and a concept album, to promote the show, were planned for September 1999.

'It keeps getting bigger that we thought,' said Donna. 'Between that and getting the basic script down, it's like, aaarrrggggh! Who said I wanted to do this?!'

In April 2000, the fate of *Ordinary Girl* was reported to be 'in limbo'.

'The musical, *Ordinary Girl*, is still in the works and, hopefully, we will work out all the rough spots and get it up and running,' stated Donna, in a message to her fans in December 2002. 'Still working on the book portion, but Michael Omartian, Al Kasha, Bruce Sudano and myself have written excellent songs, of which 20-23 songs have been finished, so far. When it does hit the stage, I hope you all come and see it, and hopefully meet all your expectations (and mine).'

Speaking in February 2008, Donna said, 'Unfortunately, every time I get revved up to do it, something else sideswipes me and it goes on hold. A couple of years ago, we were gearing up to get involved with it, and we had some personal traumas in our families we just couldn't get out of. A friend said, "Donna, you have to give something like a musical ten to fifteen years to get going", and I said, 'Are you kidding me?" So, we'll see what happens.'

As well as hits like *Hot Stuff* and *Last Dance*, songs written especially for the musical – some of which Donna performed live in concert – are known to include:

- *Arms And Legs*
- *Be Rich*
- *Begin Again*
- *Bitter End*
- *Chairman Of The Board*
- *Gotta Have A Dress*
- *I Found A Star*
- *If There Is Music There*
- *My Dream Is For You*
- *My Life*
- *No Ordinary Love Song*
- *Rain, Rain*
- *This Forbidden Fruit*

TV Series & TV Films

Donna made her TV debut, as an actress, when she briefly appeared in a German TV mini-series.

11 UHR 20

This mini-series – a spy drama – aired on German TV in January 1970, spread over three episodes:

- Episode 1: *Mord Am Bosporus* (Murder At Bosphorus) – aired 8th January 1970.

- Episode 2: *Flucht In Die Sahara* (Escape In The Sahara) – aired 9th January 1970.

- Episode 3: *Tod In Der Kasbah* (Death In The Kasbah) – aired 11th January 1970.

The mini-series was written by Herbert Reinecker, and was directed by Wolfgang Becker. The cast of the mini-series included:

- Joachim Fuchsberger as Thomas
- Wassem
- Gila von Weitershausen as Maria
- Wassem
- Nadja Tiller as Maja
- Esther Ofarim as Miriam
- Friedrich Joloff as Dr Arnold Vogt
- Christiane Kruger as Andrea
- Werner Bruhns as Minotti

- Peter Carsten as Korska.

Donna made a 50 second, uncredited cameo appearance in Episode 3, as a scantily clad Kasbah singer – she was seen singing *Black Power*.

Another song Donna recorded as Donna Gaines, *If You Walkin' Alone*, featured in the mini-series as background music.

The mini-series has been released on DVD in Germany.

VAN OEKEL'S DISCOHOEK (VAN OEKEL'S DISCO CORNER)

This Dutch TV series, a music programme loosely modelled on *Toppon* (the Dutch equivalent to the UK's *Top Of The Pops*), ran from May 1974 to April 1975.

The series featured a 'disco corner', and Donna appeared in three of the twelve episodes:

- Episode 4 – aired 1st August 1974.
- Episode 5 – aired 22nd August 1974.
- Episode 12 – aired 29th April 1975.

On her first two appearances, Donna sang *The Hostage*, which became a no.2 hit in the Netherlands. On her third and last appearance, she visited Sjef van Oekel, to pass on her thanks for making her a success in the Netherlands – this time, she sang *Love To Love You*.

Donna's performances of *The Hostage* were so popular, the episodes featuring them were repeated several times on Dutch TV.

The series was directed by Ellen Jens, Wim van der Linden & Wim T. Schippers, and the regular cast included:

- Dolf Brouwers as Sjef van Oekel
- Jaap Bar as Ir. Evert van der Pik
- I.J.F. Blokker as Barend Servet
- Gerard Schiering as Ds. Bongers
- Cees Schouwenaar as Nep da Vinci

As well as Donna, other artists to appear on the show included Paul da Vinci, Alvin Stardust and Shakin' Stevens.

VAN OEKEL BLIKT TERUG (VAN OEKEL LOOKS BACK)

This Dutch TV movie was created by the same people who directed the TV series,

Van Oekel's Discohoek – the regular cast was the same, and archive footage from the TV series was incorporated into the film.

Donna's popular performance of *The Hostage* was featured, as was her follow-up, *Lady Of The Night*.

The film premiered on Dutch TV on 31st December 1974 – Donna's 26th birthday.

Both the TV series and TV movie have been released in the Netherlands, as a four DVD box-set.

FAMILY MATTERS

This popular American sitcom, which focused on a middle class African-American family living in Chicago, ran from September 1989 to July 1998 – a total of 215 episodes, spread over nine seasons.

The sitcom was created by William Bickley & Michael Warren, and the regular cast included:

- Reginald VelJohnson as Carl Otis Winslow
- JoMarie Payton as Harriette Winslow
- Rosetta LeNoire as Estelle Winslow
- Jaleel White as Steven 'Steve' Quincy Urkel.
- Darius McCrary as Edward 'Eddie' Winslow
- Kellie Shanygne Williams as Laura Lee Winslow
- Bryton James as Richie Crawford

Donna played the character Aunt Oona – from Altoona – in two episodes, three years apart:

- Season 5, Episode 23: *Aunt Oona* – directed by Gary Menteer, the episode aired on 6th May 1994.

- Season 8, Episode 22: *Pound Foolish* – directed by Jason Bateman, the episode aired 25th April 1997.

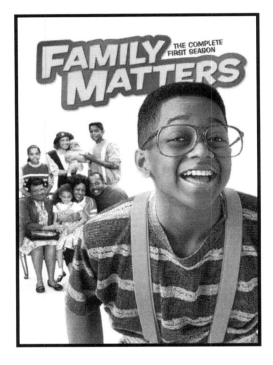

In Season 5, the shy Aunt Oona visits her nephew, Steve, and to help her break out of her shell it is suggested she goes to a karaoke bar – where she sings *Last Dance*.

Three years on, in Season 8, Aunt Oona visits again – only this time, she's embarrassed by how much weight she has gained. She's so desperate to lose weight, to impress the Reverend Fuller (played by Rif Hutton), she agrees to try out her nephew's weight loss machine – from which she emerges amazingly slim. But, as she fronts the church choir to sing *Amazing Grace*, Aunt Oona suddenly starts to balloon again – and, subsequently, she discovers the Reverend prefers big woman, when he asks her out on a date.

As well as *Amazing Grace*, Donna sang two other songs during the show: *Rejoice!* with the church choir, and as a finale, her own *She Works Hard For The Money*.

To date, only the first season of *Family Matters* has been released on DVD.

THE DONNA SUMMER SPECIAL

This 60 minute TV special – also called a TV movie – was Donna's first, and was filmed in 1979.

As well as Donna, the show featured:

- Robert Guillaume as an Angel
- Twiggy as a Bad Girl
- Pat Ast as a Bad Girl
- Debralee Scott as a Bad Girl
- Mimi Sommer as herself

The special was written by Ernest Chambers & Rod Warren, and directed by Don Mischer, with Donna as executive producer.

During the special, the following songs featured:

- *Bridge Over Troubled Water*

- *Try Me, I Know We Can Make It*
- *Hot Stuff*
- *Sunset People*
- *Bad Girls*
- *Dim All The Lights*
- *Once Upon A Time*

Robert Guillaume sang Simon & Garfunkel's *Bridge Over Troubled Water* to Donna – she joined him towards the end of the song.

The special aired in the States on 27th January 1980, but it has never been released on home video.

Posting on the Internet Movie Database in 2003, Terry Climer stated:

'I fully believe that if the Powers-that-be would allow, the Donna Summer Special could be released from original 2-inch edited-master videotape in true stereo remix with about a month's work.

'I edited the special during the last three months of 1979 and know for a fact that although it was mixed in mono (widespread use of stereo TV was five years in the future at the time), all of the original audio tracks were simultaneously recorded and saved on either 16 or 24 tracks from the Hollywood Bowl or 8 track one-inch tape at ABC/Prospect Avenue …

Donna Summer

Beautiful both to look at and listen to, Donna Summer lifts her voice in song in her brand new music special.

'The legal hoops would be the biggest hassle in getting the material together to reconstruct the show for DVD, but I feel strongly that it would stand up beautifully against today's standards, both in video and audio quality.'

TELEVISED CONCERTS

Several of Donna's concerts have been recorded and televised over the years, usually as 60 minute specials, including:

- *Donna Summer Live At Bossoladamani, Viareggio* – televised in Italy in 1977.

- *Live In Japan: Queen Of Disco Tour* – televised in Japan in 1979.

- *A Hot Summer Night* – televised by HBO in the States on 22nd October 1983, and subsequently released as a home video.

- *Donna Summer At Nuovo Teatro* – televised in Italy in 1987.

- *Donna Summer: Live From Brazil* – televised in Brazil in 1992.

- *Live & More Encore!* – televised by VH1 in the States on 20th June 1999.

Films & Short Films

Even before she travelled to Munich, to join the German production of *Hair*, one of Donna's ambitions was to become a film actress – someone like Judy Garland.

Although she sang on stage in musicals, and appeared in several TV shows, Donna didn't make her big screen debut until 1978.

THANK GOD IT'S FRIDAY

Donna's film debut was written by Armyan Bernstein, and produced by Casablanca and Motown, for Columbia Pictures.

The film, which had a budget of $2.2 million, was originally titled 'After Dark'. It was set in *The Zoo*, a fictional Los Angeles nightclub. Robert Klane directed, and the film was produced by

Neil Bogart (of Casablanca Records), Rob Cohen & Phillip Goldfarb.

A real nightclub – *Osko's* in Los Angeles – was used for the film, as *The Zoo*.

Donna played the part of Nicole Sims, an aspiring singer who goes to *The Zoo*, in the hope of getting the chance to showcase her talent at a live radio broadcast – which, finally, she does when she performs *Last Dance*.

The Commodores also appeared in the film, and sang their hit *Too Hot Ta Trot*, a R&B chart topper in the States in early 1978.

As well as Donna, the film starred:

- Valerie Landsburg as Frannie

- Terri Nunn as Jeannie
- Jeff Goldblum as Tony
- Paul Jabara as Carl
- Chick Vennera as Marv
- Ray Vitte as Bobby
- Mark Lonow as Dave
- Andrea Howard as Sue
- Robin Menken as Maddy
- Debra Winger as Jennifer
- John Friedrich as Ken
- Mews Small as Jackie
- DeWayne Jessie as Malcolm

The film premiered in the States on 19th May 1978, in New York City.

The accompanying soundtrack, a double album with a bonus 12" single, was considerably more successful than the film.

'In spite of all the accolades for *Last Dance*, filming *Thank God It's Friday* was a disappointing experience for me,' admitted Donna. 'In truth, there was virtually no acting required for me. After that experience, I knew the only types of roles I was going to be offered would be the *Fun In Acapulco* variety. I decided to give up any further attempts at a movie career. Hollywood saw me as a singer, and I was never going to shake that image by doing films like *Thank God It's Friday*.'

SHORT FILMS / MUSIC VIDEOS

Lady Of The Night (1975).
Love To Love You Baby (1975).
Try Me, I Know We Can Make It (1976).
Could It Be Magic (1976).
Spring Affair (1976).
Autumn Changes (1976).
Winter Melody (1976).
The Wanderer (1980).
Love Is On Control (Finger On The Trigger) (1982).
State Of Independence (1982).
The Woman In Me (1982).
Romeo (1983).
She Works Hard For The Money (1983).
Unconditional Love (1983).
Supernatural Love (1984).
There Goes My Baby (1984).
Dinner With Gershwin (1987 / unreleased version).
Dinner With Gershwin (1987).
All Systems Go (1987).
The Planet Is Alive (1987).
Spirit Of The Forest (1989).
This Time I Know It's For Real (1989).
Love's About To Change My Heart (1989).
I Don't Wanna Get Hurt (1989).

When Love Takes Over You (1990).
Work That Magic (1991).
Melody Of Love (Wanna Be Loved) (1994).
Endless Summer Medley (1994)
I Feel Love (Remix) (1995).
Whenever There Is Love (1996).
My Prayer For You (1999).
I Will Go With You (Con Te Partiró) (1999).
I Will Go With You (Con Te Partiró) (Big Red Remix) (1999).
Stamp Your Feet (2008).
Mr Music (2008).
The Queen Is Back (2008).
Fame (The Game) (2009).

The music video for *Romeo* comprised clips from the film, *Flashdance*, and didn't feature Donna at all.

PART 5:
THE CONCERTS

By 1976, thanks to the success of *Love To Love You Baby*, Donna was opening for some of the most popular acts at the time, including the (Detroit) Spinners and the Temptations.

Donna, unlike some artists, has always endeavoured to perform songs she has recorded, pretty much as she recorded them.

'I don't change the way they're done,' she stated. 'I make them longer or shorter, but I find that people like to sing along, and it's not fair when you switch up on them. When you see people in Vegas or Jersey, some old star of theirs and they used to sing it this way, and now they're snappin' their fingers and going "Yeah! Yeah!" I hate that – I can't handle it.'

Donna once described choosing which songs to include in a show as 'seriously hard'.

'After doing songs for years, you know what works,' she said. 'Sometimes, you have to remove something you know works for something you're not sure works in the context you want to use it … When you come onstage, they want to hear your hits. Simple, it's just a simple fact. And if you have a brand new song out that's a big hit, you're not going to sing that right off bat.

'You'll sing your old songs first, because they'll like those, but you save what they're waiting for, for last. Then put a little new stuff in, and some things they wouldn't necessarily hear you sing someplace else – broaden their scope, and their idea of how you sing. It's a whole psychology to doing it, but I think it works quite well.'

One of Donna's first concerts, as the headline act, took place at New York's Radio City Music Hall, on 3rd July 1976.

Where known, dates and venues given – but regrettably for many tours, especially for tours outside the States, this information isn't known.

1977-78:
ONCE UPON A TIME TOUR

The principal aim of this tour was to promote Donna's album of the same name.

Set List:
(San Carlos, California, on 22 July 1978)
*Could It Be Magic/Try Me, I Know I Can
Make It/Only One Man/I Remember
Yesterday/Love's Unkind/My Man
Medley (The Man I Love/I Got It Bad
(And That Ain't Good)/Some Of These
Days)/The Way We Were/If You Got It
Flaunt It/A Man Like You/Once Upon A
Time/Fairy Tale High/Faster And Faster
To Nowhere/Spring Affair/Winter
Melody/I Love You/Happily Ever After/
Love To Love You Baby/I Feel Love/Last
Dance/Rumour Has It/A Song For You*

Venues included:

- Philadelphia, Pennsylvania
- Baltimore, Maryland
- Columbia, Maryland
- Jones Beach, New York
- New York City, New York
- Boston, Massachusetts
- Cherry Hill, New Jersey
- Miami, Florida
- Atlanta, Georgia
- Las Vegas, Nevada
- Lake Tahoe, Nevada
- Los Angeles, California
- San Carlos, California
- Chicago, Illinois
- Niles, Illinois
- Highland Heights, Ohio
- East Troy, Wisconsin

Donna's series of shows at the Universal Amphitheatre, Los Angeles, in June 1978 were recorded, and were released as the album, *LIVE AND MORE*.

Donna played San Carlos on 22nd July 1978, and Philadelphia on 13th, 14th & 15th November 1978.

Outside the States, Donna played her first UK dates – initially, in July, it was announced she would play three concerts in September 'probably all in London.'

'I am definitely planning to spend six weeks touring Europe in the autumn,' said Donna. 'I can't afford to bring my Stateside set.' Donna said she would bring her own five piece band, and use British musicians in the orchestra.

Donna's European tour focused on Italy, and a concert staged in Rome was televised on Italian TV. Donna also played two UK dates, in Manchester and at the London Rainbow on 23rd October –

where she added *Down, Deep Inside (Theme From The Deep)* to her set list.

1978:
Mexico, South America & Europe.

Donna's concert at the Universal Amphitheater, Los Angeles, was recorded and released as the live album, *LIVE AND MORE*.

She played Pittsburgh, Pennsylvania on 30th March 1978, Buffalo, New York, on 25th October.

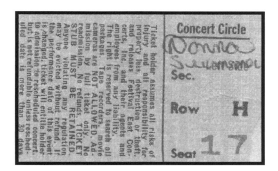

1979: BAD GIRLS TOUR

Set List:
Once Upon A Time/Fairy Tale High/ Faster And Faster To Nowhere/I Remember Yesterday/The Way We Were/ 1960s Medley/I Love You/Dim All The Lights/My Man Medley (The Man I Love/ I Got It Bad (And That Ain't Good)/Some Of These Days)/Love To Love You Baby/I Feel Love/Heaven Knows/Hot Stuff/Bad Girls/Last Dance/MacArthur Park

The *1960s Medley* featured the same songs Donna performed with Brooklyn Dreams, when they appeared on *The Midnight Special* on 26th May 1978, namely: *So Fine, Maybe, My Girl, My Guy, The Way You Do The Things You Do, Good Lovin', I Heard It Through The Grapevine* and *Heat Wave*.

Venues included:

- Columbia, Maryland
- Los Angeles, California
- Hollywood, California
- Flushing, New York
- Philadelphia, Pennsylvania
- Miami, Florida
- Cuyahoga Falls, Ohio
- Chicago, Illinois
- Japan

1981: THE WANDERER TOUR

Having cancelled her 1980 tour, as she was expecting her second child and fighting a lawsuit against her former record label, Casablanca, Donna rescheduled many of the dates for 1981.

On the tour, now she was born again, Donna faced a dilemma, over which songs she would perform and which songs she might leave out.

'If I have to perform *those* songs,' she said, 'it's part of the weight I have to carry because of the wrong I've done. I have to acknowledge that I built this bed and I've got to lay in it. There will come a time when I won't have to ever do those things again, but it's like the old remnants that you still have to clear out of your house. You can't clean your house in one day, so I'm going about it methodically.'

Initially, the concert tour was aimed at promoting Donna's new album, *I'M A RAINBOW* – which her new record Geffen company rejected. Instead, the tour was re-vamped, to promote Donna's 1980 album, *THE WANDERER*.

Donna did include one song she had recorded for her shelved album in the set list, namely *Don't Cry For Me Argentina*.

Set List:
Dim All The Lights/Love To Love You Baby/I Feel Love/Don't Cry For Me Argentina/On The Radio/The Way We Were/Oldies Medley/Cold Love/The Wanderer/No More Tears (Enough Is Enough)/Bad Girls/Sunset People/Hot Stuff/Last Dance/I Believe In Jesus/ MacArthur Park

Venues included:

- Merrillville, Indiana
- Concord, California
- Pine Knob, Kentucky
- Columbia, Maryland
- Atlantic City, New Jersey
- New York City, New York
- Cleveland, Ohio
- Hoffman Estates, Illinois
- Chicago, Illinois
- Detroit, Michigan
- San Francisco, California
- Los Angeles, California
- Las Vegas, Nevada

Donna played several dates at Atlantic City's Resorts International between 3rd to 9th August.

The Money/A Song For You-How Great
Thou Art

This was the last tour for many years on which Donna included her first international hit, *Love To Love You Baby*, in the set list. 'Never again,' she told one reporter. 'I just hate it!

June ~ September 1983:
HARD FOR THE MONEY TOUR

Donna performed two songs she had recorded for her shelved album, *I'M A RAINBOW*, on the tour: *Don't Cry For Me Argentina* and *Romeo*.

Set List (1st Leg):
MacArthur Park/Medley (Dim All The Lights/Sunset People/Bad Girls/Hot Stuff)/No More Tears (Enough Is Enough)/Don't Cry For Me Argentina/ On The Radio/Unconditional Love/ Forgive Me/The Woman In Me/Love Is In Control (Finger On The Trigger)/ Woman/Last Dance/She Works Hard For

Dates and venues included:

17 June	Del Mar, California
21 June	Toronto, Canada
22 July	Los Angeles, California
18 August	Hollywood, Florida
20 August	Biloxi, Mississippi
21 August	Memphis, Tennessee
22 August	Boston, Massachusetts
28 August	Atlantic City, New Jersey

3 September Mashantucket, Connecticut

Set List (2nd Leg):
MacArthur Park/Love Is In Control (Finger On The Trigger)/No More Tears (Enough Is Enough)/Unconditional Love/ Romeo/Don't Cry For Me Argentina/On The Radio/Forgive Me/Woman/Medley (Dim All The Lights/Sunset People/Bad

Girls/Hot Stuff)/Last Dance/She Works Hard For The Money/State Of Independence

Donna's concert at the Universal Amphitheatre, Los Angeles, on 22nd July was released on a home video titled *A Hot Summer Night* – however, Donna's performance of *No More Tears (Enough Is Enough)* was omitted from the home video.

Donna was joined by Musical Youth, to sing *Unconditional Love*, and her daughter Mimi sang the opening lines, then joined her mother, on *State Of Independence*.

Three performances from the same concert, *MacArthur Park*, *On The Radio* and *Last Dance*, were also included on Donna's 1994 home video, *Endless Summer*.

1984: THE RAINBOW TOUR

Having given birth to two daughters, Brooklyn and Amanda Grace, in 1981 and 1982, Donna understandably cut back on touring in the early-to-mid 1980s. Concerts she did play tended to be at casino showrooms, where the industry standard at the time was for a one hour show, which suited Donna.

Set List:
I'm A Rainbow/Medley (I Feel Love/Dim All The Lights/Bad Girls/Hot Stuff/ Heaven Knows)/MacArthur Park/Medley (There's No Business Like Show Business/Love Is Here To Stay/The Man I Love)/Romeo/Supernatural Love/Medley (Amazing Grace/Operator/How Great Thou Art)/Love Has A Mind Of Its Own/ There Goes My Baby/On The Radio/No More Tears (Enough Is Enough)/She Works Hard For The Money/Over The Rainbow
Venues included:

- Universal City, California
- Atlantic City, New Jersey

Donna played several concerts at Atlantic City's Resorts International between 8th and 15th September.

1986: SILVER GIRL TOUR

Once again, for her 1986 dates, Donna chose to focus on one hour concerts in casino showrooms.

Set List:
On The Radio/No More Tears (Enough Is Enough)/Romeo/I Got It Bad (And That Ain't Good)/Supernatural Love/(Medley

(Amazing Grace/How Great Thou Art/ Operator)/Medley (I Feel Love/Dim All The Lights/Bad Girls/Hot Stuff/Heaven Knows)/MacArthur Park/Silver Girl/ America The Beautiful/Last Dance

The set list included two songs Donna hadn't recorded or performed on previous tours, the patriotic *America The Beautiful* and Survivor's *Silver Girl*, after which the tour was named.

Venues included:

- Universal City, California
- Lake Tahoe, Nevada
- Atlantic City, New Jersey

Donna played concerts at Atlantic City's Resorts International between 20th and 22nd June, Harrah's Lake Tahoe through 18th September, and at Caesars Atlantic City between 29th and 31st October.

1987-88: ALL SYSTEMS GO TOUR

As her daughters grew older, so Donna embarked on her first overseas tour.

Set List:
MacArthur Park/Dim All The Lights/ Love Shock/Bad Girls/Hot Stuff/All Systems Go/God Bless The Child/ Jeremy/Amazing Grace/Celebrate Me Home/On The Radio/She Works Hard For The Money/Last Dance/The Impossible Dream
The set list included three songs Donna hadn't recorded or performed on previous tours: *God Bless The Child, Celebrate Me Home* and *The Impossible Dream.*

1987:

12 &
13 September Los Angeles, California

Towards the end of the year, Donna played several European dates, including Italy, France and the UK, and visited Japan.

20 November Manchester, England
22 November London, England
23 November Paris, France

1988:

21 ~ 26 April   Las Vegas, Nevada

1990-94:

Donna played a number of concerts in the early 1990s, however, most of the dates and venues are not known.

She is known to have visited Japan in 1991, Italy, Spain and Brazil in 1992 and 1993, and Chile in 1994.

23 March 91   Yokohama, Japan

Set List:
MacArthur Park/All Systems Go/No More Tears (Enough Is Enough)/This Time I Know It's For Real/Once Upon A Time (Theme)/Heaven's Just A Whisper Away/ On The Radio/Heaven Knows/Romeo/Dim All The Lights/Let There Be Peace/ Say A Little Prayer/She Works Hard For The Money/State Of Independence/Bad Girls/Hot Stuff/Last

*Dance/Do You Wanna Dance/
Breakaway/Work That Magic/The Girl
From Ipanema/The Impossible Dream*

Donna also sang *Send In The Clowns* at
some concerts, and she performed Gloria
Estefan's *Anything For You* at her
Spanish dates.

16 February 1994 Viña del Mar, Chile

1995: ENDLESS SUMMER TOUR

Set List:
*Dim All The Lights/On The Radio/This
Time I Know It's For Real/MacArthur
Park/My Man Medley (The Man I Love/I
Got It Bad (And That Ain't Good)/Some
Of These Days)/Don't Cry For Me
Argentina/Spring Affair/Summer Fever/
Heaven Knows/No More Tears (Enough
Is Enough)/New York Minute/She Works
Hard For The Money/I Feel Love/Bad
Girls/Hot Stuff/Could It Be Magic/Last
Dance*

The set list included only one song
Donna hadn't performed on previous
tours, Don Henley's *New York Minute*.

23, 24 &	
29 May	São Paulo, Brazil
26 & 27 May	Rio de Janeiro, Brazil
28 May	Ribeirão Preto, Brazil
31 May	Belo Horizonte, Brazil
2 June	Salvador, Brazil
3 June	Recife, Brazil
6 June	Fortaleza, Brazil
8 June	São Luís, Brazil
9 June	Belém, Brazil
10 June	Manaus, Brazil

1 July	Danbury, Connecticut
3 July	Philadelphia, Pennsylvania
5 ~ 9 July	Atlantic City, New Jersey
11 July	Cleveland, Ohio
12 July	Pine Knob, Michigan
14 July	Memphis, Tennessee
19 July	Jones Beach, New York
20 July	Westborough, Massachusetts
22 July	Klamath Falls, Oregon
25 July	Wallingford, Pennsylvania
26 July	Holmdel, New Jersey
28 July	Washington, D.C.
29 July	Boston, Massachusetts

3 August	San Diego, California
4 August	Los Angeles, California
10 August	Milwaukee, Wisconsin
11 August	Minneapolis, Minnesota
27 ~	
29 August	Ledyard, Connecticut

Other American dates, and dates outside Brazil and the States, are not known.

1996-97: MID SUMMER NIGHTS DREAM TOUR

On this tour, for the first time, the staging included some of Donna's paintings.

'For a long time,' she said, 'I didn't want to have an in-house exhibition while I

was performing because it felt it was too taxing. Normally, what I have done in places like Atlantic City and New York, is when I'd been performing I'd have an exhibition going on simultaneously so that I could visit, and sign autographs and pictures and so forth.

'But, now I've left the gallery I was with and have gone on my own, so I'll be in different galleries all over. In the interim, what I'm trying to do is develop a market for the younger people that come to the concerts. They collect posters, and could possibly afford lithographs, but maybe not originals. There's a market in terms of opening people's eyes to art, even people who aren't necessarily interested in art. It's all art. Music is art, so I think it's a natural marriage.'

Set List:
(Cleveland, Ohio, on 20th July 1996).
I Feel Love (Instrumental)/This Time I Know It's For Real/MacArthur Park/ Once Upon A Time/On The Radio/Part Of Your World/Fred Astaire/No Ordinary Love Song/No More Tears (Enough Is Enough)/Heaven Knows/ (Riding) Through The Storm/Swing Low, Sweet Chariot/I Don't Wanna Work That Hard/Dim All The Lights/She Works Hard For The Money/Bad Girls/Hot Stuff/Love's About To Change My Heart/Last Dance

During this tour, Donna performed the Yolanda Adams hit, *(Riding) Through The Storm*, plus two songs she'd written, but which had never appeared on one of her albums: *No Ordinary Love Song* (from her unpublished play, *Ordinary Girl*) and *I Don't Wanna Work That Hard*.

Donna's daughters Brooklyn & Amanda joined her to sing *Part Of Your World*, from the Disney film, *The Little Mermaid*. She also performed Gershwin's *Someone To Watch Over Me* at some concerts.

In performing *Dim All The Lights*, Donna told the audience how she had written the song for Rod Stewart, but chickened out of giving it to him. She sang the first half of the song as she envisioned Rod Stewart would sing it, and she sang the second half as she recorded it.

In 1995, it was reported Donna would play several concerts in the UK in early 1996, in Birmingham, Glasgow, London, Manchester and Newcastle. Ultimately, however, she played only one concert, at the capital's Royal Albert Hall. She also played in the French capital, Paris.

22 March	Paris, France
25 March	London, England

Donna also played numerous other dates outside the States, taking in venues as far apart as Holland and Brazil.

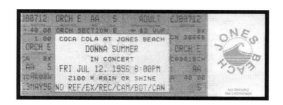

In the States, venues included:

- Ledyard, Connecticut
- Wallingford, Connecticut
- Atlantic City, New Jersey
- Holmdel, New Jersey
- Jones Beach, New York
- Hershey, Pennsylvania
- Philadelphia, Pennsylvania
- Pittsburgh, Pennsylvania
- Vienna, Virginia
- Myrtle Beach, South Carolina
- Greenville, South Carolina
- Atlanta, Georgia
- Hyannis, Massachusetts
- Boston, Massachusetts
- Warwick, Rhode Island
- Buffalo, New York
- Indianapolis, Indiana
- Merrillville, Indiana
- Columbus, Ohio
- Cleveland, Ohio
- Chicago, Illinois
- Detroit, Michigan
- San Diego, California

- Cerritos, California
- Las Vegas, Nevada

1998:

Early in the year, it was announced Donna's overseas tour would commence in the fall, with some UK dates, including London's West End. North American dates were scheduled to follow.

On 16th March, Donna made her debut at New York's Carnegie Hall – her sold out concert raised more than $400,000 for the Gay Men's Health Crisis Foundation.

'I've always wanted to play there,' said Donna, prior to her concert, 'but it's also a bit daunting for a singer, because Carnegie Hall is associated with so many other great entertainers. We'll have to play to the prestige of the hall, and I will tailor my show. It will be a little different, more stripped down. I'll do the hits and a few surprises, some standards that are befitting the evening. I can't wait!'

Other known dates are as follows:

26 April	Chicago, Illinois (1 week)
3 May	Cleveland, Ohio (2 weeks)
17 May	Miami, Florida (1 week)
31 May	Baltimore, Maryland (1 week)
7 June to 4 July	Toronto, Canada
5 July to 29 August	Boston, Massachusetts

1999: LIVE & MORE ENCORE TOUR

Set List:
I Will Go With You (Con Te Partiró)/ MacArthur Park/I Feel Love/On The Radio/This Time I Know It's For Real/ My Life/You Gotta Be Rich/If There Is Music There/Carry On/A Different Road/Dim All The Lights/No More Tears (Enough Is Enough)/She Works Hard For The Money/Bad Girls/Love To Love You Baby/Hot Stuff/Love Is The Healer/Last Dance

Known dates and venues:

4 February   New York City, New York

Donna's concert at Manhattan's Hammerstein Ballroom on 4th February 1999 was filmed for a VH1 TV special – later, it was released as a live album, *LIVE & MORE ENCORE!*, and as a similarly titled home video.

10 April	Wilmington, North Carolina
16 & 17 April	Biloxi, Massachusetts
11 June	Dallas, Texas
18 June	Chattanooga, Tennessee
23 July	Jones Beach, New York
25 July	Warwick, Rhode Island
5 August	Denver, Colorado
6 August	Phoenix, Arizona
7 August	Los Angeles, California
11 August	Cleveland, Ohio
20 November	Uncasville, Connecticut
24 &	
28 November	Atlantic City, New Jersey

Donna, during her second date at Atlantic City, treated the audience to a rare performance of *White Christmas*.

Other venues included:

- Jones Beach, New York
- Baltimore, Maryland
- Danbury, Connecticut
- Merrillville, Indiana
- Atlanta, Georgia
- Holmdel, New Jersey
- Tunica, Mississippi

2003:

| 21 August | Toronto, Canada |

2004:

Set List:
(Denver, Colorado on 18th September)
This Time I Know It's For Real/ MacArthur Park/Could It Be Magic/On The Radio/Greatest Love Of All/Someone To Watch Over Me/No More Tears (Enough Is Enough)/I Don't Wanna Work That Hard/Dim All The Lights/She Works Hard For The Money/Bad Girls/ Hot Stuff/Last Dance

Other songs Donna performed at some concerts: *Cold Love* and *Georgia On My Mind*.

27 March	Orlando, Florida
18 September	Denver, Colorado
12 November	Santa Ynez, California
13 November	Reno, Nevada
15 November	Pala, California
17 November	Phoenix, Arizona
26 November	Punta del Este, Uruguay
28 November	La Romana, Dominican Republic

Donna cancelled her December dates, including Puerto Rico on 9th December, as her father was seriously ill. Sadly, after a long illness, Andrew Gaines passed away on 14th December.

26th June ~ 25th September 2005: GREATEST HITS TOUR

24 February	Hato Rey, Puerto Rico
3 March	West Palm Beach, Florida
12 March	Melbourne, Florida
16 March	Clearwater, Florida
27 March	Orlando, Florida

Donna played 11 Florida dates in the spring, however, only the above dates are known.

This tour celebrated Donna's 30 years in the music business.

Set List:
She Works Hard For The Money/Once Upon A Time/I Love You/MacArthur Park/Could It Be Magic/Smile/Dim All The Lights/With A Little Help From My Friends/On The Radio/(You Make Me Feel Like A) Natural Woman/Le Imagine Café/My Man Medley (The Man I Love/I Got It Bad (And That Ain't Good)/Some Of These Days)/No More Tears (Enough Is Enough)/Nights In White Satin/Medley (Try Me, I Know We Can Make It/I Feel Love/Love To Love You Baby)/Cold Love/ Boogie Oogie Oogie/Pearls/Bad Girls/ Hot Stuff/Last Dance

Donna also performed *Don't Cry For Me Argentina* on selected dates, and she sang *State Of Independence* at Universal City's Gibson Amphitheatre (formerly the Universal Amphitheatre) only.

As well as some of her own 'greatest hits' Donna performed Charlie Chapin's *Smile*, Lennon & McCartney's *With A Little Help From My Friends*, Aretha Franklin's *(You Make Me Feel Like A) Natural Woman*, the Moody Blues' *Nights In White Satin*, A Taste Of Honey's *Boogie Oogie Oogie* and Sade's *Pearls*.

Donna's husband, Bruce Sudano, performed *Le Imagine Café*.

5 May	Vienna, Virginia

26 June	Prior Lake, Minnesota
28 June	Chicago, Illinois
30 June	Toronto, Canada
2 & 3 July	Atlantic City, New Jersey
5 July	Wolf Trap, Washington, DC
7 July	Boston, Massachusetts
9 July	Jones Beach, New York
22 July	Hidalgo, Texas
23 July	Houston, Texas
24 July	Dallas, Texas
27 & 29 July	Atlanta, Georgia
30 July	Kettering, Ohio
31 July	Sterling Heights, Michigan

Donna sang an *a cappella* version of *Wasserman* (*Aquarius*) in German on 29th July in Atlanta, and a short version of *You Are So Beautiful* at Holmdel on 6th August.

4 August	Uncasville, Connecticut
5 August	Bethlehem, Pennsylvania
6 August	Holmdel, New Jersey
24 August	San Diego, California
26 August	Universal City, California
28 August	Saratoga, California
30 August	Livermore, California

1 September	Anaheim, California
3 & 4 September	Las Vegas, Nevada

In Las Vegas, Donna performed *Amazing Grace* – she dedicated it to everyone who suffered from Hurricane Katrina, and asked people give and pray to help the recovery effort.

25 September	Las Vegas, Nevada

Donna attended, and performed at, the European *Nights Of The Proms*, staged in Antwerp, Belgium, between 14 October and 12th November 2005.

2006:

Set List:
(Fort Lauderdale, Florida on 26th May)
*She Works Hard For The Money/
MacArthur Park/Could It Be Magic/
Once Upon A Time/I Love You/Smile/
(You Make Me Feel Like A) Natural
Woman/My Man Medley (The Man I
Love/I Got It Bad (And That Ain't
Good)/Some Of These Days)/No More
Tears (Enough Is Enough)/On The
Radio/ With A Little Help From My
Friends/You Are So Beautiful* (a few
lines only)/ *Pearls/Dinner With
Gershwin/Dim All The Lights/Bad
Girls/Hot Stuff/Last Dance*

21 February	Clearwater, Florida
24 May	Sarasota, Florida
26 & 27 May	Fort Lauderdale, Florida
28 May	Clearwater, Florida
16 & 17 June	Westbury, New York
23 & 24 June	Las Vegas, Nevada
25 June	San Diego, California
28 June	Saratoga, California
2 July	Jacksonville, Canada
7 & 8 July	Toronto, Canada
12 July	Uncasville, Connecticut
14 & 15 July	Atlantic City, New Jersey
1 October	Los Angeles, California
24 & 25 November	Nashville, Tennessee

2007:

10 February	Orlando, Florida
3 March	San Juan, Puerto Rico

Donna appeared at the Dance To Erase MS (Multiple Sclerosis), staged at the Hyatt Regency Century Plaza, Los Angeles, on 13th April. She performed *Bad Girls*, *Hot Stuff* and *Last Dance* – as her band wasn't present, she was backed by Earth, Wind & Fire.

On 2nd June, she appeared at Disney's One Mighty Party, at Orlando, Florida, where she sang *MacArthur Park*, *On The Radio*, *She Works Hard For The Money*, *Bad Girls*, *Hot Stuff* and *Last Dance*.

20 & 21 July   Mashantucket, Connecticut

Towards the end of the year, Donna appeared at the Dutch *Night Of The Proms* concerts, staged in Rotterdam, on the 15th, 16th, 17th, 22nd, 23rd, 24th & 25th November.

2008: CRAYONS TOUR

Set List:
(Vienna, Virginia on 5th July)
*The Queen Is Back/I Feel Love/Dim All
The Lights/I Will Go With You (Con Te
Partiró)/I'm A Fire/Sand On My Feet/On
The Radio/Crayons/Mr Music/No More
Tears (Enough Is Enough)/MacArthur
Park/Be Myself Again/Stamp Your Feet/
Slide Over Backwards/Selah/She Works
Hard For The Money/Science Of Love/
Bad Girls/Hot Stuff/Last Dance*

Donna performed *No More Tears (Enough Is Enough)* with her sister, Mary, who also performed *Selah*.

Other songs Donna performed at select dates include *Could It Be Magic, Love To Love You Baby, Drivin' Down Brazil,*

Bring Down The Reign, Stamp Your Feet and *Fame (The Game)*.

A couple of years earlier, Donna make a conscious decision to go back on the road, and try to reconnect with her audience.

'I was sitting around on stage,' she explained, 'like I say on stage, and fast becoming a desperate housewife. I asked myself, "What am I going to do? What do I like?" I needed to feel like I could connect again with the audience, fully be there … I wanted to get an honest relationship going. And once I did that, I felt like I could put another record out.

'It really is difficult after so long to define yourself, when people have such a definite past image of you. You need to drop that image somewhat and move on into the future. It's not easy to find a way to bridge the gap between the old and the new, and still not lose the audience and make them feel you've deserted them, from who you used to be.'

Although the tour officially kicked off in Vienna, Virginia, on 5th July, Donna also played several earlier dates.

3 June	New York, New York
24 June	Nashville, Tennessee
26 June	Marksville, Louisiana
27 & 28 June	Lake Charles, Louisiana

1 July	Atlanta, Georgia
3 July	Newport News, Virginia
5 July	Vienna, Virginia
8 July	Gilford, New Hampshire
9 July	Uncasville, Connecticut
11 July	Bethel, New York
12 July	Boston, Massachusetts
16 July	Baltimore, Maryland
18 July	Holmdel, New Jersey
19 July	Jones Beach, New York
20 July	Salamanca, New York
22 & 23 July	Rama, Canada
25 & 26 July	Atlantic City, New Jersey
27 July	Westhampton Beach, New York

| 6 August | Seattle, Washington |
| 8 & 9 August | Vancouver, Canada |

10 August	Spokane, Washington
13 August	Saratoga, California
15 August	Reno, Nevada
16 August	Oakland, California
17 August	Santa Rosa, California
20 August	Alpine, California
22 &	
23 August	Los Angeles, California
27 &	
28 August	Windsor, Canada
30 August	Highland Park, Illinois
31 August	Prior Lake, Minnesota

29 August	Atlantic City, New Jersey
25 September	Los Angeles, California
10 &	
11 November	São Paulo, Brazil

2009:

17 May	Hollywood, Florida
25 June	Santa Ynez, California
7 July	Paris, France
30 July	Berlin, Germany

At her Paris show, Donna added *Smile* to the set list, and before she dedicated it to him, she paid a warm tribute to the Michael Jackson, who died on 25th June.

In Berlin, Donna treated her fans to an Anglo-German rendition of *Wassermann (Aquarius)* – she was accompanied by several members of the original Munich cast of *Haare (Hair)*.

1 August	Lokeren, Belgium
20 &	
21 August	Niagara Falls, Canada
22 August	Windsor, Canada
23 August	Hammond, Indiana
27 August	Coney Island, New York
28 August	Mashantucket, Connecticut

2010: EYELASH TOUR

Set List:
(Vienna, Virginia, on 29th August 2010)
The Queen Is Back/Dim All The Lights/ Love To Love You Baby/I Feel Love/ Could It Be Magic/I'm A Fire/To Paris With Love/Crayons/No More Tears (Enough Is Enough)/On The Radio/ Smile/MacArthur Park/Don't Rain On My Parade/Stamp Your Feet/She Works Hard For The Money/Bad Girls/Hot Stuff/Last Dance

There were two notable additions to the set list, *Don't Rain On My Parade*, from the musical *Funny Girl*, and Donna's new single, *To Paris With Love*, which she performed for the first time at her concert in Boston on 27th August – plus, for the first time in a long time, Donna sang *Love To Love You Baby* at most dates.

'I didn't used to perform *Love To Love You Baby* because when I did,' said Donna, 'it would create pandemonium. I stopped doing that for many years, but this last tour I started singing it again. Now I feel like it's OK to do it again, it's sweet and fun. People usually sing the whole song with me anyway.'

| 17 June | Del Mar, California |
| 19 June | Indio, California |

18 August	Hollywood, Florida
20 August	Biloxi, Massachusetts
21 August	Memphis, Tennessee
22 August	Atlanta, Georgia
25 August	Morristown, New Jersey
27 August	Boston, Massachusetts
29 August	Vienna, Virginia
31 August	Binghamton, New York

| 3 September | Mashantucket, Connecticut |
| 4 September | Atlantic City, New Jersey |

'The audience has been great,' said Donna, at the end of August. 'I like to try to give people some of what they came for right off top, such as two or three hits to open the show, and then go into maybe some material that's newer, and then get back to the hits. I sort of go in and out of the hits, so that it's not a long wait for them to come. There's talk and interaction with the audience in between, there's dancers, background singers, the band and some visual effects – there's a plethora of little things going on. For performers, live shows these days are a lot easier than when I was first staring out. As a singer, you used to have to sing against an entire band, and they were a lot louder than you were. Today, everyone wears in-ear monitors and I think, actually, it's helped a lot of singers retain their voices longer, because you can hear yourself. It's very important to be able to hear yourself.'

On 15th October, Donna appeared at the *David Foster & Friends* concert, staged at the Mandalay Bay Events Center, Las Vegas – with Seal, she sang *On The Radio*, Seal's *Crazy* and Toni Braxton's hit, *Un-Break My Heart*.

| 16 October | Phoenix, Arizona |

At 'The Concert And The Encore' concert in Phoenix, Donna was joined by the Phoenix Symphony, with Michael Christie conducting the orchestra.

2011:

Donna made her first ever appearance in Switzerland in February, when she performed at *Art On Ice*, along with numerous world class ice skaters.

| 3 ~ 6 February | Zurich, Switzerland |
| 8 & 9 February | Lausanne, Switzerland |

Two days after her final appearance in Lausanne, Donna returned to the States, where she been scheduled to perform at *the MusiCare Person of the Year Gala* at the Los Angeles Convention Center – Barbra Streisand was honoured as the Person of the Year. However, due to her busy working schedule, Donna cancelled her appearance.

PART 6:
THE AUTOBIOGRAPHY

Donna's autobiography, *Ordinary Girl: The Journey*, was published in the States by Villard/Random House in October 2003.

The book, which Donna co-wrote with Marc Eliot, was timed to coincide with a two disc compilation, *THE JOURNEY: THE BEST OF DONNA SUMMER*.

'This book came about in a kind of obscure way,' said Donna. 'I wasn't planning on writing a book, but I decided that I would do it at this point, because I felt that I needed to go to another level. I just was bored with everything so, you know, time to move. So I also had written the music to *Ordinary Girl*, a musical, and we needed a book to go with it so they could do the stage production.

'I felt that writing my own story might help someone else, that I could be like a mirror. So many diverse things have happened in my life, and what I know is that we are all similar in our essence. I thought that when people read the book, they could relate and be emphatic, especially if they may feel there's no hope, no future – that they've come to the end of the proverbial road.'

Having taken the decision to write about her life, Donna bravely decided to make her story as honest and personal as she possibly could. 'It was cathartic for me to speak about the fears and circumstances I had,' she said. 'There are so many things I could have held back. So writing was way more painful than I thought it would be. There was a lot of crying and some physical pain. There were some things I never grieved about, like the death of my brother-in-law and having to go onstage and do four shows in Las Vegas. That experience just about broke me. In civilian life, you may get the chance to take some time out to grieve. When you're on the road, you have to put the pain on hold … I've heard people say how painful books would be, but I didn't think it would be that painful. Going into your own past is difficult. Normally in your life, you live out a bad experience – you have it and it's bad and it's gone. In a book, you consolidate a series of things you wouldn't ever live through at one single time.'

On the front cover of the Advance Uncorrected Copy of the book, it stated: "Will include a CD with new original songs by Donna Summer from her autobiographical musical, *Ordinary Girl*."

THE JOURNEY: THE BEST OF DONNA SUMMER did feature a couple of new songs, *That's The Way* & *Dream-A-Lot's Theme (I Will Live For Love)*, however, neither came from Donna's musical – suggesting, originally, Donna may have planned or wanted to release an *ORDINARY GIRL* album to accompany her autobiography.

ORDINARY GIRL

THE JOURNEY

Donna
Summer

WITH MARC ELIOT

VILLARD

Donna's autobiography, unlike some, was remarkably candid – for example, she admitted being unfaithful to her first husband, Helmuth Sommer, and many critics who reviewed the book were quick to pick up on her attempted suicide toward the end of 1976.

Donna, at the time, was struggling to come to terms with her new found success; she was in an abusive relationship and her first husband had just appeared in the States, to demand custody of their daughter, Mimi. Her life, she felt, was in a mess, and she felt truly and completely alone, and utterly desperate. Things came to a head when she was staying at New York's Navarro Hotel.

'Those dark thoughts forced me out of bed,' she wrote. 'I walked over to the big, heavy hotel window, threw it open, and hoped the weight of my loneliness would send me crashing eleven stories to the sidewalk below.'

But Donna's foot got caught up in the drapes and, as she tried to free it, the maid walked into her room – and unwittingly stopped Donna from taking her own life. Badly shaken, and shocked to realise what she had been about to do, Donna sought professional help, and she went on to continue her world tour which finally ended in 1977.

PART 7:
CHARTOGRAPHY & CHART RUNS

This chartography focuses on Donna's chart successes in five countries: USA (Pop and R&B charts), the UK, Germany, the Netherlands & Australia.

Chartography:

The following charts are covered:

- USA: Hot 100 Singles/Tracks & 'Bubbling Under' Top 25, Billboard 200 Albums, Top 100 R&B Singles/Tracks, 'Bubbling Under' Top 25 & Top 100 R&B Albums.
- UK: Top 200 Singles & Top 200 Albums (Top 50s in early 1970s).
- Germany: Top 100 Singles & Top 100 Albums (Top 40s in early 1970s).
- Netherlands: Top 100 Singles & Top 100 Albums (Top 40s in early 1970s).
- Australia: Top 100 Singles & Top 100 Albums (Top 50s before 1990).

Key:

Date = earliest date of chart entry in the USA or UK (or any of the other countries, for titles that didn't chart in the USA or UK).

USA = Pop charts in USA, R&B = R&B chart in USA, UK = United Kingdom, Ger = Germany, Ned = the Netherlands, Aus = Australia, tip = chart breaker in the Netherlands.

Throughout the chartography, singles are listed in lower case and ALBUMS in capitals.

DONNA SUMMER: 1969 ~ 1976

Date	USA	R&B	UK	Ger	Ned	Aus	Title
Mar 69				4			*HAARE* (HAIR, Cast Recording)
Aug 74					2		The Hostage
Sep 74					tip		Denver Dream
Dec 74				7	4		Lady Of The Night
Feb 75					27		LADY OF THE NIGHT
Mar 75					17		Love To Love You
Oct 75	11	6	16	23		7	LOVE TO LOVE TOU BABY
Dec 75	2	3	4	6		4	Love To Love You Baby
Mar 76	21	16	41	24		32	A LOVE TRILOGY
Apr 76	52	21	40	23	2		Could It Be Magic
Jun 76	80	35		42	tip		Try Me, I Know We Can Make It
Nov 76	29	13		31			FOUR SEASONS OF LOVE
Dec 76	47	24			tip		Spring Affair

282

DONNA SUMMER: 1976 ~ 1984

Date	USA	R&B	UK	Ger	Ned	Aus	Title
Dec 76	43	21	27				Winter Melody
Jun 77	18	11	3	7	11	4	I REMEMBER YESTERDAY
Jun 77		20					Can't We Just Sit Down (And Talk...)
Jul 77	70					63	THE DEEP (Soundtrack)
Jul 77	6	9	1(4)	3	1(1)	1(1)	I Feel Love
Aug 77			5	25	6	70	Down, Deep Inside (Theme From...)
Sep 77			14		24		I Remember Yesterday
Nov 77	26	13	24			44	ONCE UPON A TIME
Dec 77			3	18	32		Love's Unkind
Dec 77	37	28	10			47	I Love You
Jan 78			4		30		THE GREATEST HITS OF
Feb 78	53	21	19	21	22		Rumour Has It
Apr 78			29				Back In Love Again
May 78	10	6	40	34	17	21	THANK GOD IT'S FRIDAY (S'track)
May 78	3	5	51		8	69	Last Dance
Sep 78	1(3)	8	5	39	9	8	MacArthur Park
Sep 78	1(1)	4	16		17	27	LIVE AND MORE
Jan 79	4	10	34			15	Heaven Knows
Apr 79	1(3)	3	11	5	14	1(1)	Hot Stuff
May 79	1(6)	1(3)	23	7	8	6	BAD GIRLS
May 79	1(5)	1(1)	14	9	7	14	Bad Girls
Aug 79	2	13	29	25	tip		Dim All The Lights
Oct 79	1(2)	20	3	31	20	8	No More Tears (Enough Is Enough)
Nov 79	1(1)	4	24	42	21	16	ON THE RADIO - GREATEST HITS...
Jan 80	5	9	32	34	20	36	On The Radio
Jun 80			46		tip		Sunset People
Sep 80	36	35					Walk Away
Sep 80	3	13	48		26	6	The Wanderer
Oct 80	50	54					WALK AWAY
Nov 80	13	12	55	54		18	THE WANDERER
Nov 80	33		44				Cold Love
Feb 81	40					100	Who Do You Think You're Foolin'
Jun 82	10	4	18		6	17	Love Is In Control (Finger On ...)
Jul 82	20	6	13	37	3	45	DONNA SUMMER
Oct 82	41	31	14		1(1)	30	State Of Independence
Dec 82			21				I Feel Love (Remix)
Dec 82	33	30	62		7		The Woman In Me
May 83						16	GREATEST HITS VOLS 1 & 2
May 83	3	1(3)	25	11	17	4	She Works Hard For The Money
Jul 83	9	5	28	14	11	21	SHE WORKS HARD FOR THE MONEY
Sep 83	43	9	14		tip	57	Unconditional Love
Dec 83	70	35					Love Has A Mind Of Its Own

DONNA SUMMER: 1984 ~ 2012

Date	USA	R&B	UK	Ger	Ned	Aus	Title
Jan 84			57				Stop, Look And Listen
Aug 84	21	20	99		31	52	There Goes My Baby
Sep 84	40	24	69	39	15	91	CATS WITHOUT CLAWS
Nov 84	75	51					Supernatural Love
May 85			97				Eyes
Aug 87	48	10	13		34		Dinner With Gershwin
Oct 87	122	53			49		ALL SYSTEMS GO
Jan 88			54				All Systems Go
Feb 89	7		3	15	5	34	This Time I Know It's For Real
Mar 89	53	71	17	49	19	95	ANOTHER PLACE AND TIME
May 89			7	25	30		I Don't Wanna Get Hurt
Aug 89	85		20		tip	83	Love's About To Change My Heart
Nov 89			72				When Loves Takes Over You
Nov 90			45				State Of Independence (reissue)
Nov 90			24	76	43		THE BEST OF
Jan 91			49				Breakaway
Aug 91	77	18					When Love Cries
Oct 91		97					MISTAKEN IDENTITY
Nov 91			74				Work That Magic
Nov 94			21				Melody Of Love (Wanna Be Loved)
Nov 94			37		75		ENDLESS SUMMER
Sep 95			8		28		I Feel Love (1995 Remix)
Apr 96			13				State Of Independence (1996 Remix)
Dec 96	109						Whenever There Is Love
Jul 98			65				Carry On
Jul 99	79		44		59		I Will Go With You (*Con Te Partiró*)
Jul 99	43	33		75			LIVE & MORE ENCORE!
Oct 03	111	65	6		57		THE JOURNEY: THE VERY BEST OF
Jun 08				88			Stamp Your Feet
Jun 08	17	5		73			CRAYONS
							Posthumous Hits
May 12			45				I Feel Love
May 12			111		93		Hot Stuff
May 12					97		Last Dance
May 12			114				This Time I Know It's For Real
May 12			138		90		Love To Love You Baby
May 12			143		55		State Of Independence
May 12					69		MacArthur Park
May 12					81		Could It Be Magic
May 12	88		67				THE JOURNEY: THE VERY BEST OF
May 12	90		154				ENDLESS SUMMER
Jun 12	73						GREATEST HITS VOLS 1 & 2

DONNA SUMMER: 2012 onwards

Date	USA	R&B	UK	Ger	Ned	Aus	Title
Jun 12	194						GREATEST HITS
Nov 13	97						LOVE TO LOVE YOU DONNA

In the States, Donna is also one of the most successful artists of all-time on Billboard's Hot Dance Club Play/Songs chart, with 17 chart toppers:

- *Love To Love You Baby.*
- *Try Me, I Know We Can Make It / Wasted.*
- *FOUR SEASONS OF LOVE* (all cuts).
- *I REMEMBER YESTERDAY* (all cuts).

- *ONCE UPON A TIME* (all cuts).
- *Last Dance.*
- *MacArthur Park.*
- *Hot Stuff / Bad Girls.*

- *No More Tears (Enough Is Enough).*
- *Melody Of Love (Wanna Be Loved).*
- *I Will Go With You (Con Te Partiró).*
- *Love Is The Healer.*

- *I'm A Fire.*
- *Stamp Your Feet.*
- *Fame (The Game).*
- *To Paris With Love.*
- *MacArthur Park 2013.*

The Laidback Luke Remix of *MacArthur Park*, taken from the remix album *LOVE TO LOVE YOU DONNA*, meant the song had hit no.1 on two separate occasions, and it gave Donna her first posthumous chart topper.

On the same chart, *The Power Of One* hit no.2, and the following songs all achieved no.3: *Could It Be Magic, Down, Deep Inside (Theme From 'The Deep'), Love Is On Control (Finger On The Trigger), She Works Hard For The Money* and *Love's About To Change My Heart.*

Chart Runs

Here are the complete chart runs for Donna's singles, albums and home videos, on the following charts:

- USA Hot 100 singles chart (and, for singles that didn't make the Hot 100, the Top 25 'Bubbling Under' section of the chart).
- USA Billboard 200 albums chart.
- USA Top 40 Music Videos chart.
- UK Singles chart (currently Top 200, but only a Top 50 in the mid-1980s).
- UK Albums chart (currently Top 200, but only a Top 50 in the mid-1980s).

Key: HP = highest position achieved on the chart.
  Weeks = total number of weeks spent on the chart.

The date is the date of chart entry (or re-entry).

USA SINGLES

Love To Love You Baby HP: 2 Weeks: 18
6.12.1975: 55-45-27-15-11-9-7-4-3-**2-2**-4-11-15-29-37-66-97

Could It Be Magic HP: 52 Weeks: 5
1.05.1976: 85-74-64-**52-52**

Try Me, I Know We Can Make It HP: 80 Weeks: 4
10.07.1976: 88-84-**80-80**

Spring Affair HP: 47 Weeks: 8
18.12.1976: 80-70-70-60-60-58-52-**47**

Winter Melody HP: 43 Weeks: 6
12.02.1977: 88-77-66-56-46-**43**

I Feel Love HP: 6 Weeks: 23
6.08.1977: 86-64-52-44-40-29-23-16-14-13-9-8-7-7-**6**-12-16-28-51-57-65-65-100

I Love You HP: 37 Weeks: 11
17.12.1977: 87-77-77-63-52-47-40-**37-37**-51-80

Rumour Has It HP: 53 Weeks: 9
4.03.1978: 83-73-61-55-55-55-**53**-68-100

Last Dance HP: 3 Weeks: 21
13.05.1978: 85-75-67-38-29-23-20-17-13-10-5-4-4-**3-3**-10-20-46-55-98-98

MacArthur Park HP: **1(3)** Weeks: 20
9.09.1978: 85-75-50-25-21-11-8-4-2-**1-1-1**-2-2-10-15-15-38-56-97

Heaven Knows (& Brooklyn Dreams) HP: 4 Weeks: 19
13.01.1979: 77-40-26-18-17-15-11-6-5-**4-4-4**-14-26-30-64-98-98-94

Hot Stuff HP: **1(3)** Weeks: 21
21.04.1979: 79-29-20-3-2-2-**1**-2-**1-1**-2-3-3-3-4-9-9-19-43-71-100

Bad Girls HP: **1(5)** Weeks: 20
26.05.1979: 55-46-28-11-5-3-2-**1-1-1-1-1**-4-5-11-21-31-52-98-98

Dim All The Lights HP: 2 Weeks: 21
25.08.1979: 70-57-46-39-27-19-10-8-6-4-3-**2-2**-4-8-19-36-50-50-98-98

No More Tears (Enough Is Enough) (& Barbra Streisand) HP: **1(2)** Weeks: 15
20.10.1979: 59-33-10-7-3-**1-1**-2-6-8-8-21-24-38-94

On The Radio HP: 5 Weeks: 17
12.01.1980: 86-49-35-16-14-9-7-6-**5-5**-6-16-22-31-42-86-95

Walk Away HP: 36 Weeks: 11
13.09.1980: 82-60-49-42-40-**36-36**-52-66-82-97

The Wanderer HP: 3 Weeks: 20
20.09.1980: 43-30-21-18-11-7-6-5-**3-3-3**-13-36-37-60-60-60-66-73-93

Cold Love HP: 33 Weeks: 12
29.11.1980: 81-72-61-54-41-41-37-**33-33**-43-51-76

Who Do You Think You're Foolin' HP: 40 Weeks: 11
21.02.1981: 84-74-64-53-43-**40-40**-51-59-82-97

Love Is In Control (Finger On The Trigger) HP: 10 Weeks: 18
26.06.1982: 79-65-51-36-27-23-16-14-12-12-12-12-11-**10**-59-85-94-95

State Of Independence HP: 41 Weeks: 10
2.10.1982: 70-59-49-45-43-**41-41**-80-91-95

The Woman In Me HP: 33 Weeks: 16
18.12.1982: 78-60-60-55-48-44-42-40-39-37-**33-33-33**-62-91-97

She Works Hard For The Money HP: 3   Weeks: 21
28.05.1983: 67-55-42-34-30-25-18-14-10-8-**3-3-3**-4-5-7-11-18-24-34-73

Unconditional Love HP: 43   Weeks: 8
3.09.1983: 82-69-61-52-47-**43-43**-92

Love Has A Mind Of Its Own (& Matthew Ward) HP: 70   Weeks: 4
14.01.1984: 86-82-**70**-96

There Goes My Baby HP: 21   Weeks: 14
11.08.1984: 59-47-42-37-33-30-26-23-22-**21**-33-55-78-97

Supernatural Love HP: 75   Weeks: 5
10.11.1984: 84-77-**75-75**-92

Dinner With Gershwin HP: 48   Weeks: 11
22.08.1987: 85-76-62-58-55-50-**48**-54-61-76-99

This Time I Know It's For Real HP: 7   Weeks: 17
22.04.1989: 88-57-45-41-28-23-16-14-9-**7-7**-14-22-40-51-65-82

Love's About To Change My Heart HP: 85   Weeks: 3
16.09.1989: 89-**85**-98

When Love Cries HP: 77   Weeks: 5
17.08.1991: 92-80-**77-77**-93

Whenever There Is Love (& Bruce Roberts) HP: 109
7.12.1996: 122-116-x-**109**-125

I Will Go With You (*Con Te Partiró*) HP: 79   Weeks: 9
24.07.1999: 85-83-**79-79-79-79-79**-87-99

USA ALBUMS

LOVE TO LOVE YOU BABY HP: 11   Weeks: 30
1.11.1975: 190-155-94-77-64-52-40-31-27-23-21-18-16-15-13-**11-11**-33-40-45-76-106-
   133-133-121-110-102-116-153-196

A LOVE TRILOGY HP: 21   Weeks: 27
27.03.1976: 181-75-59-49-42-38-34-30-26-22-**21**-28-26-33-42-71-91-111-108-115-115-
   115-123-123-125-122-196

FOUR SEASONS OF LOVE HP: 29 Weeks: 26
6.11.1976: 56-42-34-30-30-**29**-62-52-52-42-37-52-52-55-53-58-58-53-51-47-46-54-97-
107-127-127

I REMEMBER YESTERDAY HP: 18 Weeks: 40
4.06.1977: 80-50-39-35-33-28-26-24-24-27-39-43-43-43-41-36-32-30-25-23-21-19-**18**-41-
38-77-77-73-73-73-73-145-145-143-147-147-147-150-151-160

THE DEEP (Soundtrack) HP: 70 Weeks: 10
2.07.1977: 99-87-74-**70**-93-93-85-119-135-165

ONCE UPON A TIME HP: 26 Weeks: 58
26.11.1977: 48-40-36-31-29-29-27-**26-26**-30-29-43-89-130-130-126-120-115-111-109-
107-104-104-99-97-95-93-89-104-104-108-108-105-102-100-100-98-96-92-93-105-102-
194-183-167-167-140-130-130-130-110-110-108-117-121-183-185-185

THANK GOD IT'S FRIDAY (Soundtrack) HP: 10 Weeks: 27
13.05.1978: 74-40-34-29-23-17-13-12-12-11-**10-10-10**-21-21-30-47-47-66-91-82-101-
121-131-142-165-197

LIVE AND MORE HP: **1(1)** HP: 75
16.09.1978: 30-24-17-12- 9-6-5-3-**1**-2-2-2-4-4-8-8-13-16-24-24-23-22-21-19-18-14-12-12-
19-27-31-37-57-56-57-57-57-56-54-53-63-66-62-76-77-80-76-86-88-92-101-101-103-
103-103-98-105-127-126-125-123-135-146-143-139-137-136-136-133-143-143-143-
164-174-171

BAD GIRLS HP: **1(6)** Weeks: 49
12.05.1979: 39- 10-5-3-3-**1**-2-2-**1-1-1-1-1**-2-2-4-9-16-16-19-18-17-16-17-26-28-43-73-94-
92-92-88-92-92-82-82-86-86-97-97-96-106-102-111-133-142-160-161-192

ON THE RADIO – GREATEST HITS VOLUMES I & II HP: **1(1)** Weeks: 40
3.11.1979: 53- 8-5-5-2-2-2-2-2-**1**-2-2-4-7-7-7-6-6-6-17-17-20-21-24-51-60-70-90-90-94-
96-97-113-127-144-158-165-178-178
2.06.2012: 73

WALK AWAY – THE BEST OF 1977-1980 HP: 50 Weeks: 15
11.10.1980: 177-114-105-95-56-**50-50**-55-96-102-113-131-131-132-198

THE WANDERER HP: 13 Weeks: 18
8.11.1980: 35-14-**13-13-13**-33-32-40-40-53-53-51-68-77-104-177-177-183

DONNA SUMMER   HP: 20   Weeks: 37
14.08.1982: 48-34-30-26-22-**20-20-20-20-20**-47-47-46-46-63-86-98-126-126-126-126-
   125-124-123-125-131-130-129-128-125-164-159-159-157-187-187-200

SHE WORKS HARD FOR THE MONEY   HP: 9   Weeks: 32
16.07.1983: 81-23-19-16-12-11-**9**-14-14-18-24-26-27-27-29-31-42-45-49-58-75-74-84-95-
   95-100-96-106-112-138-159-175

CATS WITHOUT CLAWS   HP: 40   Weeks: 17
22.09.1984: 106-53-43-**40-40**-43-61-86-91-89-97-114-134-142-142-173-174

ALL SYSTEMS GO   HP: 122   Weeks: 6
10.10.1987: 165-135-130-**122-122**-182

ANOTHER PLACE AND TIME   HP: 53   Weeks: 20
20.05.1989: 125-66-63-56-56-**53-53**-63-70-83-88-92-103-123-125-165-181-193-195-200

LIVE & MORE ENCORE!   HP: 43   Weeks: 13
10.07.1999: **43**-47-51-61-74-74-90-107-96-110-137-155-179

THE JOURNEY – THE VERY BEST   HP: 88   Weeks: 6
18.10.2003: 111-164-143-178
2.06.2012: 95-x-**88**

CRAYONS   HP: 17   Weeks: 5
7.06.2008: **17**-44-108-187
21.03.2009: 191

ENDLESS SUMMER   HP: 90   Wks: 1
2.06.2012: **90**

GREATEST HITS   HP: 194   Wks: 1
2.06.2012: **194**

LOVE TO LOVE YOU DONNA   HP: 97   Wks: 1
9.11.13: **97**

USA MUSIC VIDEOS

Endless Summer   HP: 37   Weeks: 1
18.03.1995: **37**

Live & More Encore! HP: 8   Weeks: 12
10.07.1999: 15-18-26-33-x-39
9.06.2012: 25-**8**-12-22-25-26-24

The Best Of – The DVD Collection HP: 22   Weeks: 1
13.03.2004: **22**

UK SINGLES

Love To Love You Baby HP: 4   Weeks: 10
17.01.1976: 37-16-6-**4**-5-6-12-21-28
26.05.2012: 138

Could It Be Magic HP: 40   Weeks: 7
29.05.1976: 45-44-44-**40**-44-44-49

Winter Melody HP: 27   Weeks: 6
25.12.1976: 45-45-46-29-**27**-34

I Feel Love HP: **1(4)**   Weeks: 43
9.07.1977: 15-3-**1-1-1-1**-3-5-11-26-33
4.12.1982: 42-33-22-23-23-22-21-22-33-55 (1982 remix)
9.09.1995: 8-16-28-52-67-80-105-118-147-138-160-164-134-158-159-169-194-x-186
  (1995 remix)
14.03.1998: 167 (1995 remix)
26.05.12: 45-89
9.11.13: 166

Down, Deep Inside (Theme From The Deep) HP: 5   Weeks: 10
20.08.1977: 50-21-14-**5-5-5-5**-10-15-33

I Remember Yesterday HP: 14   Weeks: 7
24.09.1977: 32-21-17-16-**14**-16-19

Love's Unkind HP: 3   Weeks: 13
3.12.1977: 36-16-13-6-6-4-**3-3-3**-6-9-29-38

I Love You HP: 10   Weeks: 9
10.12.1977: 33-25-26-26-30-**10**-16-18-40

Rumour Has It HP: 19   Weeks: 8
25.02.1978: 40-30-28-**19-19**-22-24-30

Back In Love Again   HP: 29   Weeks: 7
22.04.1978: 40-**29-29**-34-31-46-73

Last Dance   HP: 51   Weeks: 8
10.06.1978: 70-x-**51**-60-56-62-72-64-55-57

MacArthur Park   HP: 5   Weeks: 10
14.10.1978: 29-12-**5-5-5**-9-15-34-48-69

Heaven Knows (& Brooklyn Dreams)   HP: 34   Weeks: 8
17.02.1979: 48-36-35-**34**-36-47-53-74

Hot Stuff   HP: 11   Weeks: 11
12.05.1979: 55-29-24-**11-11**-12-17-28-44-59
26.05.2012: 111

Bad Girls   HP: 14   Weeks: 10
7.07.1979: 39-22-22-**14**-15-21-28-45-58-68

Dim All The Lights   HP: 29   Weeks: 9
1.09.1979: 64-47-46-38-32-32-**29**-41-66

No More Tears (Enough Is Enough) (& Barbra Streisand)   HP: 3   Weeks: 14
3.11.1979: 72-27-14-6-**3-3**-5-11-11-14-29-48-66
16.11.13: 140

On The Radio   HP: 32   Weeks: 6
16.02.1980: 54-**32**-35-37-46-60

Sunset People   HP: 46   Weeks: 5
21.06.1980: 71-52-**46**-47-63

The Wanderer   HP: 48   Weeks: 6
27.09.1980: 69-54-52-49-**48**-64

Cold Love   HP: 44   Weeks: 3
17.01.1981: 48-**44**-50

Love Is In Control (Finger On The Trigger)   HP: 18   Weeks: 12
3.07.1982: 87-67-38-32-27-22-**18**-24-23-30-36-72

State Of Independence   HP: 13   Weeks: 28
30.10.1982: 95-52-29-14-15-19-20-36-54-54-47-69
10.11.1990: 78-49-45-56 (1990 remix)

6.04.1996: **13**-26-40-45-67-101-129-147-126-160-174 (1996 remix)
26.05.2012: 143

The Woman In Me   HP: 62   Weeks: 3
26.02.1983: 84-**62**-73

She Works Hard For The Money   HP: 25   Weeks: 8
18.06.1983: 46-36-33-30-29-**25**-35-47

Unconditional Love   HP: 14   Weeks: 13
17.09.1983: 86-53-45-46-42-39-28-22-16-**14**-22-37-61

Stop, Look And Listen   HP: 57   Weeks: 3
21.01.1984: 62-**57**-86

There Goes My Baby   HP: 99   Weeks: 1
1.09.1984: **99**

Eyes   HP: 97   Weeks: 1
25.05.1985: **97**

Dinner With Gershwin   HP: 13   Weeks: 13
26.09.1987: 84-x-x-81-70-50-39-23-17-**13**-20-34-53-75-66

All Systems Go   HP: 54   Weeks: 3
23.01.1988: 59-**54**-66

This Time I Know It's For Real   HP: 3   Weeks: 15
25.02.1989: 42-30-11-4-**3**-**3**-4-8-10-19-29-35-48-73
26.05.2012: 114

I Don't Wanna Get Hurt   HP: 7   Weeks: 9
27.05.1989: 19-**7**-10-9-16-21-31-41-57

Love's About To Change My Heart   HP: 20   Weeks: 6
26.08.1989: 28-**20**-24-29-33-53

When Loves Takes Over You   HP: 72   Weeks: 2
25.11.1989: **72**-87

Breakaway   HP: 49   Weeks: 4
12.01.1991: 59-**49**-53-72

Work That Magic   HP: 74   Weeks: 1
30.11.1991: **74**

Melody Of Love (Wanna Be Loved)   HP: 21   Weeks: 13
12.11.1994: **21**-32-61-81-124-171-171-137-137-131-123-150-182

Carry On (& Giorgio Moroder)   HP: 65   Weeks: 3
11.07.1998: **65**-115-174

I Will Go With You (*Con Te Partiró*)   HP: 44   Weeks: 5
30.10.1999: **44**-99-135-170-188

UK ALBUMS

LOVE TO LOVE YOU BABY   HP: 16   Weeks: 9
31.01.1976: 43-26-**16**-18-25-23-45-39-52

A LOVE TRILOGY   HP: 41   Weeks: 9
22.05.1976: 60
11.09.1976: 57-x-**41**-45-**41**-55-49-52-59-x-54

I REMEMBER YESTERDAY   HP: 3   Weeks: 23
25.06.1977: 42-26-14-13-**3**-6-6-6-5-7-9-11-10-14-16-17-14-15-20-16-38-39-52

ONCE UPON A TIME   HP: 24   Weeks: 12
26.11.1977: 26-**24**-31-37-29-29-46-x-26-45-52-58
27.05.1978: 55

THE GREATEST HITS OF   HP: 4   Weeks: 18
7.01.1978: 29-9-5-**4**-5-**4**-5-6-9-17-27-32-34-36-32-51-37-x-43

THANK GOD IT'S FRIDAY (Soundtrack)   HP: 54   Weeks: 1
25.05.1978: **54**

LIVE AND MORE   HP: 16   Weeks: 16
21.10.1978: 35-28-24-17-**16**-21-33-37-45-61-61-61-x-45-x-58-x-65-x-74

BAD GIRLS   HP: 23   Weeks: 23
2.06.1979: 70-25-**23**-25-29-27-25-29-26-29-37-28-32-35-35-28-32-39-52-31-49-65-61

ON THE RADIO – GREATEST HITS VOLUMES I & II   HP: 24   Weeks: 22
10.11.1979: 46-**24**-28-26-33-33-43-43-50-36-32-37-39-46-41-44-43-35-41-74-55-74

THE WANDERER HP: 55 Weeks: 2
1.11.1980: 65-**55**

DONNA SUMMER HP: 13 Weeks: 16
31.07.1982: 22-15-14-**13**-14-36-46-88-99-62-59-72-79-88-100-100

SHE WORKS HARD FOR THE MONEY HP: 28 Weeks: 5
16.07.1983: **28**-32-50-55-93

CATS WITHOUT CLAWS HP: 69 Weeks: 2
15.09.1984: **69**-71

ANOTHER PLACE AND TIME HP: 17 Weeks: 28
25.03.1989**: 17-17**-23-21-33-34-41-55-75-64-41-33-32-36-41-45-55-69
2.09.1989: 67-60-67-36-19-**17**-27-30-48-72

THE BEST OF HP: 24 Weeks: 9
24.11.1990: **24-24**-40-44-54-56-58-70-73

ENDLESS SUMMER HP: 37 Weeks: 13
26.11.1994: **37**-52-77-142
27.09.1997: 152-184
26.09.1998: 177
26.05.2012: 190-169-156-171-x-154-192

THE JOURNEY: THE VERY BEST OF HP: 6 Weeks: 18
26.06.2004: 16-**6**-18-28-41-53-81-95-105-100-122-182-198
2.04.2005: 87-97-153
26.05.2012: 67-153

PART 8: USA DISCOGRAPHY

As well as commercially released albums and singles, this discography also includes known promo/test pressings which, for whatever reason, were never officially released in any format. Significant re-issues only are listed.

Albums

LOVE TO LOVE YOU BABY (1975) Oasis OCLP 5003
A LOVE TRILOGY (1976) Oasis OCLP 5004
FOUR SEASONS OF LOVE (1976) Casablanca NBLP 7038
I REMEMBER YESTERDAY (1977) Casablanca NBLP 7056
ONCE UPON A TIME (1977) Casablanca NBLP 7078
THE DEEP (Soundtrack, 1977) Casablanca NBLP 7060 – translucent blue vinyl
THANK GOD IT'S FRIDAY (Soundtrack, 1978) Casablanca NBLP 7099
LIVE AND MORE (1978) Casablanca NBLP 7119
THE BEST OF LIVE AND MORE (1978) Casablanca NBPIX 7119 – promo picture disc
BAD GIRLS (1979) Casablanca NBLP 7150
ON THE RADIO: GREATEST HITS VOLUMES I & II (1979) Casablanca NBLP 7191
WALK AWAY – THE BEST OF 1977-1980 (1980) Casablanca NBLP 7244
THE WANDERER (1980) Geffen GHS 2000
DONNA SUMMER (1982) Geffen GHS 2005
SHE WORKS HARD FOR THE MONEY (1983) Mercury 821 265
CATS WITHOUT CLAWS (1984) Geffen GHS 24040
THE SUMMER COLLECTION (1985) Mercury 826144-1 – promo
ALL SYSTEMS GO (1987) Geffen GHS 24102
THE DANCE COLLECTION (1987) PolyGram 2LP – 830 534
ANOTHER PLACE AND TIME (1989) Atlantic 81917
MISTAKEN IDENTITY (1991) Atlantic 82285
THE ANTHOLOGY (1993) Casablanca 518 144-2
ENDLESS SUMMER (1994) Mercury 314 526 178-2
CHRISTMAS SPIRIT (1994) Mercury 314 522 694-2
I'M A RAINBOW (1996) Casablanca/Mercury 314 532 869-2 – recorded in 1981
GREATEST HITS (1998) Mercury 314 558 795-2
CHILD OF THE PROMISE (Cast Album, 2000) Sparrow 724385170225
THE BEST OF – THE MILLENIUM COLLECTION (2003) Mercury 440 063 609 2
BAD GIRLS (2003) Chronicles/Mercury B00000683 – deluxe edition
THE JOURNEY – THE BEST OF (2003) Mercury B0001009-02 – with bonus CD;
    Mercury 4400111737 (2004) – Limited Edition Deluxe Gift Box, with Donna's
    autobiography, Ordinary Girl: The Journey
GOLD (2005) Hip-O Records 000271902

THE BEST OF – THE CHRISTMAS COLLECTION (2005) Mercury B0005126-02 – reissue of CHRISTMAS SPIRIT

THE BEST OF – THE MILLENNIUM COLLECTION VOLUME 2 (2007) Hip-O Records 000820402

CRAYONS (2008) Burgundy 8869722992 2

PLAYLIST – THE VERY BEST OF (2013) Epic/Legacy 8888371084 2

ICON (2013) Mercury B0015598-02

LOVE TO LOVE YOU DONNA (2013) Verve B0019066-02

Box-Sets

THE BOX (1984) Geffen 9080/3 – 3CD box-set with the albums, CATS WITHOUT CLAWS, DONNA SUMMER & THE WANDERER.

A RETROSPECTIVE (1994) PolyGram BX45120 – box-set of either 9 x 7" singles or 12 x 12" singles, each with back-to-back hits

CHRONICLES (2005) Mercury B0004821-02 – 3CD box-set with the albums, LOVE TO LOVE YOU BABY, A LOVE TRILOGY & FOUR SEASONS OF LOVE

Home Videos

A Hot Summer Night (1983) RCA/Columbia

Endless Summer (1994) PolyGram 800 632 353-2

Live & More Encore! (1999) Sony 50202

The Best Of – The DVD Collection (2004) Universal B000197109

7" Singles

Love To Love You Baby (4:57)/(3:27) (1975) Oasis OC 401

Could It Be Magic/Whispering Waves (1976) Oasis OC 405

Try Me, I Know I Can Make It/Wasted (1976) Oasis OC 406

Spring Affair/Come With Me (1976) Casablanca NB 872

Winter Melody (Mono)/(Stereo) (1977) Casablanca NB 874

I Love You/Once Upon A Time (1977) Casablanca NB 907

Rumour Has It/Once Upon A Time (1977) Casablanca NB 916

Last Dance/With Your Love (1978) Casablanca NB 926

MacArthur Park/Once Upon A Time (1978) Casablanca NB 939

Heaven Knows/Only One Man (1978) Casablanca NB 959

Hot Stuff/Journey To The Centre Of Your Heart (1979) Casablanca NB 978

Bad Girls/On My Honor (1979) Casablanca NB 988

Dim All The Lights/There Will Always Be A You (1979) Casablanca NB 2201

Walk Away/Could It Be Magic (1979) Casablanca NB 2300

No More Tears (Enough Is Enough)/Barbra Streisand: Wet (1979) Columbia 11125

On The Radio/There Will Always Be A You (1979) Casablanca NB 2236

The Wanderer/Stop Me (1980) Geffen GEF 49563

Cold Love/Grand Illusion (1980) Geffen GEF 49634
Who Do You Think You're Foolin'/Running For Cover (1981) Geffen GEF 49664
Love Is On Control (Finger On The Trigger)/Sometimes Like Butterflies (1982) Geffen 29982
State Of Independence/Love Is Just A Breath Away (1982) Geffen 29895
The Woman In Me/Livin' In America (1983) Geffen 29805
She Works Hard For The Money/I Do Believe (I Fell In Love) (1983) Mercury 812 370
Unconditional Love/Woman (1983) Mercury 814 088
Love Has A Mind Of Its Own/Stop, Look And Listen (1983) Mercury 814 922
There Goes My Baby/Maybe It's Over (1984) Geffen 29291
Supernatural Love/Face The Music (1984) Geffen 29142
Dinner With Gershwin/(Instrumental) (1987) Geffen 28418
Only The Fool Survives/Love Shock (1987) Geffen 28165 – promo
This Time I Know It's For Real/If It Makes You Feel Good (1989) Atlantic 88899

12" Singles

Winter Melody/Spring Affair (1977) Casablanca NBD 100
I Feel Love/Theme From 'The Deep' (Down, Deep Inside) (1977) Casablanca NBD 20104 – one sided
Je T'Aime... Moi Non Plus (1977) Casablanca NBD 20105 DJ – one-sided promo
Rumour Has It/I Love You (1977) Casablanca NBD 20112 DJ – promo
With Your Love (1978) Casablanca NBD 20117 DJ – one-sided promo
Last Dance (1978) Casablanca NBD 20122 DJ – one sided promo
MacArthur Park Suite (1978) Casablanca NBD 20148 DJ – one-sided promo
MacArthur Park/I Feel Love (Original) (1979) Casablanca DS 12006
Hot Stuff/Bad Girls (1979) Casablanca NBD 20167
Dim All The Lights (1979) Casablanca NBD 20193 DJ – one-sided promo
Walk Away (12" Extended Version) (1979) Casablanca NBD 20226 DJ – one-sided promo
No More Tears (Enough Is Enough) (1979) Casablanca NBD 20199 – one-sided
The Wanderer (Mono)/(Stereo) (1980) Warner Bros PRO 910 – promo
Cold Love/Looking Up/Who Do You Think You're Foolin' (1980) Warner Bros PRO 925
Love Is In Control (Finger On The Trigger) (Dance Remix)/(Instrumental) (1982) Geffen 29938
State Of Independence/Protection (1982) Geffen PRO 1048 – promo
She Works Hard For The Money (Club Mix)/(Instrumental) (1983) Mercury MK 249 – promo
Unconditional Love (Club Mix)/She Works Hard For The Money (Club Mix) (1983) Mercury 814 592
There Goes My Baby/Maybe It's Over (1984) Geffen PRO 2180 – promo
Supernatural Love (Extended Dance Remix)/Face The Music (1984) Geffen 20273
Dinner With Gershwin (Extended Version)/(Instrumental) (1987) Geffen 20635
All Systems Go (Dance Mix)/Fascination (1987) Geffen PRO 3036 – promo
Hot Stuff/Bad Girls/I Feel Love (1989) Casablanca 874 127-1

This Time I Know It's For Real (Extended Remix)/If It Makes You Feel Good/ (Instrumental) (1989) Atlantic 86415

Love's About To Change Mt Heart (PWL 12" Mix)/(PWL 7" Mix)/(Clivilles & Cole 12" Mix)/(Dub 2)/(Clivilles & Cole 7" Mix) (1989) Atlantic 86309

Breakaway (Extended Power Mix)/(Power Radio Mix)I Don't Wanna Get Hurt (12" Version) (1989) Atlantic 86255

Dim All The Lights (The 100 Watt Mix)/(The 50 Watt Radio Edit)/(The Kilowatt Radio Edit)/(The 75 Watt Dub) (1991) Hearsay HEAR 101

Work That Magic (Extended ISA Remix)/(ISA Remix)/(Capricorn Remix)/Let There Be Peace (1991) Atlantic 85925

When Love Cries (Vocal Club Dub)/(Radio)/(Club Mix)/(Instrumental) (1991) Atlantic 85961

Melody Of Love (Wanna Be Loved) (Classic Club Mix)/(Boss Mix)/(Epris Mix)/ (Mijangos Powertools Trip #1) (1994) Casablanca 856 357-1

Whenever There Is Love (Club Mix)/(Club Dub)/(Riff Dub)/(Tribal Beats)/(Instrumental)/ (7") (1996) Universal TA41

Someday (Cox Euro Disney Mix)/(Swingin' In The Summer Mix)/(Gypsy Classic Extended Mix)/(Donna's 5AM Deep Mix) plus five mixes by other artists (1997) Wonderland/Disney 050086034819 – promo double pack

I Will Go With You (Con Te Partiró) (Hex Hector Extended Vocal Mix)/(Club 69 Future Mix)/(Rosabel Main Vox)/(Richie Santana Virus Dub) (1999) Epic 49 79202

I Will Go With You (Con Te Partiró) (Club 69 Underground Anthem Mix)/(Rosabel Dark Dub)/(Warren Rigg Summer Dub)/(Club 69 Trippy Dub) (1999) Epic 49 79226

Love Is The Healer (Album Version)/(Eric Kupper's I Feel Healed 12" Mix)/(Thunderpuss 2000 Club Mix)/(Eric Kupper's I Feel Healed 7" Mix) (1999) Epic 668308 8

You're So Beautiful (Tony & Mac's Dancefloor Journey Mix)/(Friscia & Lamboy Beautiful Vocal Mix) (2003) UTV UTVF05126-1 – promo

Dream-A-Lot's Theme (I Will Live For Love) (12" Extended Remix)/(Dub Mix)/LP Version) (2004) UTV UTVF05128-1 – promo

Power Of Love (Hani's Extended Mix)/(Album Mix)/(Hani Mixshow Edit)/(Power Keys)/ (Hani Mixshow Instrumental) (2005) J Records 82876 74077 1 – promo

I Feel Love (MezzoForte's Tribute To Patrick Cowley Mix)/(Patrick Cowley Original Remix) (2007) Vicious VIC-0058 – red vinyl promo

Bad Girls (Classic NYC 12" Mix)/Now I Need You (2009) East End Music EA 33189

CD Singles

This Time I Know It's For Real (Album Version)/(Extended Remix)/(Instrumental) (1989) Atlantic PR 2718 – promo

Love's About To Change My Heart (PWL 7" Mix)/(Clivilles & Cole 7" Mix)/(Album version)/(PWL 12" Mix)/(Clivilles & Cole 12" Mix) (1980) Atlantic PR 2876 – promo

Breakaway (1989) Atlantic PR 3003 – promo

When Love Cries (Radio Edit)/(Summertime Remix)/(12" Mix) (1991) Atlantic PRCD 4163 – promo

Don't Cry For Me Argentina (Edit)/(Album Version) (1993) Casablanca CDP 1023 – promo

Melody Of Love (Wanna Be Loved) (Original Version)/(Classic Club Mix)/(Boss Mix)/ Epris Mix)/(AJ & Humpty's Anthem Mix)/(Epris Radio Mix)/On The Radio/The Christmas Song (1994) Casablanca 856 367-2

Any Way At All (1994) Casablanca CDP 1417 – promo

Christmas Spirit Sampler: The Christmas Song/Christmas Medley/Christmas Is Here) (1994) Mercury SACD 958 – promo

Lamb Of God (1994) Mercury – promo

Whenever There Is Love (Club Mix)/(Club Dub)/(Riff Dub)/(Tribal Beats)/(Instrumental)/ (7") (1996) Universal U5P-1130

Someday (Cox Euro Disney Mix)/(Swingin' In The Summer Mix)/(Gypsy Classic Mix)/ (Cox Euro Disney Club Mix)/(Swingin' In The Summer Club Mix) (1997) Wonderland/ Disney 03MS 27300 – promo

I Will Go With You (Con Te Partiró) (Radio Edit)/(Club 69 Future Radio Edit)/(Rosabel Radio Remix)/(Welcome Downtempo Radio Mix)/(Hex Hector Extended Vocal Mix – Cold End)/Love On & On (Hex Hector 7" Remix) (1999) Epic 34K 79201

I Will Go With You (Con Te Partiró) (Radio Edit)/(Club 69 Radio Mix)/(Rosabel Radio Remix)/(Welcome Downtempo Radio Mix)/(Warren Rigg Radio Edit – Cold End)/ (Skillmasters Remix)/(Hex Hector Extended Vocal Mix)/(Club 69 Future Mix)/Love On & On (Hex Hector 7" Remix) (1999) Epic 49K 79202

Love Is The Healer (Album Version)/(Thunderpuss 2000 Club Mix)/(Eric Kupper's I Feel Healed 7" Mix) (1999) Epic 668308 1

The Power Of One/Talley Sherwood: The Legend Comes To Life From 'The Power Of One' Score (2000) Atlantic 83370-2

Power Of Love (Hani's Extended Mix)/(Radio Mix)/(Hani's Mixshow Edit)/(Power Keys)/ (Hani's Mixshow Instrumental) (2005) J Records

Stamp Your Feet (Jason Nevins Radio Edit)/(Escape/Coluccio Radio Edit)/(Ranny's Radio Edit)/(Jason Nevins Extended Mix)/(Escape/Coluccio Club Mix)/(Ranny's Big Room Mix)/(Granite & Sugarman Club)/(Granite & Sugarman Mixshow)/(DiscoTech Mix) (2008) Sony BMG

I'm A Fire (Baggi Begovic Soul Conspiracy Original Mix)/(Baggi Begovic Mixshow)/ (Matty's Soulflower Club Mix)/(Matty's Sunflower Reprise)/(Matty's Sunflower Beats)/(Matty's Sunflower Acapella)/(Roca Sound Original Album Mix)/(Craig C Mixshow)/(Lost Daze Remix) (2008) Sony BMG – promo

I'm A Fire (Solitaire Club Mix)/(Solitaire Instrumental)/(Craig C Burnin' Club Mix)/ (Craig C Burnin' Vocal Mastermix)/(Rod Carrillo Groove Dub)/(Redtop Extended Mix)/(Redtop Dub) (2008) Sony BMG – promo

Fame (The Game) (Album Version)/(Ralphi Rosario Radio)/(Extended Ultimix Album Version)/(Ralphi Rosario Club)/(Ralphi Radio) (2008) Sony BMG – promo

Fame (The Game) (Dave Aude Radio)/(Dave Chase Radio)/(Dave Aude Club)/(Dave Aude Dub)/(Dave Aude Dub Instrumental)/(Dave Chase Full Vocal)/(Dave Chase Dub)/(Dave Chase Instrumental) (2008) Sony BMG – promo

PART 9: UK DISCOGRAPHY

As well as commercially released albums and singles, this discography also includes known promo/test pressings which, for whatever reason, were never officially released in any format. Significant re-issues only are listed.

Albums

LOVE TO LOVE YOU BABY (1975) GTO GTLP 008
A LOVE TRILOGY (1976) Casablanca 2055
FOUR SEASONS OF LOVE (1976) GTO GTLP 018
I REMEMBER YESTERDAY (1977) GTO GTLP 025
ONCE UPON A TIME (1977) Casablanca CALD 5003
THE GREATEST HITS OF (1977) GTO GTLP 028
THE DEEP (Soundtrack, 1977) Casablanca CAL 2018
THANK GOD IT'S FRIDAY (Soundtrack, 1978) Casablanca TGIF 100
LIVE AND MORE (1978) Casablanca CALD 5006
BAD GIRLS (1979) Casablanca CALD 5007
ON THE RADIO: GREATEST HITS VOLUMES I & II (1979) Casablanca NB 7070
THE WANDERER (1980) Geffen K99124, Driven By The Music DBTMCD001 (2014) – remastered reissue with bonus tracks
DONNA SUMMER (1982) Warner Bros K99163, Driven By The Music DBTMCD002 (2014) – remastered reissue with bonus tracks
SHE WORKS HARD FOR THE MONEY (1983) Mercury MERL21
CATS WITHOUT CLAWS (1984) Warner Bros 250 806, Driven By The Music DBTMCD003 (2014) – remastered reissue with bonus tracks
THE SUMMER COLLECTION (1985) Mercury MERH 84
ALL SYSTEMS GO (1987) Warner Bros 252 953, Driven By The Music DBTMCD004 (2014) – remastered reissue with bonus tracks
ANOTHER PLACE AND TIME (1989) Warner Bros 255 976, Driven By The Music DBTMCD305 (2014) – remastered reissue with 2CDs of bonus tracks
THE BEST OF (1990) Warner Bros WX 397
MISTAKEN IDENTITY (1991) Warner Bros 75159, Driven By The Music DBTMCD006 (2014) – remastered reissue with bonus tracks
THE ANTHOLOGY (1993) Casablanca 518 144-2
THIS TIME I KNOW IT'S FOR REAL (1993) WEA 9548-31823-2
ENDLESS SUMMER (1994) Mercury 526 217-2
I'M A RAINBOW (1996) Casablanca/Mercury 314 532 869-2 – recorded in 1981, Driven By The Music DBTMCD207 (2014) – remastered reissue on 2CDs
CHRISTMAS SPIRIT (1999) Spectrum 522 6942
BAD GIRLS (2003) Universal 9860357 – deluxe edition

THE JOURNEY – THE BEST OF (2003) Mercury 0602498491904 – single CD edition; 0602498628584 – with bonus CD
GOLD (2005) Almighty CDALMY 120
CRAYONS (2008) Burgundy 8869730725 2
CLASSIC (2009) Spectrum UMC 5424
LOVE TO LOVE YOU BABY / I REMEMBER YESTERDAY (2010) Commercial Marketing 5325945
I FEEL LOVE – THE COLLECTION (2013) Spectrum SPECXX 2105
LOVE TO LOVE YOU DONNA (2013) Verve 0602537506552

Box Sets

THE VINYL COLLECTION (2014) Driven By The Music DBTMLPBOX01 (2014) – seven LP box-set with remastered albums, THE WANDERER, DONNA DUMMER, CATS WITHOUT CLAWS, ALL SYSTEMS GO, ANOTHER PLACE AND TIME, MISTAKEN IDENTITY & I'M A RAINBOW (double album)
THE CD COLLECTION (2014) Driven By The Music DBTMCDBOX01 – 10CD box-set of remastered albums with bonus tracks: THE WANDERER, DONNA DUMMER, CATS WITHOUT CLAWS, ALL SYSTEMS GO, ANOTHER PLACE AND TIME, MISTAKEN IDENTITY & I'M A RAINBOW (2CD), plus two bonus CDs of remixes from ANOTHER PLACE AND TIME

Home Videos

A Hot Summer Night (1983) Channel 5 CFV 00242
Endless Summer (1994) PolyGram 632 352-3
Live & More Encore! (1999) Sony 201982 9

7" Singles

The Hostage/Let's Work Together Now (1974) People PEO 115 – demo
Love To Love You Baby/Need-A-Man Blues (1975) GTO GT 17
Could It Be Magic/Whispering Waves (1976) GTO GT 60
Winter Melody/Wasted (1976) GTO GT 76
I Feel Love/Can't We Just Sit Down (And Talk It Over) (1977) GTO GT 100
I Remember Yesterday/Spring Affair (1977) GTO GT 107 – issued with blue or red label
Love's Unkind/Autumn Changes (1977) GTO GT 113
Down, Deep Inside (Theme From 'The Deep')/John Barry: Theme From 'The Deep' (Instrumental) (1977) Casablanca CAN 111
I Love You/Once Upon A Time (1977) Casablanca CAN 114
Rumour Has It/Once Upon A Time (1977) Casablanca CAN 122
Back In Love Again/Try Me, I Know I Can Make It/Wasted (1977) GTO GT 117
Last Dance/With Your Love (1978) Casablanca TGIFS 2
MacArthur Park/Once Upon A Time (1978) Casablanca CAN 131

Heaven Knows/Only One Man (1979) Casablanca CAN 141
Hot Stuff/Journey To The Centre Of Your Heart (1979) Casablanca CAN 151
Bad Girls/On My Honor (1979) Casablanca CAN 155
On My Honor/With Your Love (1979) Casablanca CANP 155 – promo
Dim All The Lights/There Will Always Be A You (1979) Casablanca CAN 162
No More Tears (Enough Is Enough)/My Baby Understands (1979) Casablanca CAN 174
Sunset People/Our Love (1980) Casablanca CAN 198
On The Radio/There Will Always Be A You (1979) Casablanca NB 2236
The Wanderer/Stop Me (1980) Geffen K79180
Cold Love/Grand Illusion (1980) Geffen K79193
Who Do You Think You're Foolin'/Running For Cover (1981) Geffen K79201
Love Is In Control (Finger On The Trigger)/Sometimes Like Butterflies (1982) Warner
  Bros K79302
State Of Independence/Love Is Just A Breath Away (1982) Warner Bros K79344
I Feel Love (Part 1)/(Part 2) (1982) Casablanca FEEL 7
The Woman In Me/Livin' In America (1983) Warner Bros U9983
She Works Hard For The Money (Special Long Version)/I Do Believe (I Fell In Love)
  (1983) Mercury DONNA 1
Unconditional Love/Woman (1983) Mercury DONNA 2
Stop, Look And Listen/Tokyo (1983) Mercury DONNA 3
Love Has A Mind Of Its Own/People, People (1984) Mercury DONNA 4
There Goes My Baby/Maybe It's Over (1984) Warner Bros U9438
Supernatural Love (Remix)/Suzanna (1984) Warner Bros U9254
Eyes (Edit)/It's Not The Way (1985) Warner Bros U9103
Dinner With Gershwin/(Instrumental) (1987) Warner Bros U8237
All Systems Go (Edit)/Bad Reputation (1988) Warner Bros U8122
I Feel Love/Love To Love You Baby (1988) Old Gold OG 9771
This Time I Know It's For Real/Whatever Your Heart Desires (1989) Warner Bros U7780
This Time I Know It's For Real/Whatever Your Heart Desires (1989) Warner Bros
  U7780P – limited edition heart shaped picture disc
I Don't Wanna Get Hurt/(Instrumental) (1989) Warner Bros U7567
Work That Magic/Let There Be Peace (1991) Warner Bros U5937
Melody Of Love (Wanna Be Loved) (West End 7" Radio Mix)/On The Radio (1994)
  Mercury MERJB 418

12" Singles

Love To Love You Baby (Come On Over To My Place Version)/(Come Dancing Version)
  (1982) Casablanca CANX 1014
Back In Love Again/Try Me, I Know I Can Make It/Wasted (1977) GTO GT 117 – special
  limited edition
Last Dance/With Your Love (1978) Casablanca TGIFL 2
MacArthur Park Suite (1978) Casablanca CALD 5006 – one-side promo

Hot Stuff/Journey To The Centre Of Your Heart (1979) CANL 151 – also released as a limited edition red vinyl single

Bad Girls/On My Honor (1979) Casablanca CANL 155

Dim All The Lights/There Will Always Be A You (1979) Casablanca CANL 162

No More Tears (Enough Is Enough)/Barbra Streisand: Wet (1979) CBS S CBS 13 8000

Sunset People/Our Love (1980) Casablanca CANL 198

On The Radio/There Will Always Be A You (1979) Casablanca NBL 2236

Love Is On Control (Finger On The Trigger) (Extended Remix)/(Instrumental) (1982) Warner Bros K79302T

State Of Independence/Love Is Just A Breath Away/State Of Independence (Edit) (1982) Warner Bros K79344T

I Feel Love (Mega Mix)/(Mega Edit) (1982) Casablanca FEEL 12

The Woman In Me/Livin' In America/The Wanderer (1983) Warner Bros U9983CT – translucent blue vinyl

She Works Hard For The Money (Special Long Version)/(Instrumental) (1983) Mercury DONNA 12

Unconditional Love (Extended Version)/(Instrumental)/Woman (1983) Mercury DONNA 212

Stop, Look And Listen (Extended Remix)/Tokyo (1983) Mercury DONNA 312

Love Has A Mind Of Its Own/She Works Hard For The Money/People, People (1984) Mercury DONNA 412

There Goes My Baby/Maybe It's Over/Face The Music (1984) Warner Bros U9438T

Supernatural Love (Extended Dance Remix)/Suzanna (1984) Warner Bros U9254T

Eyes (Extended Mix)/I'm Free/It's Not The Way (1985) Warner Bros U9103T

Dinner With Gershwin (Extended Version)/(Album Version)/Tearin' Down The Walls (1987) Warner Bros U8237T

Dinner With Gershwin (Extended Version)/(Album Version)/Tearin' Down The Walls (1987) Warner Bros U8237TP – picture disc

This Time I Know It's For Real (Extended Version)/Whatever Your Heart Desires/This Time I Know It's For Real (Instrumental) (1989) Warner Bros U7780T

I Don't Wanna Get Hurt (Extended Versions)/(Instrumental)/Dinner With Gershwin (1989) Warner Bros U7567T

Love's About To Change Your Heart (Extended Remix)/(Instrumental)/Jeremy (1989) Warner Bros U7494T

Love's About To Change Your Heart (Clivilles & Cole 12" Mix)/(Dub 2)/(Clivilles & Cole 7" Mix) (1989) Warner Bros U7494TX

When Love Takes Over You (Extended Remix)/(Instrumental)/Bad Reputation (1989) Warner Bros U7361T

State Of Independence/(Edit)/Love Is Just A Breath Away (1990) Warner Bros U2857T

State Of Independence (New Bass Mix)/(No Drum Mix)/(N-R-G Mix) (1990) Warner Bros U2857TX

Breakaway (Remix Full Version)/(Remix Edit)/Love Is In Control (Finger On The Trigger) (1991) Warner Bros U3308T

Work That Magic (Extended ISA Remix)/(Capricorn ISA Remix)/Let There Be Peace (1991) Warner Bros U5937T

Melody Of Love (Wanna Be Loved) (Classic Club Mix)/(Boss Mix)/(Epris Mix)/Mijangos Powertools Trip #1)/(West End 7" Radio Edit) (1994) Mercury MERX 418

I Feel Love (Rollo & Sister Bliss Monster Mix)/(Masters At Work 86th St. Mix)/(Summer '77 Re-EQ '95)/Melody Of Love (Junior Vasquez DMC Mix) (1995) Manifesto/Mercury FESX 1

State Of Independence (DJ Dero Vocal Mix)/(Jules & Skins)/(Murk Club Mix)/(Murk-A-Dub Mix) (1996) Manifesto FESX 7

State Of Independence (Jules & Skins Vocal Mix)/(Jules & Skins Dub Mix)/(DJ Dero Vocal Mix) (1996) Manifesto INDDJ 2

CD Singles

Love's About To Change My Heart (Extended Remix)/(Instrumental)/Jeremy (1989) Warner Bros U7494CD

State Of Independence (Edit)/State Of Independence/Love Is Just A Breath Away (1990) Warner Bros U2857CD

Breakaway (Remix Full Version)/(Remix Edit)/Love Is In Control (Finger On The Trigger) (1991) Warner Bros U3308CD

Work That Magic (ISA Full Length Remix)/This Time I Know It's For Real/Dinner With Gershwin/State Of Independence (1991) Warner Bros U5937CD

Melody Of Love (Wanna Be Loved) (Epris Mix)/(Classic Club Mix)/(Mijangos Powertools Trip #1)/(AJ & Humpty's Anthem Mix) (1994) Mercury MERDD 418

I Feel Love (Rollo & Sister Bliss Monster Mix)/(Masters At Work 86th St. Mix)/(Summer '77 Re-EQ '95)/Melody Of Love (Junior Vasquez DMC Mix) (1995) Manifesto/Mercury FESCD 1

State Of Independence (New Radio Millennium Mix)/(Creation Mix)/(Original Album Version)/(DJ Dero Vocal Mix)/(Murk Club Mix)/(Jules & Skins Vocal) (1996) Manifesto FESCD 7

I Will Go With You (Con Te Partiró) (Radio Edit)/(Groove G Club Mix)/(Hex Hector Extended Vocal Mix) (1999) Epic 668209 2

I Will Go With You (Con Te Partiró) (Radio Edit)/(Club 69 Future Mix)/(Rosabel Radio Remix)/(Video) (1999) Epic 668209 5

Stamp Your Feet (Original Album Version)/(Jason Nevins Radio Edit) (2008) Sony BMG 88697316772

About the author

Craig Halstead began writing about music in 1990, when he launched a writing partnership with Chris Cadman; together, they compiled 'The Complete Michael Jackson Solo Discography 1972-90' for Adrian Grant's official fan magazine, *Off the Wall*.

Chris launched his own fanzine *Jackson* in 1995, with Craig as contributor, proof reader and eventual co-editor (*Jackson* is no longer published). Craig and Chris's first two books, *Michael Jackson – The Early Years* and *Michael Jackson – The Solo Years*, were published in 2002 and 2003, respectively. *Jacksons Number Ones* followed later in 2003, and their first non-Jackson book, *ABBA Gold Hits*, was published in 2004.

The first edition of the best-selling *Michael Jackson: For The Record*, was published in 2007 – this was followed two and a half years later by the revised and expanded 2nd edition, in September 2009. Their most recent book, *Janet Jackson: For The Record*, was published in 2010. *Whitney Houston: For The Record*, the first music book Craig researched and wrote solo, was also published in 2010, and he followed it with *Michael, Janet & The Jackson Family – All The Top 40 Singles*, *Michael, Janet & The Jackson Family – All The Top 40 Albums* and *ABBA – All The Top 40 Hits*. His most recent book is *Carpenters – All The Top 40 Hits*.

Craig was born in June 1959 in Rochdale, England. He studied Applied Chemistry and Biochemistry at Huddersfield, gaining a B.Sc. (honours), but since November 1986 he has worked as a Community Worker at a small, multi-cultural Community Centre. He also writes fiction and is the author of three novels, *The Secret Library*, *Shadow Of Death* and *Tyranny* (which was originally published as *Ribbon Of Darkness*). He lives in the North West of England with his teenage son, Aaron.

Acknowledgements

Thanks, as always, to my writing partner Chris Cadman – your interest, encouragement and support is greatly appreciated. I'm looking forward to working with you again in the near future, on projects old and new.

Cathy Hawkins, your donna-tribute.com site is a credit to both you and Donna, many thanks for taking the time to respond to my queries and fill gaps in my knowledge. Many thanks, Chris Kimberley, for your ongoing support and friendship. I would also like to acknowledge the online music community who share information so selflessly, most notably, the music forums at ukmix, buzzjack & haven.

A big and heartfelt thank you to Richard Fitt and the team at Authors Online who helped to turn Chris and I into published writers ~ we were shocked and saddened to hear of your company's demise, and wish you and everyone involved with Authors Online best wishes for the future.

Printed in Great Britain
by Amazon